IMAGES
of America

BURTON

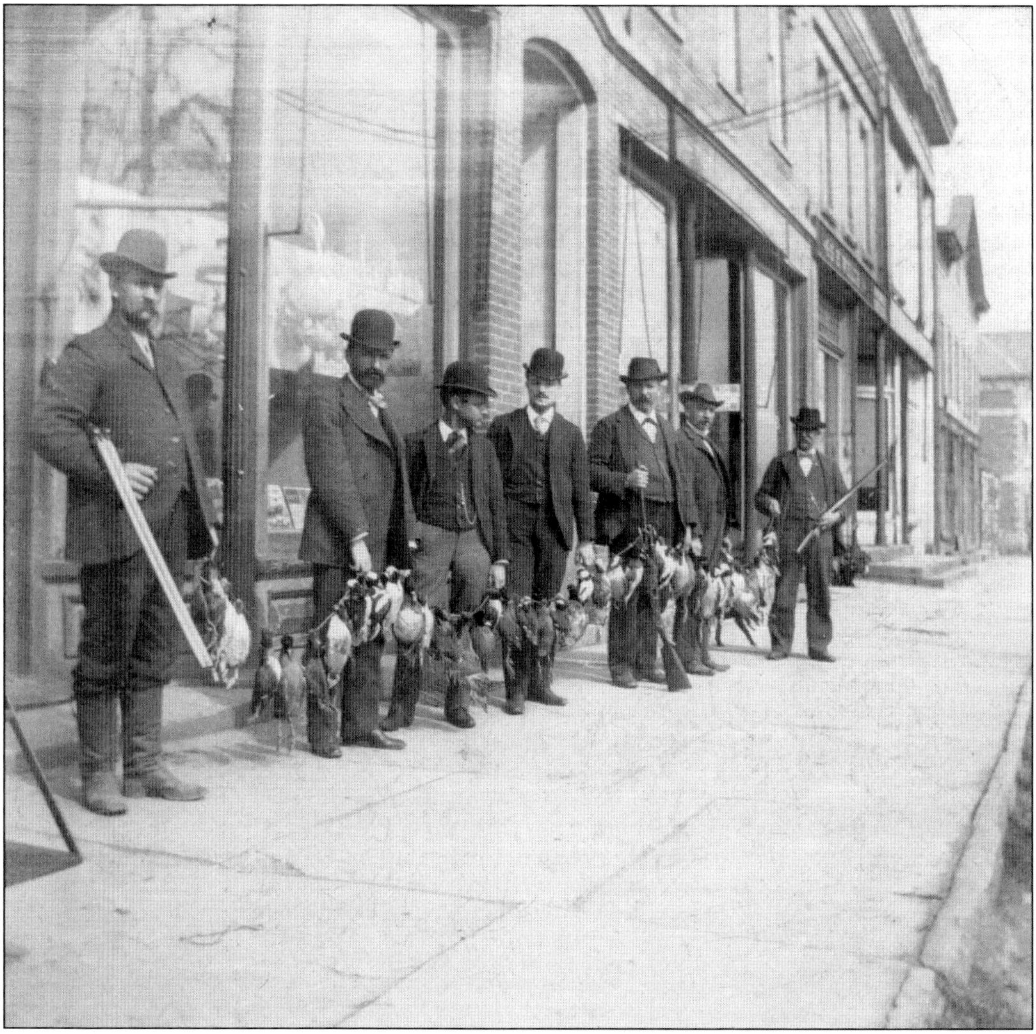

A group of men stands in front of Parmalee Bros. Hardware on North Cheshire Street after a hunt in 1889. For more than 150 years, North Cheshire Street has also been called Main Street by residents, as well as on maps, and is the main commercial district in the village. The hunters could have been Burton residents, but they were just as likely from Cleveland; many of the wealthier residents of Cuyahoga County used the less-populated Geauga County as a weekend retreat during that era. (Courtesy of Geauga County Historical Society's Shanower Library.)

On the Cover: Burton Park was established by the founders of Burton in 1803 and still remains at the center of the community. On May 30, 1901, the Burton Citizen Band, formed in 1877, gathers in the park. The band consisted of drum major C.L. Brown and, from left to right, (first row) L.J. Ford, Frank Carey, Fred Crittenden, and Doc Crittenden; (second row) W.B. Canfield, Elmer Warner, George Fenn, and Shirl Charter; (third row) P.W. Hicks, Art Brown, R.H. Hicks, and P.W. Dayton; (fourth row) Noel Hick (clarinet), C.O. Dayton, Frank Rice, R.W. Ford, and H.D. Rex; (fifth row) Archie Latham (bass drum), Elmer Charter (snare drum), and Louie Reed (cymbals). (Courtesy of Geauga County Historical Society's Shanower Library.)

IMAGES
of America

BURTON

Calvin Rydbom and Thomas Kubat
on behalf of the Burton Public Library
and the Burton Historic District Association

ARCADIA
PUBLISHING

ISBN 978-0-7385-9412-5

Published by Arcadia Publishing
Charleston, South Carolina

Printed in the United States of America

Library of Congress Control Number: 2012938486

For all general information, please contact Arcadia Publishing:
Telephone 843-853-2070
Fax 843-853-0044
E-mail sales@arcadiapublishing.com
For customer service and orders:
Toll-Free 1-888-313-2665

Visit us on the Internet at www.arcadiapublishing.com

To the founders and first settlers of Burton

Contents

ACKNOWLEDGMENTS

Burton has a long and rich history, as evidenced by the variety of photographs contained within this book, many of which came from the personal collections of Burton residents and were collected by the Burton Public Library. Special thanks needs to be given to Holly Lynn Manning, the library director, for managing the collection of so many photographs, as well as giving us a place to call home during our project. The Burton Historic District Association and particularly Jacqueline Samuel provided considerable aid during this project, especially in tracking down pieces of information and forgotten facts we needed to explain some of the images.

Many images and considerable assistance also came from the Cleveland Press Collection at the Michael Schwartz Library at Cleveland State. Without the help of Bill Barrow, Lynn Duchez Bycko, Kiffany Francis, and Joanne Cornelius, the completion of this book would not have been possible.

Thanks to Geauga County Historical Society's Shanower Library for providing numerous photographs. The Shanower Library houses Geauga County records, diaries, genealogical material, and photographs from as early as the 18th century.

We would also like to thank all those who added their personal photographs and professional research to this project. This book would not have come about without every one of you. And lastly, thank you to our families and friends, whose support is always appreciated.

INTRODUCTION

This book looks at the many significant historical moments and residents in Burton's history while taking time to also focus on the people, places, and events that shaped the community and made it what it is today. And what it is today is not only "Where History Lives," but also a very nice place to live. Through these images, the book will trace the community from its founding as the first settlement in Geauga County up through its position in the current world.

Arriving in the spring of 1798, the first settlers had a difficult life in the beginning, dealing with isolation, harsh weather, wildlife, and occasional issues with the Native Americans who called the area home. Many of the early settlers wrote of having a good relationship with the Native Americans, even dining and socializing with them in the early days, but they also wrote of having to be on the lookout for and be weary of a chief becoming enamored with their daughter and making an offer to buy her. What really jumps out from the pages of the letters and diaries of the settlers, who had left the already-settled Connecticut behind, is how much they seemed to ignore all these hardships and truly celebrate the home they were creating.

The history of Burton started with the surveying and purchase of Town Seven, Range Seven within the Connecticut Western Reserve. It continued with the arrival of some of the men who made the purchase, as well as others, in 1798. The founders wasted very little time in turning Town Seven, Range Seven into something much more than a group of settlers—a community. The first road, which allowed easy travel for an entire two miles, was cut into the landscape within a month of their arrival, and both a sawmill and a gristmill were built and functioning by 1800.

The Umberville Coffee House opened in 1798, and Gideon Finch opened a competing establishment shortly afterwards. J.S. Cleveland arrived in Burton in 1800 and opened the first store two years later. Dr. Joseph Clark arrived to take care of the area's medical needs in 1804. While the first schoolhouse was not erected until 1803, the children of Burton attended class in a building near the Umberfield home before that. Not content with a log schoolhouse, the Burton Academy first held class in 1806. At 25 feet by 50 feet, the academy was large for its time and featured brick chimneys, fireplaces, and multiple rooms. It was considered by many to be the most impressive and elegant building in the Western Reserve. Before work on the building even began, local residents petitioned the territorial legislature to charter the academy as a college. The Burton Academy relocated to Hudson in 1826 and eventually, after a few name changes and mergers, became Case Western Reserve University.

The first church service officiated by an ordained minister was in 1802, the same year the first election was held. The Burton Congregational Church, which is still an active and vital part of the community, was established in 1808. In an amazing burst of foresight, the founders of Burton set aside an area of land and dedicated it as Burton Park. Still sitting in the center of the community and houses (among other things), it is the only municipally owned sugar camp in the country.

All this was accomplished within Burton's first decade. The following 15 years saw the first Great Geauga County Fair, held at Burton Park. The fair is still held in Burton, and a fairground has been built especially for the event, which draws over 200,000 people every year. The Domestic Arts and Flower Hall fairground buildings are listed in the National Register of Historical Places.

By the middle of the 19th century, Burton had begun to shape not only its small section of Geauga County but also the direction of the state of Ohio. Peter Hitchcock, the first instructor at the Burton Academy, served on the Ohio Supreme Court for 28 years (21 of them as chief justice) and in the Ohio Senate. In 1850, he served as a delegate to the Ohio Constitutional Convention and was often referred to as the "father of the Ohio Constitution." Not to be outdone, his nephew Seabury Ford served as the last Whig governor of Ohio in 1849 and 1850. Ohioans were deeply divided over the issue of slavery, and Ford campaigned against the expansion of slavery and for the repeal of the discriminatory Black Laws.

In 1872, the Boughton, Ford & Co. bank was formed. It was a much larger and more important financial institution than the area would suggest, flourishing for years until failing in 1903 for reasons still argued about more than 100 years later. Its problems and closing were considered important enough to be covered by the *New York Times*. The bank had a far-reaching influence on Burton; in 1877, because the bank wanted to get financial news as soon as it arrived at the railway station, the first telephone line in the state of Ohio was established.

In 1931, the Log Cabin Sugar Camp was built at the bequest of the chamber of commerce near the south end of Burton Park. It was the first municipal maple sugarhouse in the country. It remains an important fixture in Burton; maple sugar candy and pure maple spread are still sold at the cabin.

In 1941, with the help of Congresswoman Frances P. Bolton, the Geauga County Historical Society acquired the home of Eleazer Hickox, one of the earliest settlers. The Hickox home, along with 65 acres of land, became the Geauga County Historical Society and Century Village Museum. Just off Burton Park, Century Village boasts 23 historic buildings and homes in an authentic representation of a Western Reserve village in 1798, making it easy to see why Burton is known as "Where History Lives."

One

In the Beginning

In 1796, surveyors for the Connecticut Land Company, which had bought the Western Reserve from the State of Connecticut, assigned a section of land in northeast Ohio the designation Town Seven within the seventh range. This 25-square-mile township became Burton, the first settlement in Geauga County.

The original survey divided the township into tracts of 160 acres to be sold at just over 62¢ an acre. The township was purchased by a small group of men: Turhand Kirtland, Seth Hart, Benjamin Doolittle, Titus Street, William Law, Andrew Hull, Daniel Holbrook, Levi Tomlinson, and possibly a Mr. Brand. Street, one of the main investors in the group, decided to name the township after his son Burton.

The names of those in the party that came west in the spring of 1798, mostly from Cheshire, Connecticut, are still reflected in the street names, parks, and homes of Burton more than 200 years after their arrival. Thomas and Lydia (Hotchkiss) Umberfield, also referred to as "Umberville" in early records, and their five children arrived on June 21, 1798, as the first family in the area.

During the next 80 years, Burton went from a settlement of roughly 30 families in 1803 to a financial center and, in some instances, a technological one by the end of the 19th century. In between, Burton produced a governor and a chief justice of the Ohio Supreme Court. The residents built a business district, half of which burned in 1871 but was reconstructed. Shortly after that, the Baltimore & Ohio Railroad (B&O) came through Burton. A fairground was developed and still houses the oldest county fair in Ohio today. Locals erected an academy, and when it moved south, they produced a second one. Burton became not only a thriving community but also an extremely resilient one.

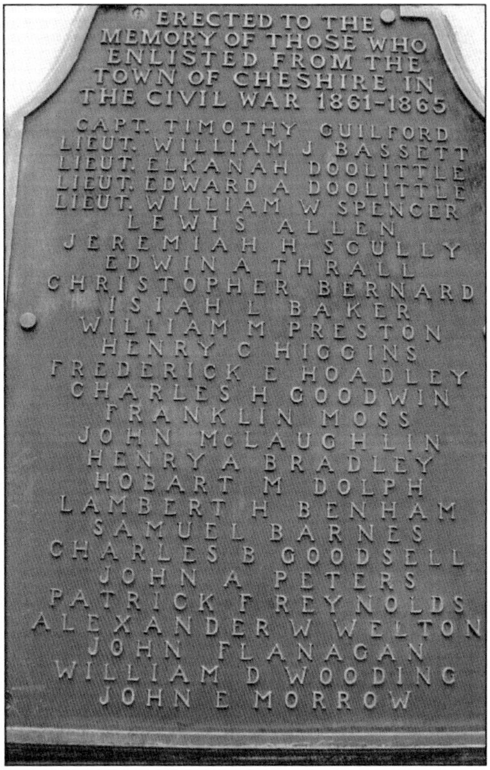

Within five years of the first arrivals, Burton's population had swelled to roughly 30 families; the majority of them were from Cheshire, Connecticut. These families, according to early chroniclers of Burton's history, brought the pilgrim spirit with them and were very concerned about their religious instruction and installing morals in the growing population. A few short years after arriving, they had established a church to meet their religious needs and the Burton Academy for education, moral and otherwise. This four-sided monument lists the men of Cheshire who served in the Civil War about 65 years after Burton was settled. Many of the surnames on the monument are the same as early Burton settlers. (Courtesy of Jacqueline Samuel.)

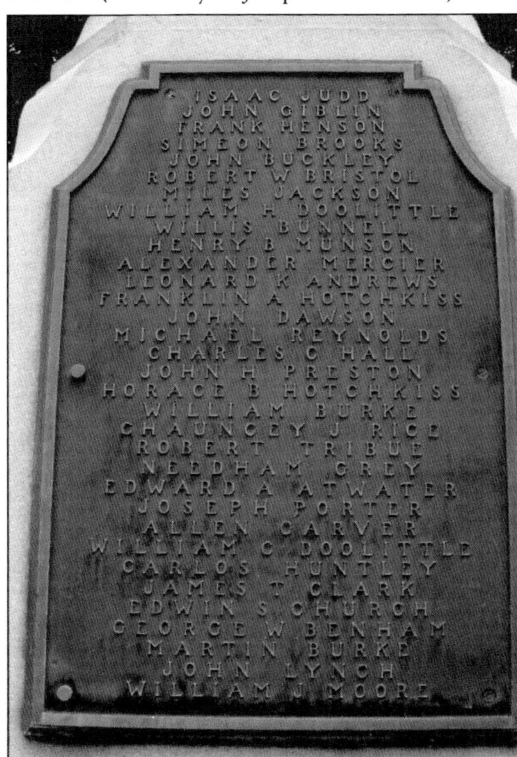

The grave sites of Thomas and Lydia Umberfield, the first husband and wife to settle in Burton, are in Memorial Cemetery, originally known as Lower Fox Valley Cemetery. The local Native American chief had become taken with their daughter's beauty and offered to buy her, but the Umberfields declined. (Courtesy of Jacqueline Samuel.)

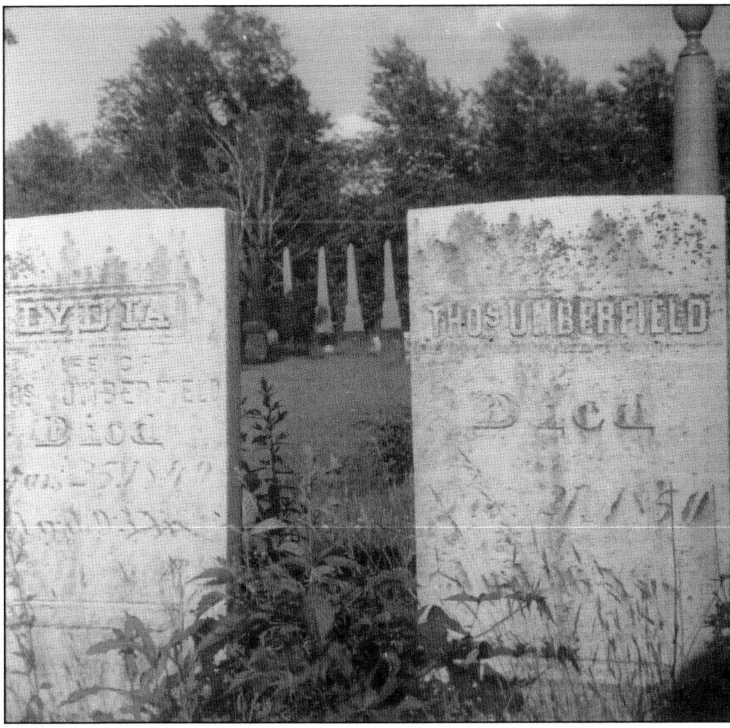

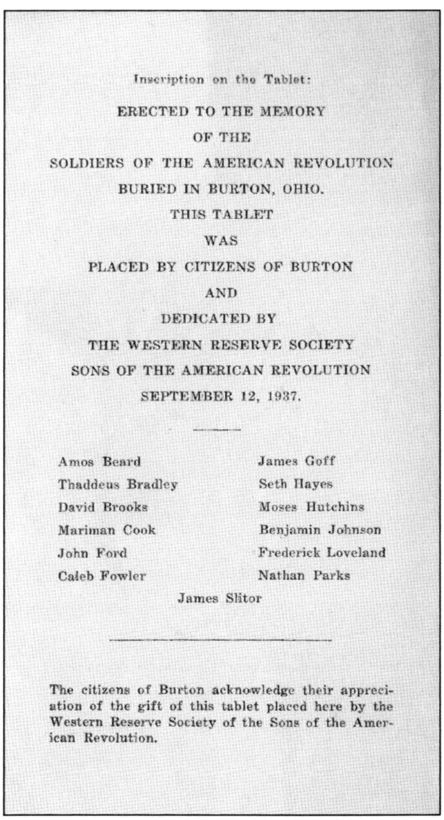

Inscription on the Tablet:

ERECTED TO THE MEMORY
OF THE
SOLDIERS OF THE AMERICAN REVOLUTION
BURIED IN BURTON, OHIO.
THIS TABLET
WAS
PLACED BY CITIZENS OF BURTON
AND
DEDICATED BY
THE WESTERN RESERVE SOCIETY
SONS OF THE AMERICAN REVOLUTION
SEPTEMBER 12, 1937.

Amos Beard	James Goff
Thaddeus Bradley	Seth Hayes
David Brooks	Moses Hutchins
Mariman Cook	Benjamin Johnson
John Ford	Frederick Loveland
Caleb Fowler	Nathan Parks

James Slitor

The citizens of Burton acknowledge their appreciation of the gift of this tablet placed here by the Western Reserve Society of the Sons of the American Revolution.

In 1937, the Western Reserve Society Sons of the American Revolution erected a tablet to commemorate the 13 early Burton settlers who fought in the Revolutionary War. The organization also placed the Joseph Badger plaque. See following page. (Courtesy of Geauga County Historical Society.)

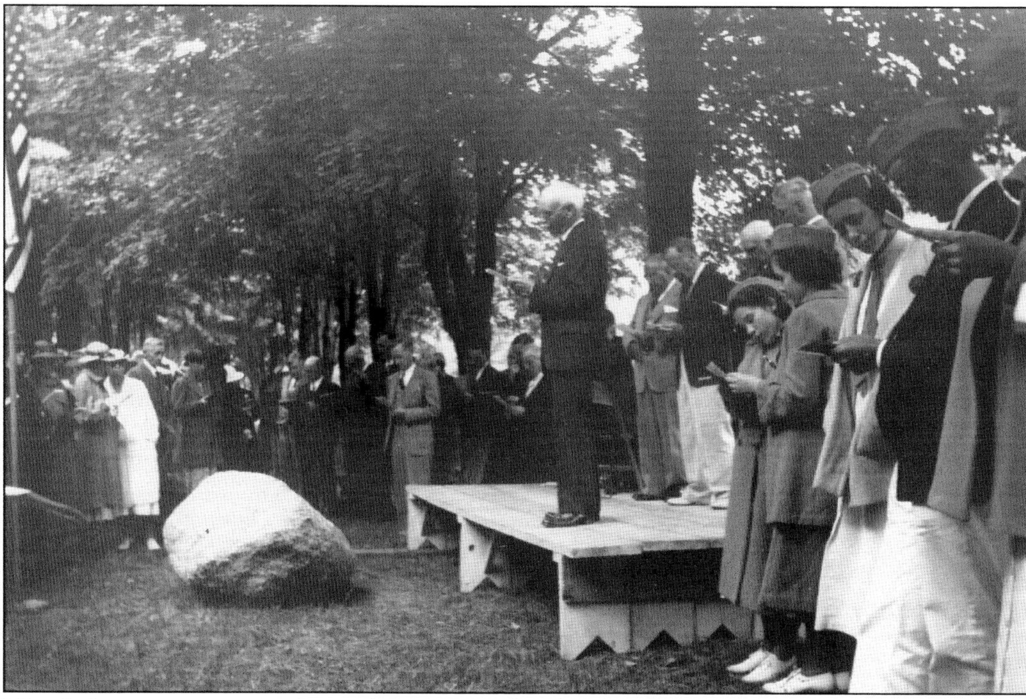

The dedication ceremony for a plaque erected to honor the Rev. Joseph Badger (1757–1846) was held on July 24, 1926, in Burton Park. The plaque is still there today. (Courtesy of Burton Public Library.)

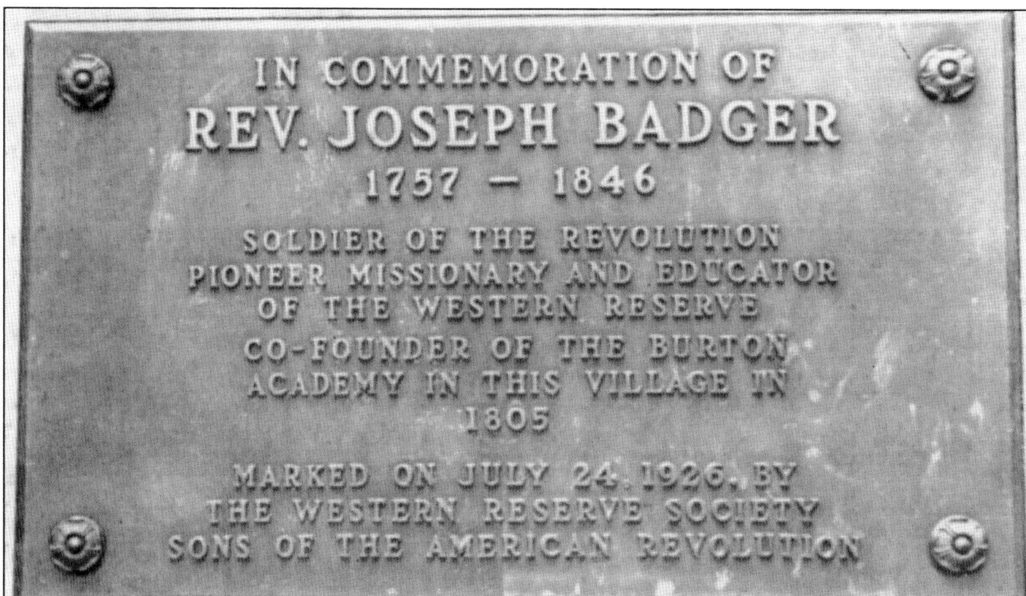

Reverend Badger, the first missionary in Burton, established the first church in what was known as the Connecticut Western Reserve. He arrived in the area in 1800 and stayed until his death in 1846. While living in Burton, he preached in practically every community in what is now Geauga County. He was also a cofounder of the Burton Academy. (Courtesy of Geauga County Historical Society.)

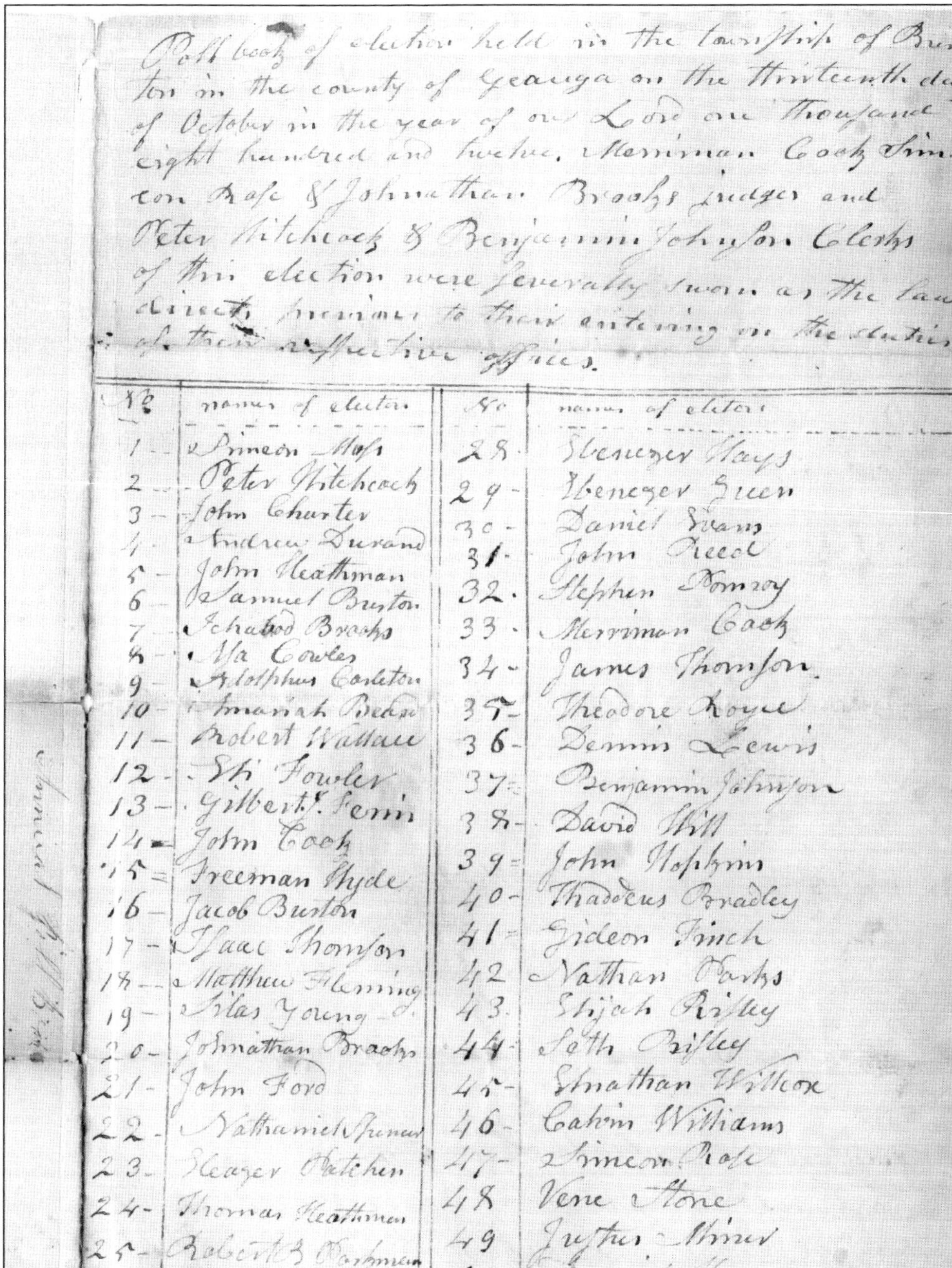

Poll book of election held in the township of Burton in the county of Geauga on the thirteenth day of October in the year of our Lord one thousand eight hundred and twelve. Merriman Cook Simeon Rose & Johnathan Brooks judges and Peter Hitchcock & Benjamin Johnson Clerks of this election were severally sworn as the law directs previous to their entering on the duties of their respective offices.

No	names of electors	No	names of electors
1	Simeon Moss	28	Ebenezer Hays
2	Peter Hitchcock	29	Ebenezer Green
3	John Charter	30	Daniel Evans
4	Andrew Durand	31	John Reed
5	John Heathman	32	Stephen Pomroy
6	Samuel Burton	33	Merriman Cook
7	Ichabod Brooks	34	James Thomson
8	Asa Cowles	35	Theodore Royce
9	Adolphus Carleton	36	Dennis Lewis
10	Amariah Beden	37	Benjamin Johnson
11	Robert Wallace	38	David Hill
12	Eli Fowler	39	John Hopkins
13	Gilbert F. Fenn	40	Thadeus Bradley
14	John Cook	41	Gideon Finch
15	Freeman Hyde	42	Nathan Parks
16	Jacob Burton	43	Elijah Risley
17	Isaac Thomson	44	Seth Risley
18	Matthew Fleming	45	Elnathan Wilcox
19	Silas Young	46	Calvin Williams
20	Johnathan Brooks	47	Simeon Rose
21	John Ford	48	Vene Stone
22	Nathaniel Spencer	49	Luther Miner
23	Eleazer Hatchet	50	Daniel Hays
24	Thomas Heathman		
25	Robert B Parkman		
[illegible]	Jacob W[illegible]		

Geauga County was organized in 1806, and Burton held its first election in April of that year. Handwritten poll books still exist for some of the first elections. This one from 1812 provides a fairly detailed account of an early election process by listing not only the winners but also the names of all the men who voted for the offices. One of the men who oversaw the election process, Judge Peter Hitchcock, collected 55 votes to his opponent's 1 and was a member of the state senate from 1812 to 1815. The term *severally sworn* refers to the fact the men who oversaw the election were sworn in separately, not en masse. (Courtesy of Geauga County Historical Society.)

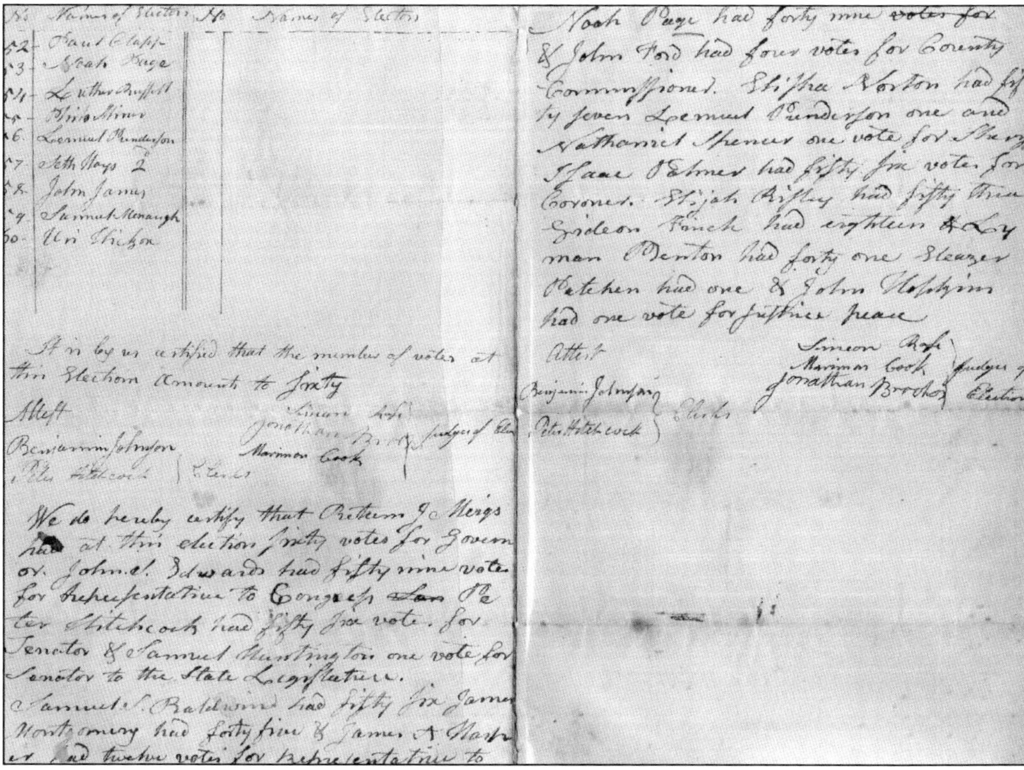

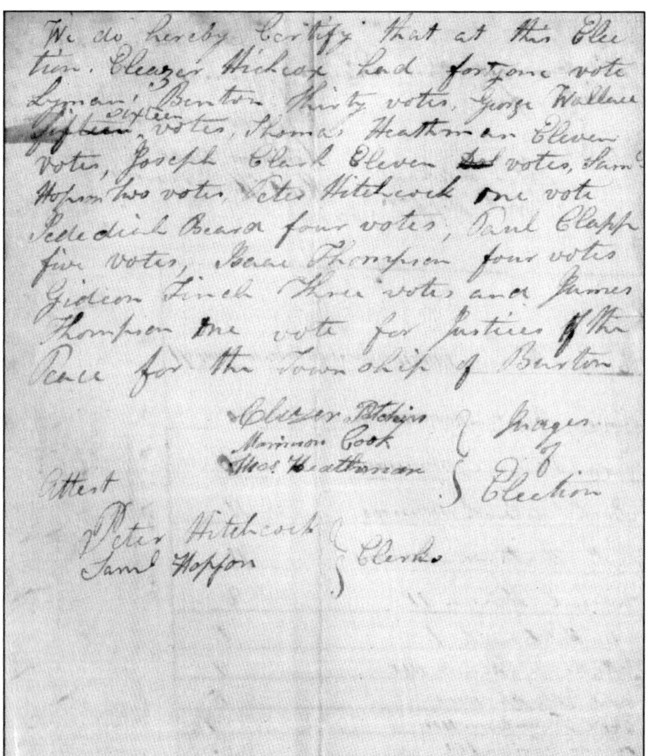

While 65 men are listed as voters in the 1809 election, only 60 were documented in 1812. The names Hitchcock, Beard, Burton, Carleton, Cook, Ford, Hickox, and Johnson are all on street signs and buildings in Burton today. One of the voters is Peter Hitchcock, who became the chief justice of the Ohio Supreme Court. The name of John Ford, father of the future Ohio governor, Seabury Ford, also appears on the document. Some of the more important Ohio politicians of the mid-19th century can be traced back to Burton poll books. (Courtesy of Geauga County Historical Society.)

Both produced around 80 years after Burton's founding, these maps illustrate how, in a relatively short time, the community grew from a small group of settlers to a well-established society. The first Geauga County Fair was held only 25 years after the first settlers arrived. The 1874 map below includes a business directory, which lists the town dentist and a hotel and boasts that the cheese factory has "the Capacity of using Milk of 600 Cows." The directory also lists a physician and surgeon, as well as a botanic physician who used herbs and roots for medicines. (Courtesy of Geauga County Historical Society.)

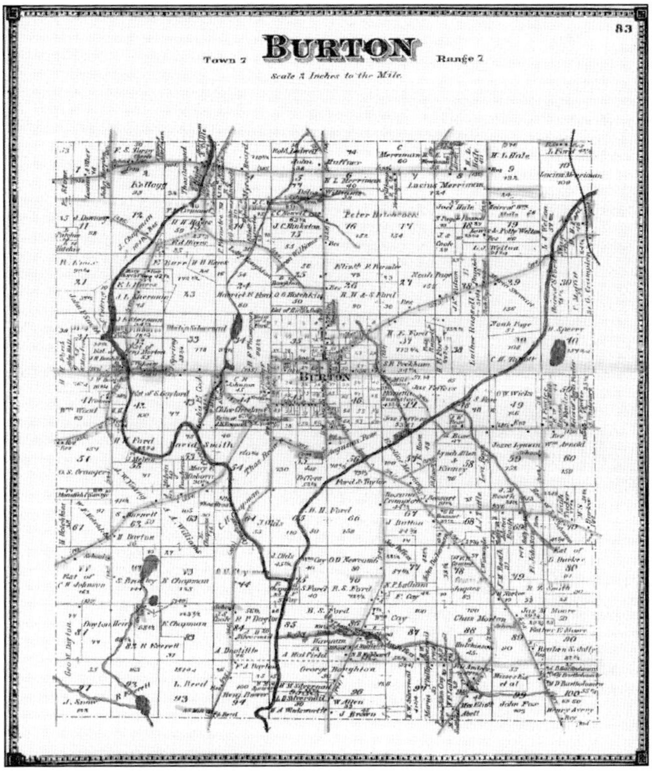

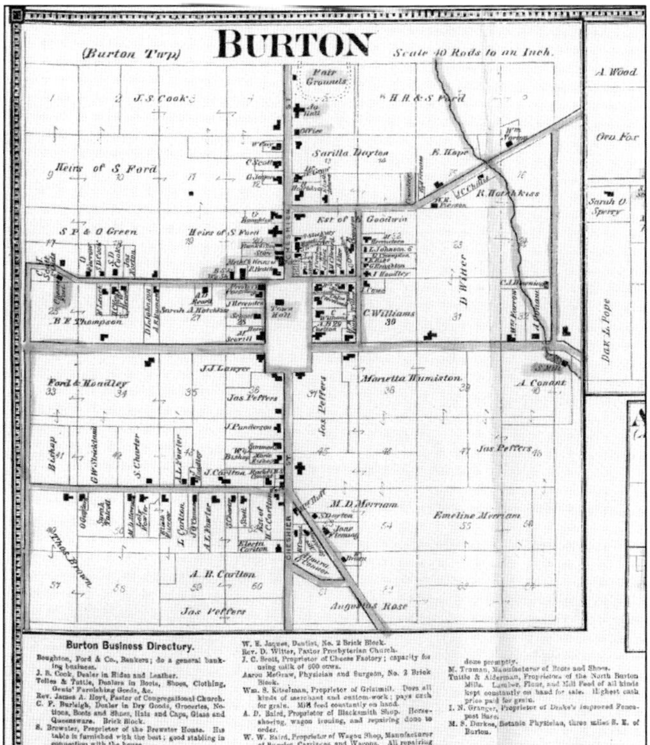

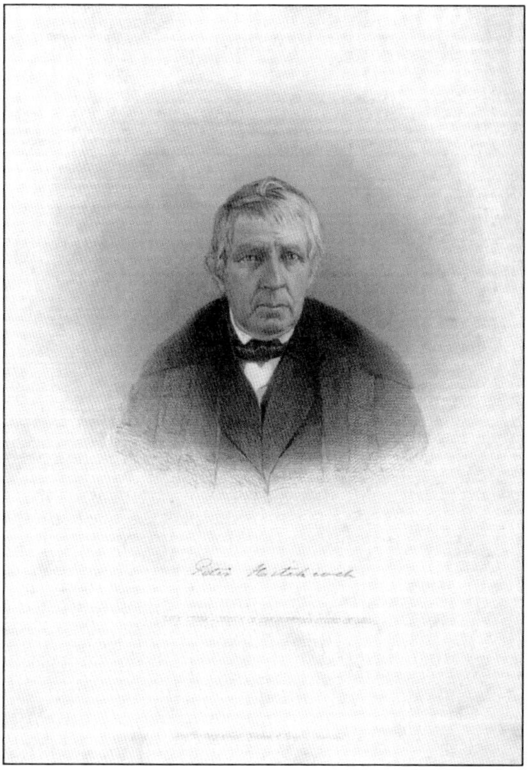

Peter Marshall Hitchcock (1781–1853) was born in Cheshire, Connecticut, and moved to Burton at an early age. He served in the Ohio House and Senate before serving 28 years on the Ohio Supreme Court, including 21 years as chief justice. He was commonly referred to as the father of the 1851 Ohio Constitution, as he was at the forefront of revising the original state constitution. (Courtesy of Geauga County Historical Society.)

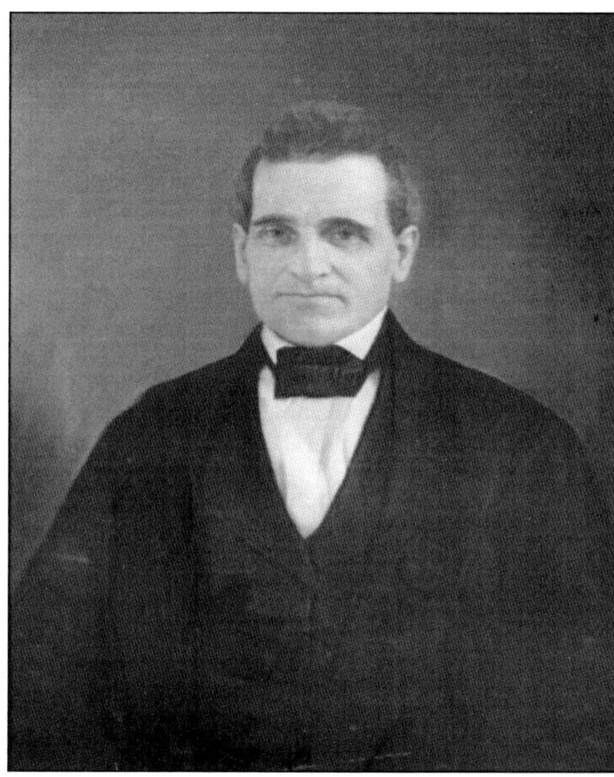

Seabury Ford (1801–1855), the nephew of Peter Hitchcock, was also born in Cheshire, Connecticut, and served in the Ohio House and Senate before serving a term as governor of Ohio in 1849 and 1850. The last Whig governor of Ohio, Ford's one great success was the repeal of the Black Laws, which discriminated against African Americans in Ohio. (Courtesy of Geauga County Historical Society.)

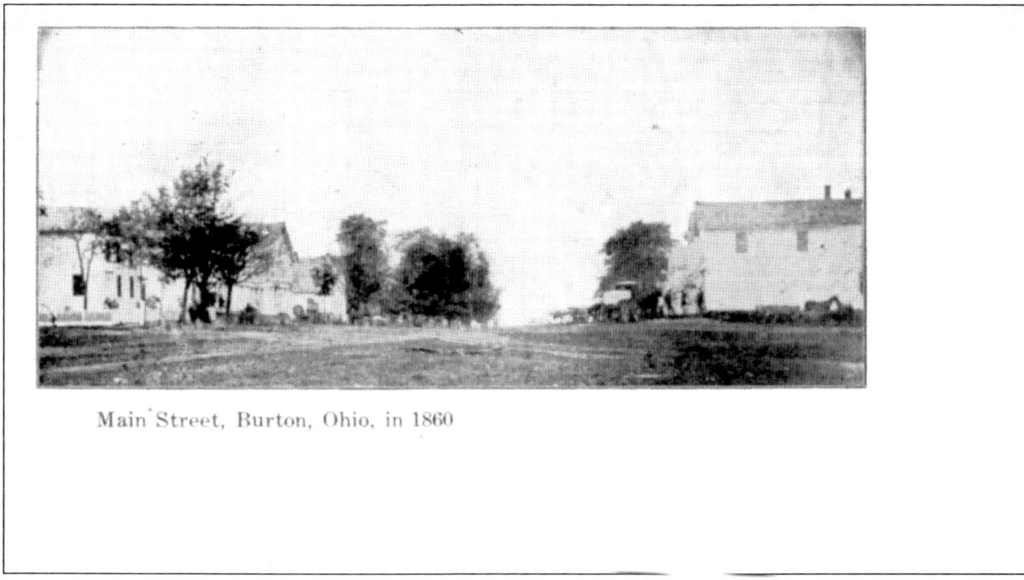

Main Street, also known as North Cheshire Street, is seen here in 1860. Called both names on maps and by locals, the street was just a few years away from becoming the main business district of Burton when this photograph was taken. Not long after the business district was established, a large part of it burned down in 1871. It was subsequently reconstructed with buildings still standing today. (Courtesy of Bill Jackson.)

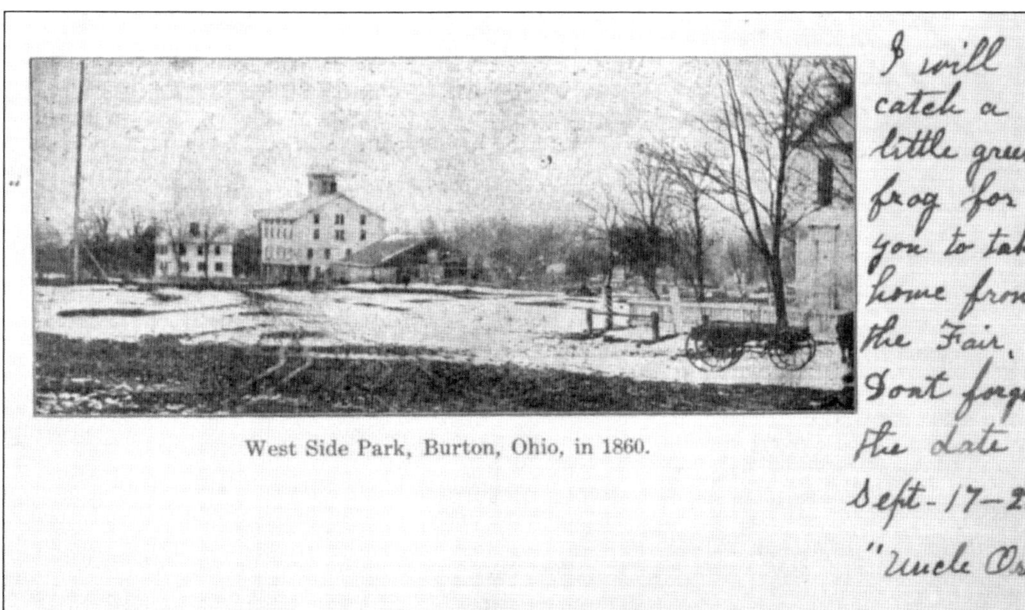

The sender of this postcard of another view of Burton in 1860 reminds a friend about the Geauga County Fair, the oldest state fair in Ohio. First held in Burton in 1823, it is still held there annually on Labor Day weekend. (Courtesy of Bill Jackson.)

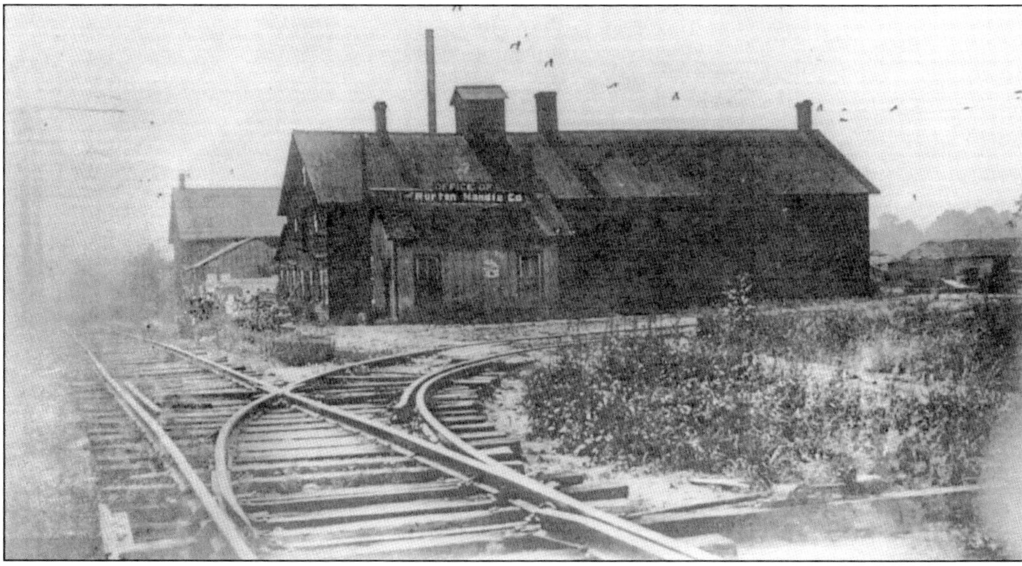

The Burton Handle Company was established in 1880 on Spring Street. The company was purported to be the largest manufacturer of plows, cultivators, handles, bobsleds, horse rakes, and castings in the country. it moved to the industrial area across from the fair grounds entrance where this photograph was taken. (Courtesy of Geauga County Historical Society.)

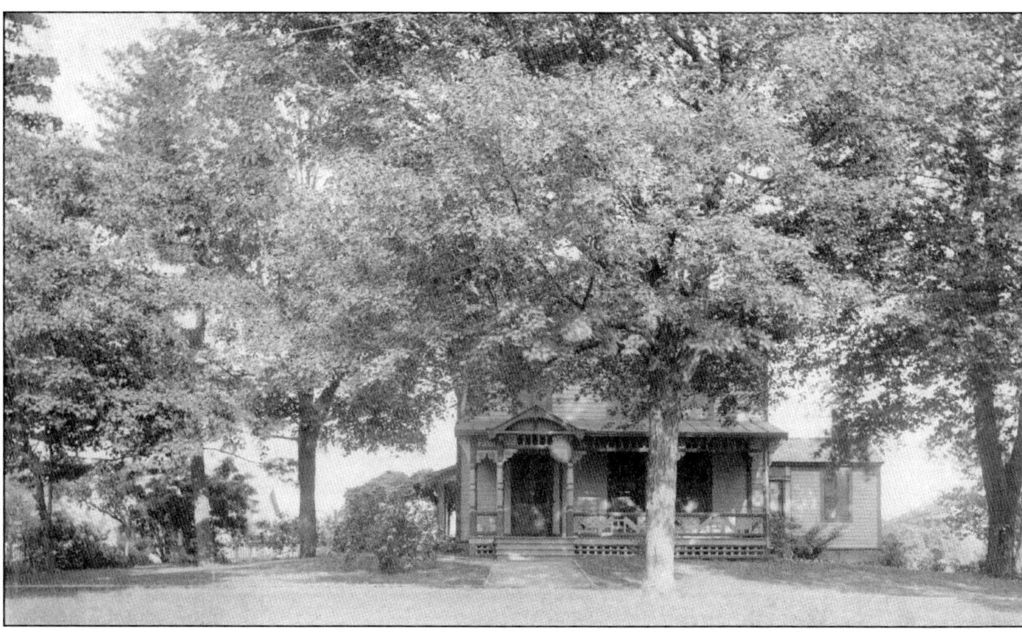

The Fords were a prominent family in Burton; there are three houses in Burton still known as the Ford home, but this one owned by Gov. Seabury Ford is no longer standing. The Fords were a prominent bank family as principles in Boughton, Ford & Co. (Courtesy of Geauga County Historical Society.)

Two

Historic Homes of Burton

The bevy of historic homes and buildings located in the village dates from 1807. The Cook home was the first frame house erected in Burton. Construction of these buildings continued through 1931, when the Log Cabin Sugar Camp was constructed. Keeping with Burton's long-standing appreciation of and devotion to its abundant history, a walking tour of 39 vital architectural structures, many of which were built by the first settlers, has been established to further the mission of the Burton Historic District Association.

The Burton Village Historic District is made up of 27 houses; eight buildings devoted to education, worship, civil service, or commerce; two commercial blocks; the town barn; and the aforementioned log cabin. Among the houses are the renowned Hickox Brick, constructed by Eleazar Hickox, a member of the state legislature in 1822 and 1823, and three homes belonging at one time to the prestigious Ford family. The district was recognized by the National Register of Historic Places in 1974.

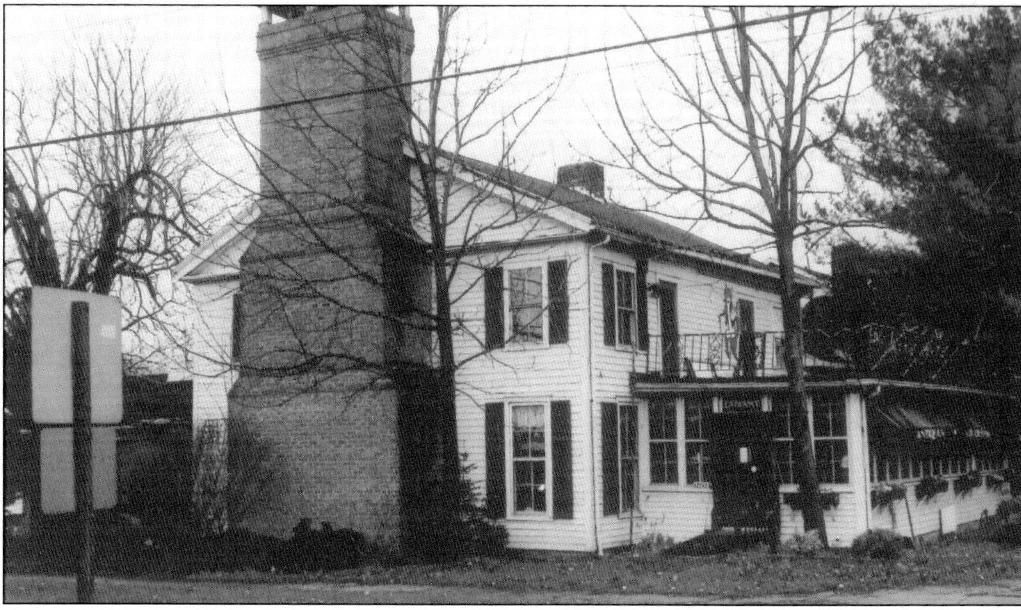

In 1840, James Peffers built this magnificent Greek Revival house 11 years after first settling in Burton. The house was greatly remodeled with a variety of modifications, including the addition of a glassed-in porch. Since 1925, the house has been maintained as the popular eating and lodging establishment Ye Olde Homestead. (Courtesy of Linda Natco on behalf of Little Pond Publishing.)

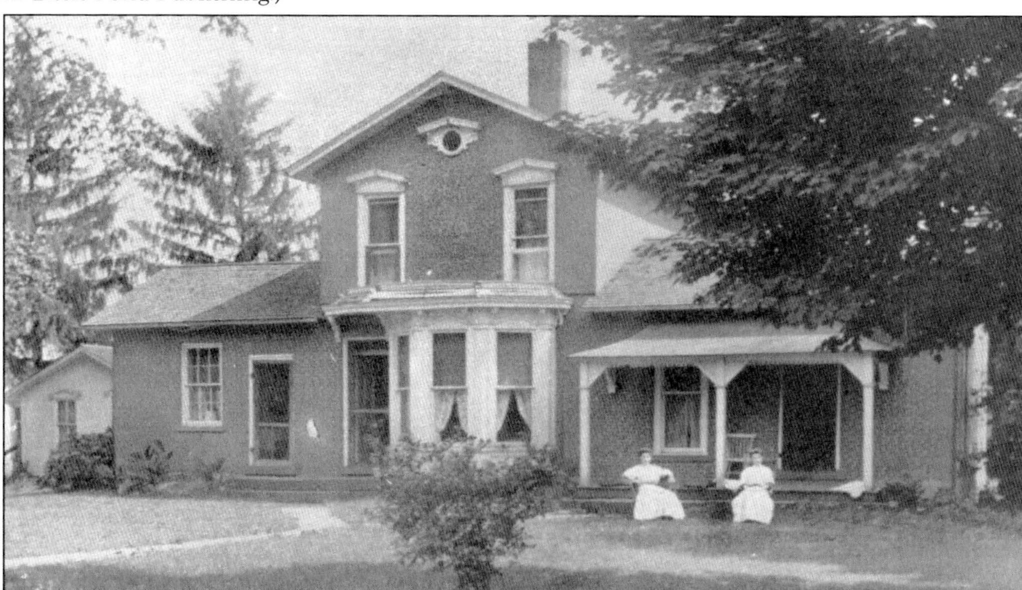

One of the most distinctive and significant houses in Geauga County, the Hickox Brick has been the home of the Geauga County Historical Society since 1941. This beautiful brick house was built in 1832 by Eleazar Hickox, one of the first settlers in Burton, who was a member of the state legislature in 1822 and 1823 and a prominent producer and distributor of goods and livestock. He lived in his store prior to the construction of the house. (Courtesy of Geauga County Historical Society.)

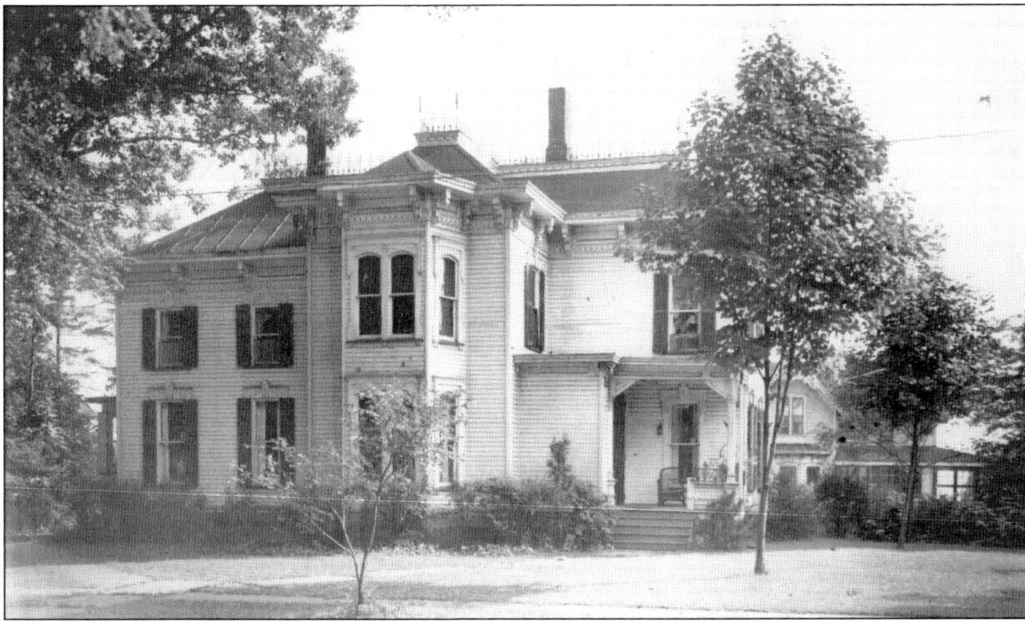

This Italianate home, currently located at 14629 East Center in Burton Village, was built by E.P. Latham. This house includes L-shaped door handles designed specifically for Latham, who had both of his arms amputated and lost sight in one eye after the overzealous celebration of a Union victory at Cumberland Gap in the Civil War. Latham operated the solid brass handles with the hooks attached to his stumps. (Courtesy of Geauga County Historical Society.)

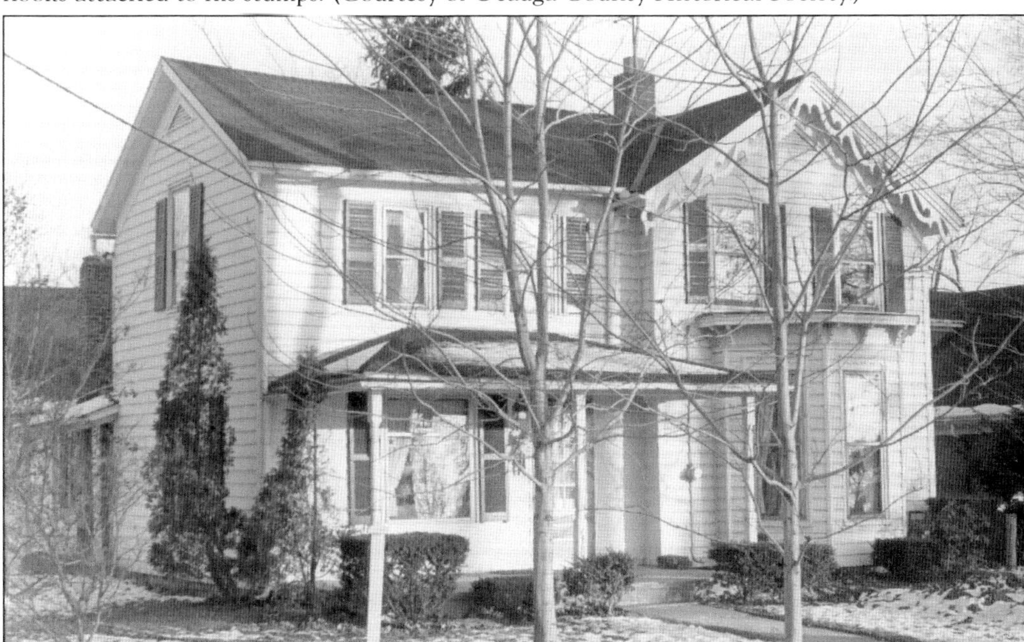

Almon B. Carlton, a carpenter by trade, built this two-story house in 1863 on the former site of Burton Academy. He was responsible for the construction of a number of houses in Burton and also had a hand in finalizing the interior of the Congregational church. (Courtesy of Geauga County Historical Society.)

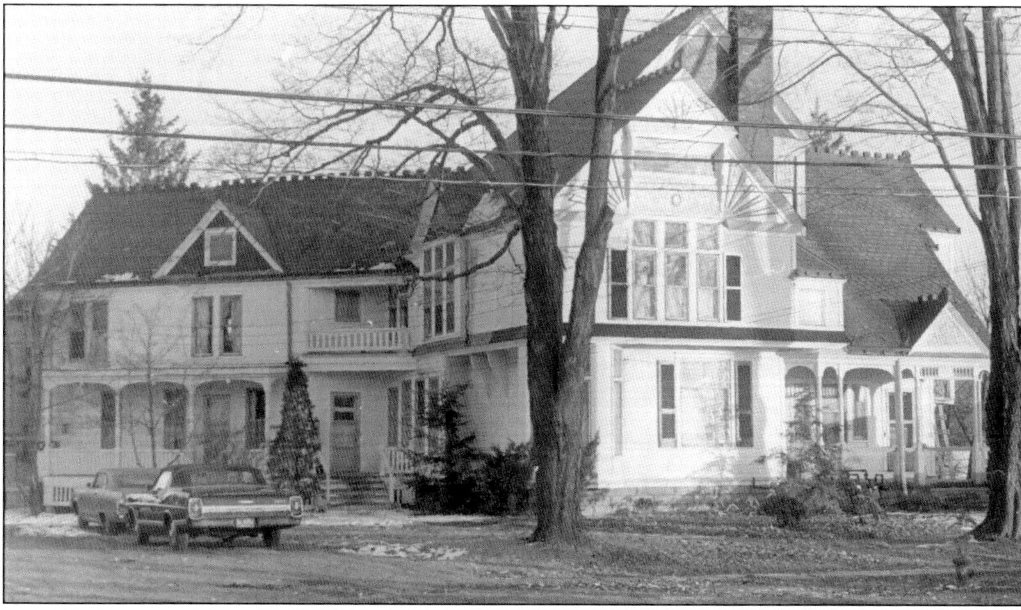

In 1891, George H. Ford built this exquisite house. The home's spacious and welcoming air was extended to numerous political personalities of the time, including William McKinley, Sen. Joseph B. Foraker, and Mark Hanna. (Courtesy of Geauga County Historical Society.)

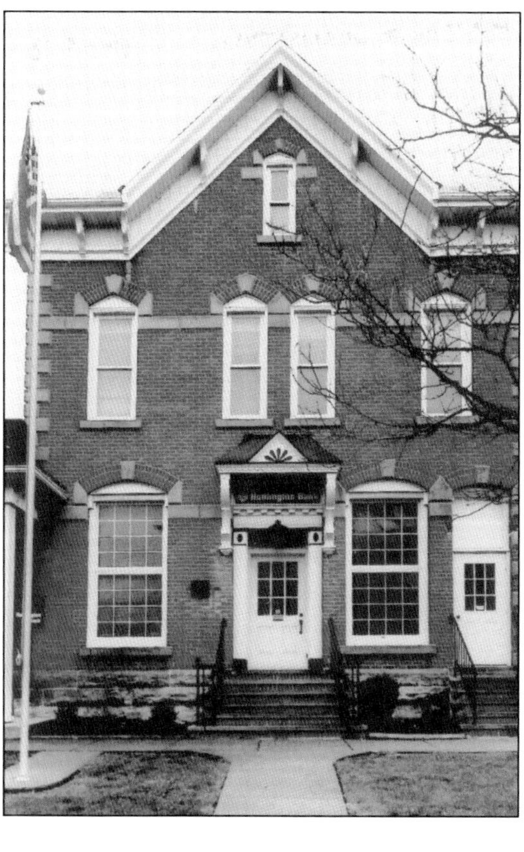

The Boughton, Ford & Co. bank opened its doors in 1871 under the governance of George Boughton, H.H. Ford, George H. Ford, and R.N. Ford. After 32 years, the bank suddenly closed in 1903. Numerous local businesses like Parmalee Bros. and the Burton Handle Company, as well as townspeople, were financially devastated by the abrupt end of the bank. Charges of embezzlement and fraud were brought against the Fords, but none could be proven. (Courtesy of Geauga County Historical Society.)

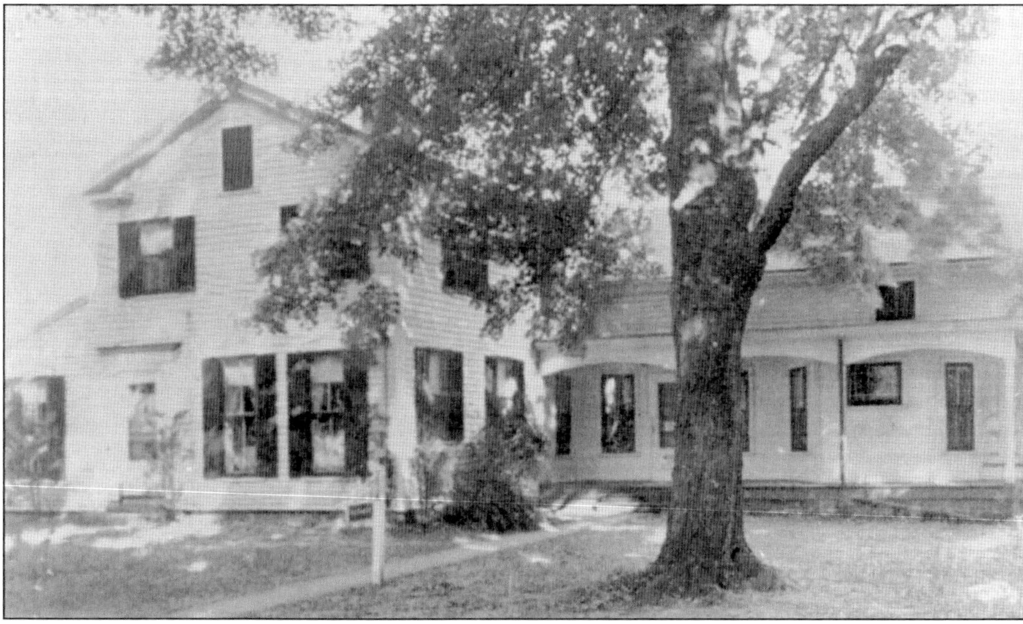

Edward Griswold and Silas Gaylord, pioneers from Cheshire, Connecticut, were business partners dealing in tinware and brass kettles. Griswold built a shop for their business on East Park in 1834, and the following year, he built this residence, which still stands today. Eventually, it was purchased by respected village physician Dr. William Albert Reed. (Courtesy of Geauga County Historical Society.)

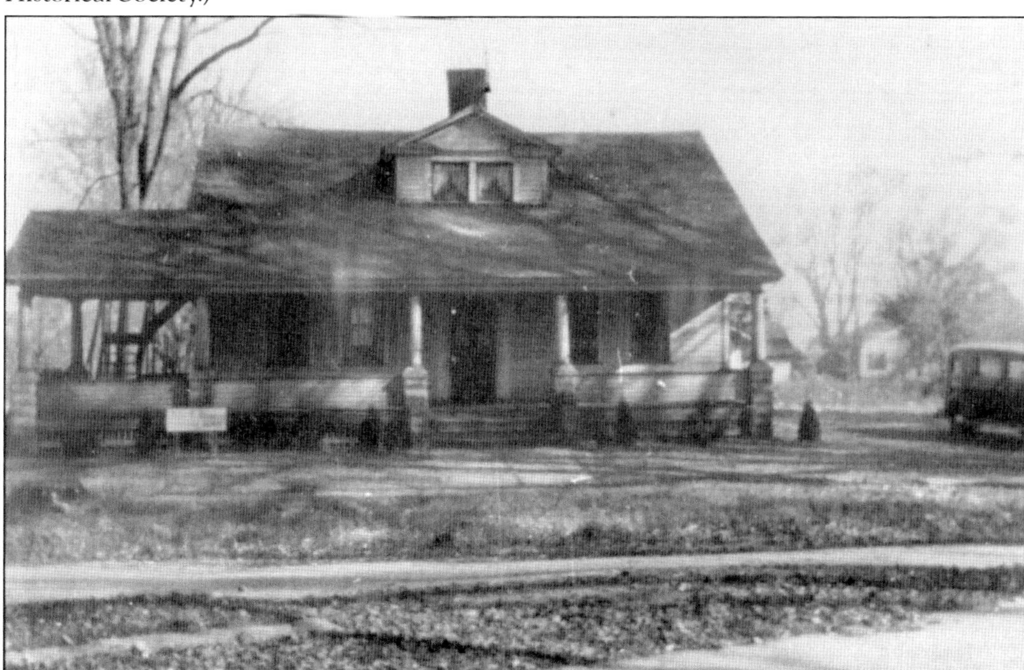

As Griswold built his house, Silas Gaylord erected his house right next door. Gaylord's house became John Dingman's home and funeral parlor in the mid-1900's. (Courtesy of Geauga County Historical Society.)

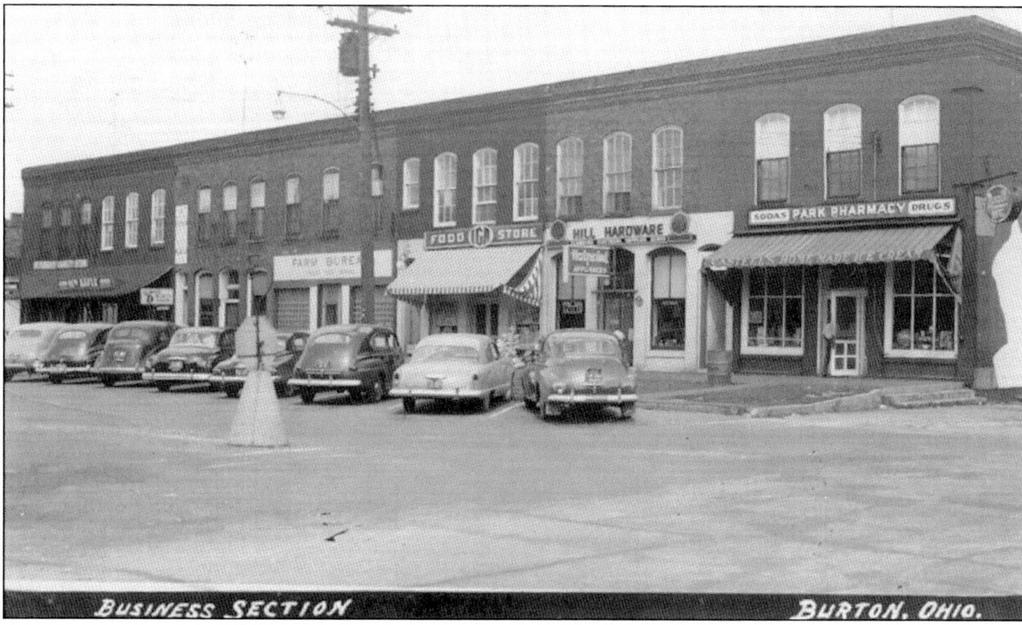

The east commercial block of North Cheshire Street (Main Street) consists of seven separate storefronts. The block as it appears today was constructed in 1872 and 1873 following a treacherous fire that eviscerated several wood-frame commercial buildings in 1871. (Courtesy of Elizabeth A. Cupp.)

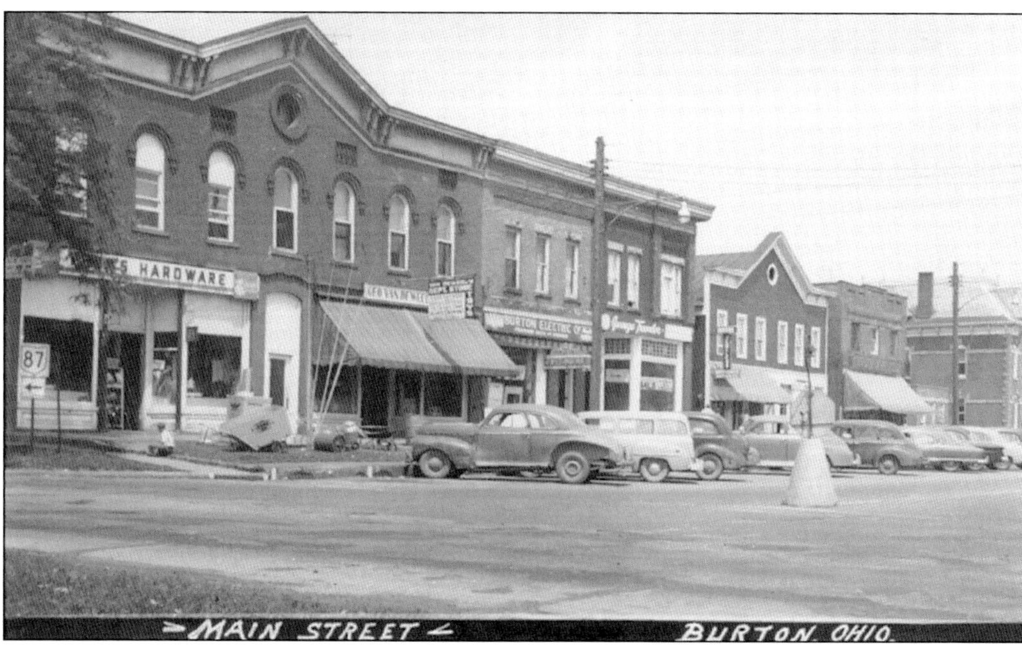

At the time this photograph was taken, only four buildings stood on the west block of North Cheshire Street. The popular Parmalee Bros. Hardware store occupied the southernmost building in 1881. Other businesses at various times included the clothier Tuttle and Thrasher, Ludlow Groceries, and another grocery owned by Fred Talcott. (Courtesy of Elizabeth A. Cupp.)

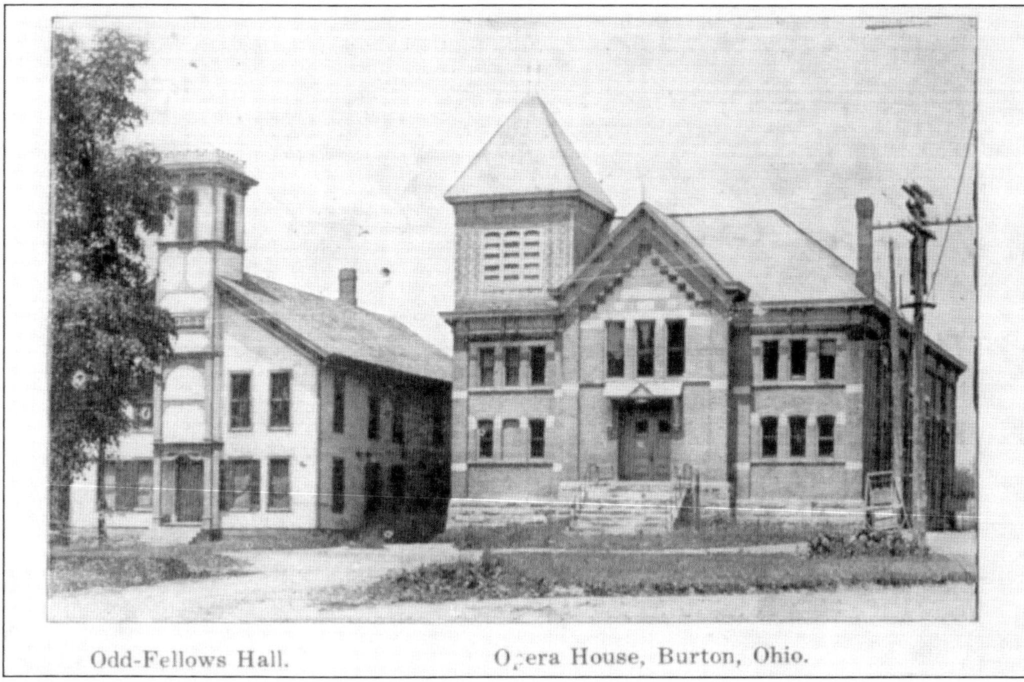

The second town hall, built in 1881, also served as an opera house. Political debates were the main event held at the town hall, but a variety of other activities transpired there, such as high school graduations and motion picture screenings. In 1957, the structure was converted into a firehouse for the Burton Fire Department, which had previously resided in the basement of the building. (Courtesy of Geauga County Historical Society.)

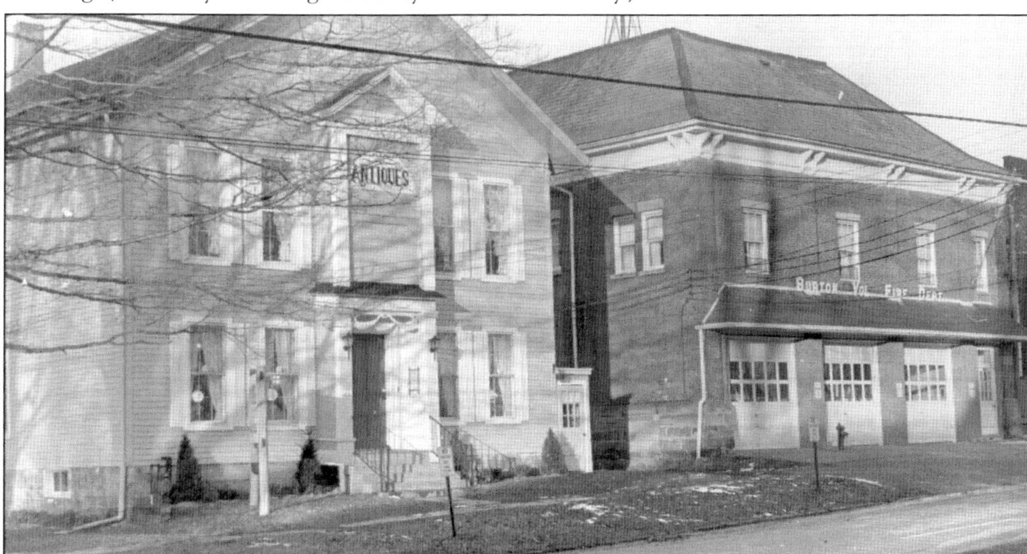

Initially constructed for use as a union school in 1868 for $4,000, this building would eventually serve as the lodge for the local chapter of the Independent Order of Odd Fellows (IOOF). Burton Central High School was established in 1866 after voters supported it in a special election. The upper story was utilized for high school, while the lower floor contained two schoolrooms used for a primary and an intermediate grade. (Courtesy of Geauga County Historical Society.)

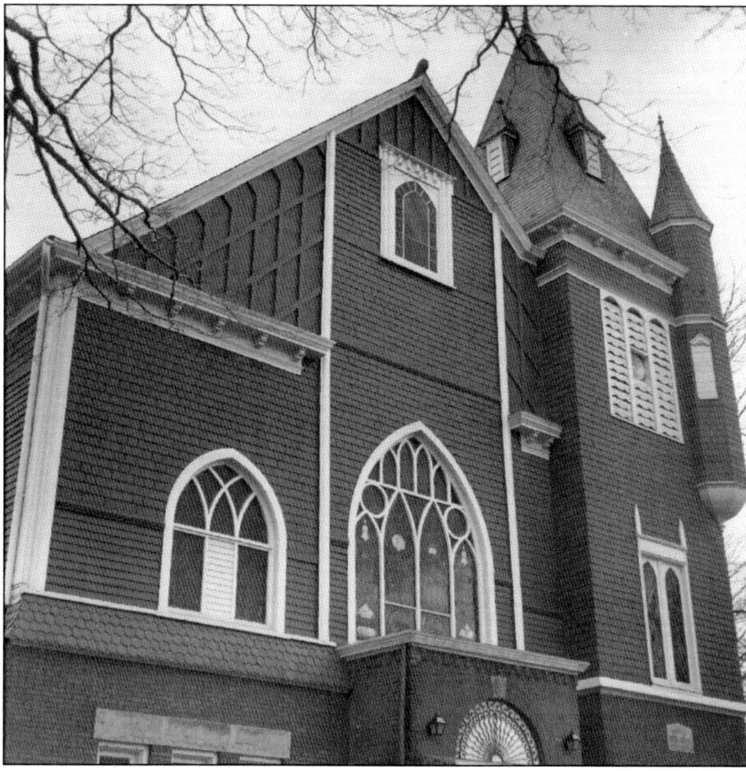

The Burton Congregational Church was organized on August 22, 1808, by Rev. Enoch Burt. The 10th Congregational church founded in Ohio, it is also one of the longest continuously running churches in the state. The church was erected in 1836 and has received numerous modifications through the years, including the addition of an educational wing in 1954. (Courtesy of Geauga County Historical Society.)

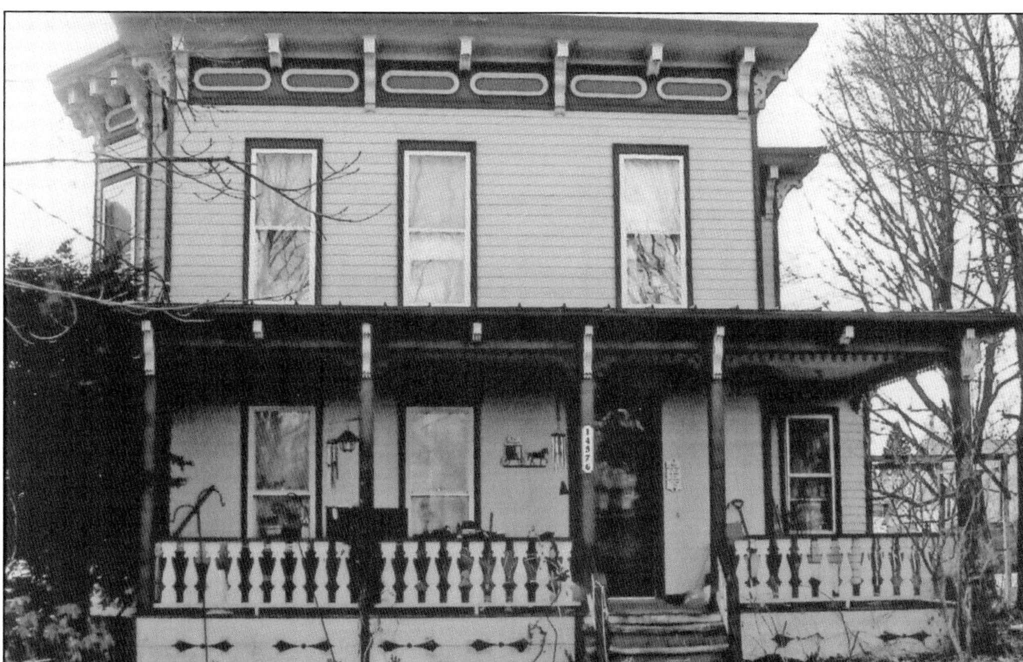

The Herenden house is next to the library on West Park Street. (Courtesy of Linda Natco on behalf of Little Pond Publishing.)

The Ohio General Assembly authorized the construction of the Central School, which was completed in 1884. For 53 years, this building was used for primary, intermediate, and high school classes. In 1936, a new high school was erected, and the Central School was converted into the Burton Public Library. (Courtesy of Special Collections, Michael Schwartz Library, Cleveland State University.)

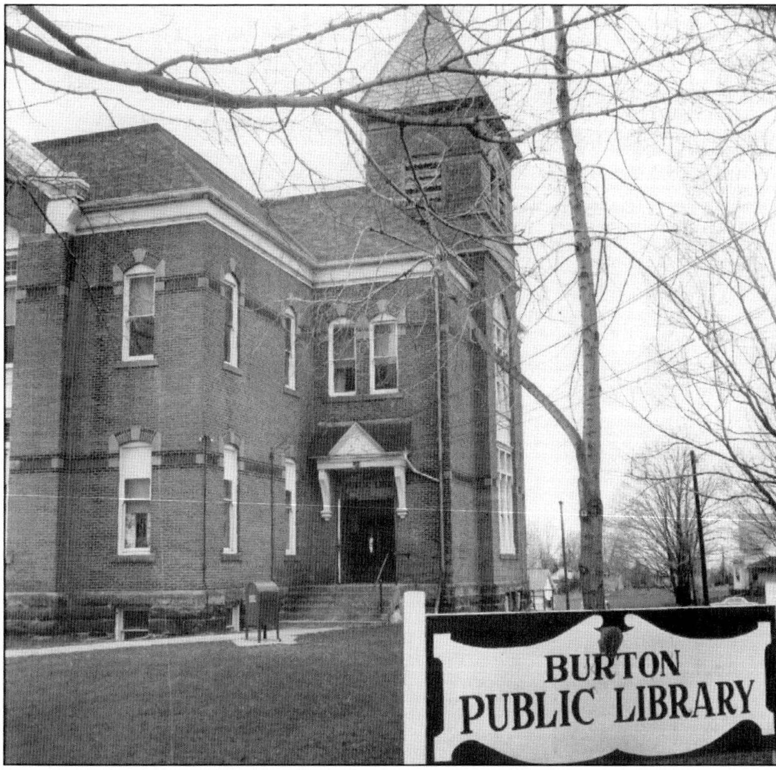

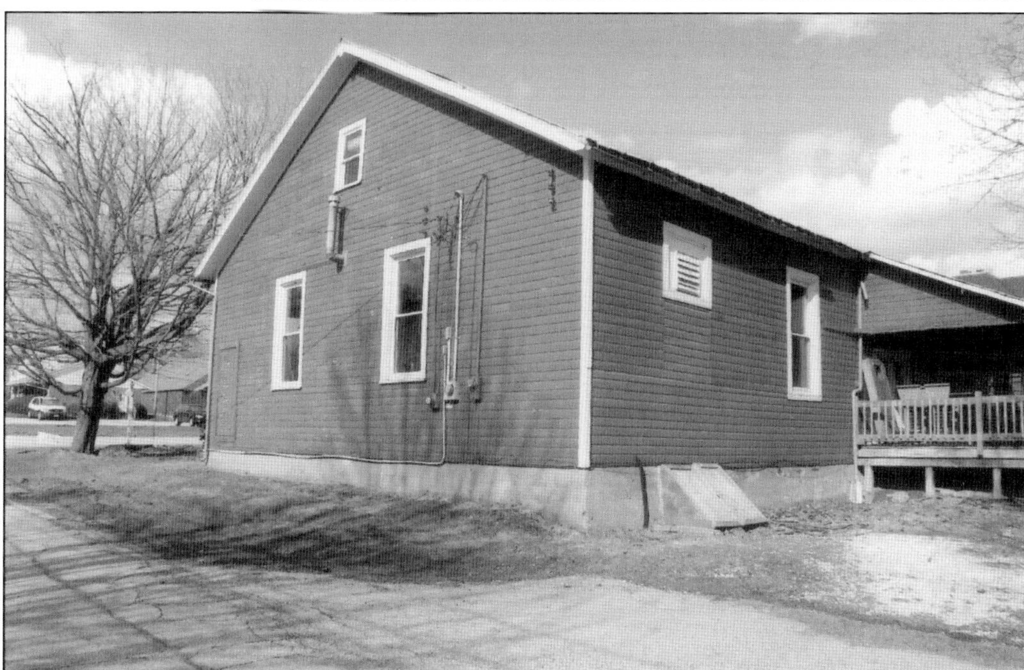

Constructed in 1920, this building was initially a school gymnasium. Today, it is the arts center located behind the Burton Public Library. (Courtesy of Linda Natco on behalf of Little Pond Publishing.)

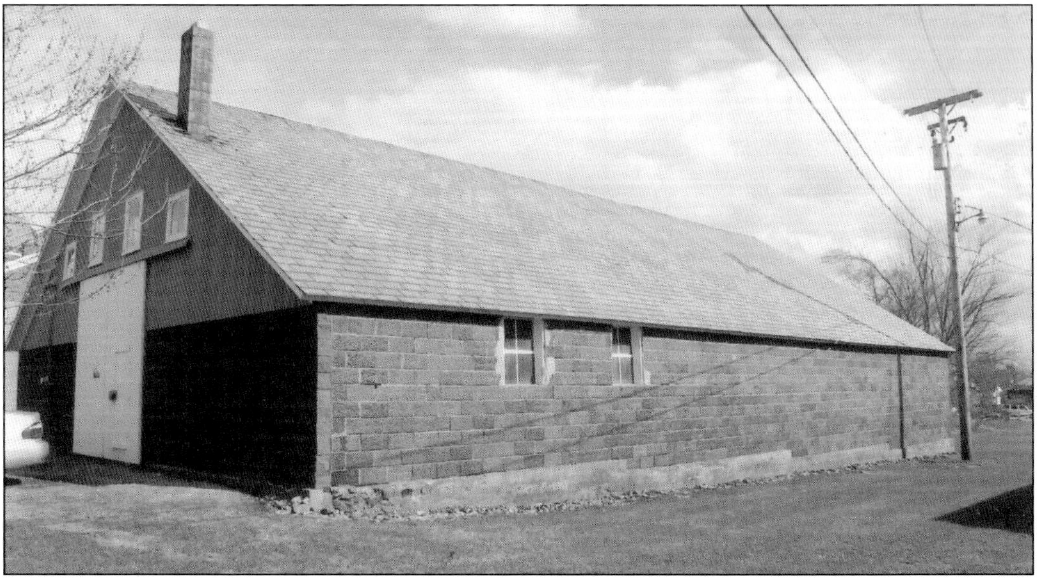

This town barn, located behind the Congregational Church, was raised in 1910 and officially dedicated on August 25. It could not have been built without the sponsorship of the Civic Improvement Society and the participation of the townspeople. The unusual barn was constructed of tile block and featured a low-gabled roof. The main purpose for the barn was to temporarily store horses while their owners shopped in the town. (Courtesy of Linda Natco on behalf of Little Pond Publishing.)

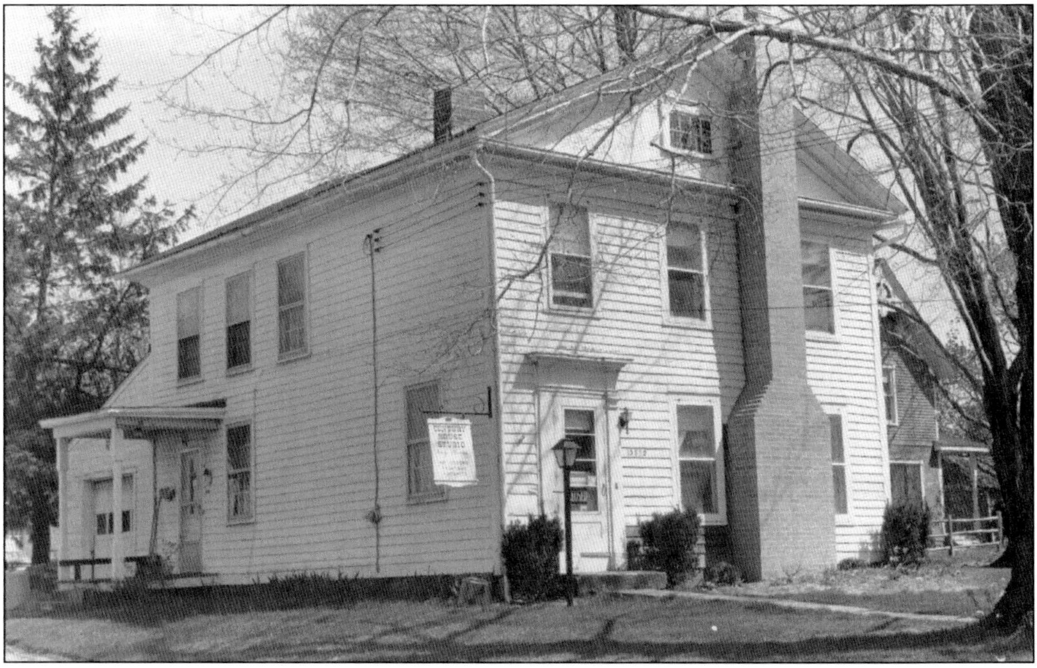

The Beach house, situated at 13810 Spring Street on the corner of Spring and Cheshire Streets, was constructed in 1832. While still at its original location, Richard Beach ran a general store in an adjoining wing that was lost in the relocation. The house was later moved father down Spring Street to its present location. (Courtesy of Geauga County Historical Society.)

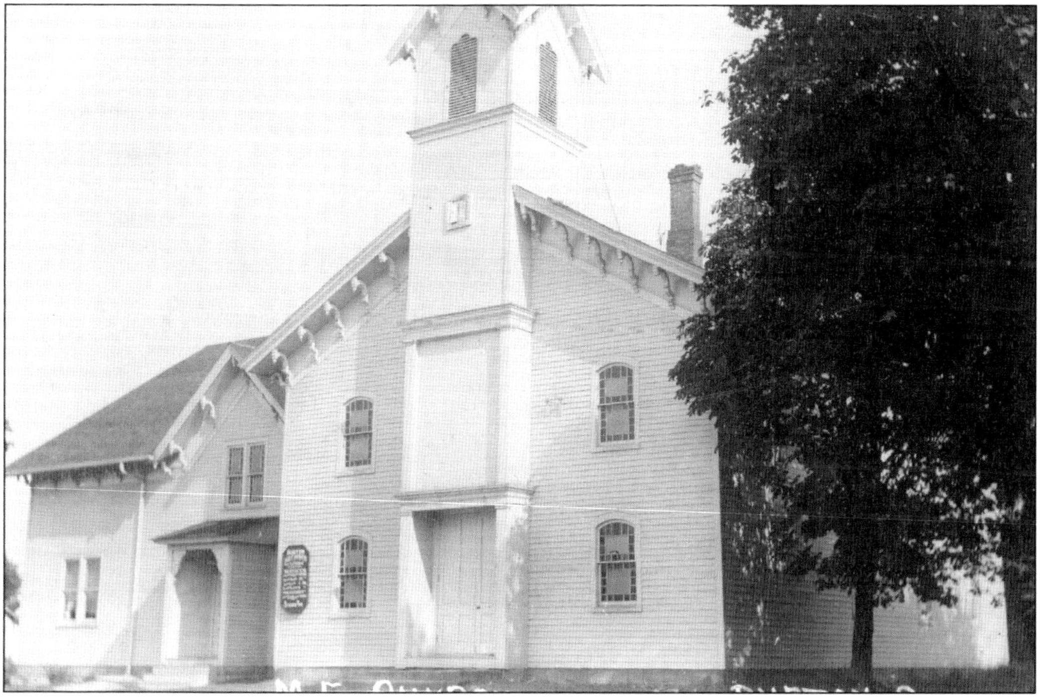

The Methodist Episcopal Church in Burton was formed between 1806 and 1811. Members of the congregation met in private homes until the church was built in 1845. The church occupied this building for exactly 100 years; Assembly of God Church made it their new home in 1945. (Courtesy of Geauga County Historical Society.)

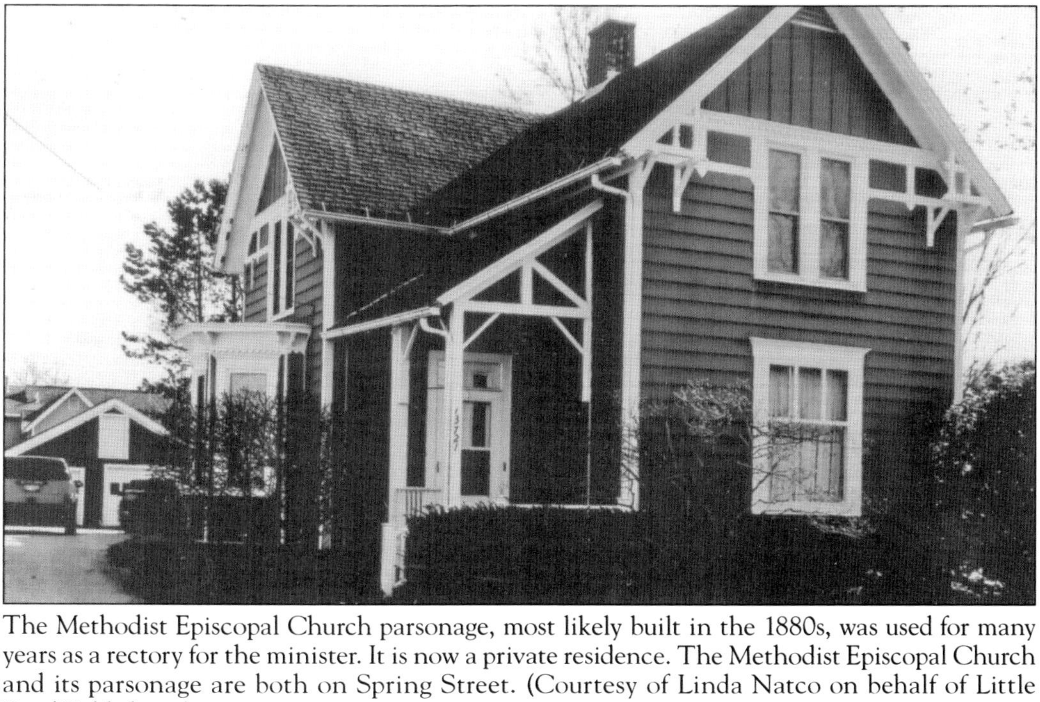

The Methodist Episcopal Church parsonage, most likely built in the 1880s, was used for many years as a rectory for the minister. It is now a private residence. The Methodist Episcopal Church and its parsonage are both on Spring Street. (Courtesy of Linda Natco on behalf of Little Pond Publishing.)

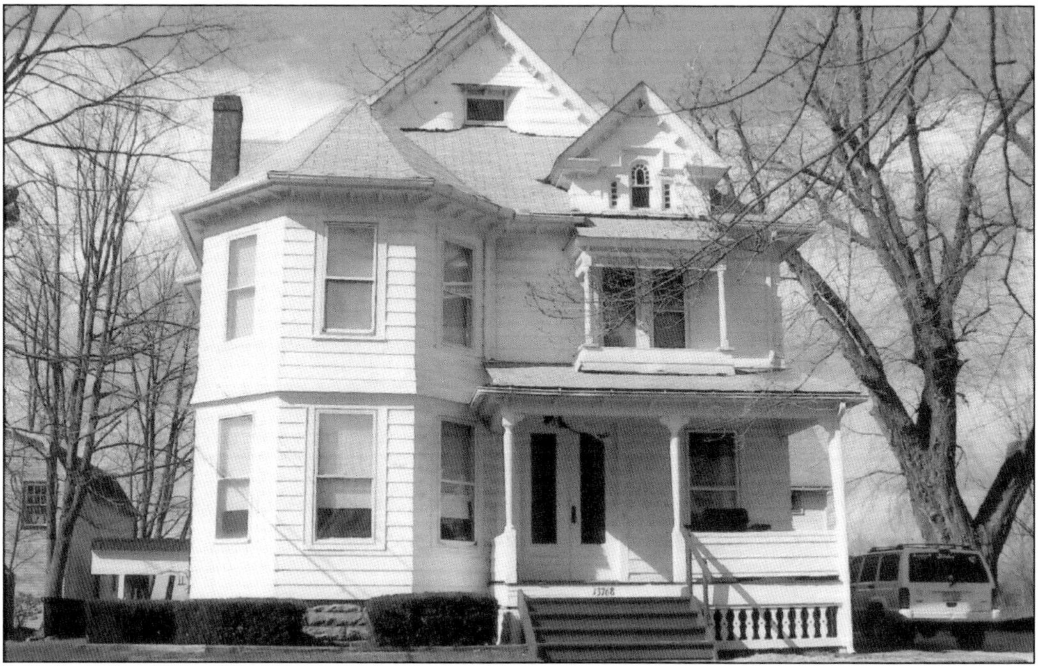

The Canfield house at 13768 Spring Street is a beautiful example of transitional Queen Anne/ Colonial Revival style. (Courtesy of Linda Natco on behalf of Little Pond Publishing.)

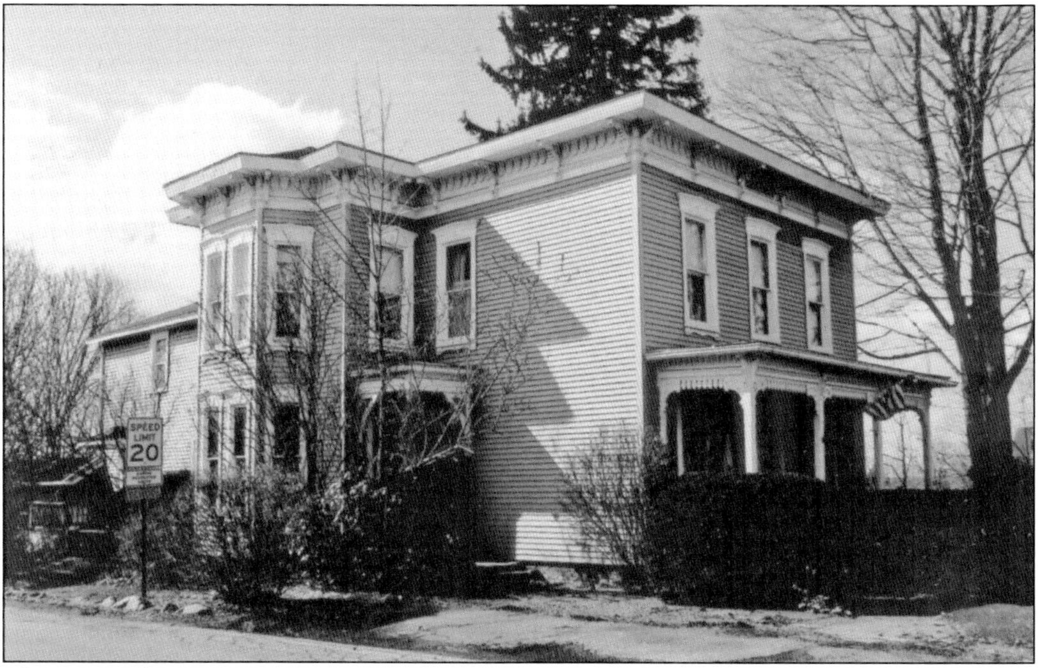

The Dayton house, an exquisite example of the Italianate architectural style, is at 14472 North Cheshire Street. The Dayton family were among the first settlers in Burton, arriving in 1805, although this house was not built until 1875. The house is on the corner of North Cheshire Street and Ford Lane. (Courtesy of Linda Natco on behalf of Little Pond Publishing.)

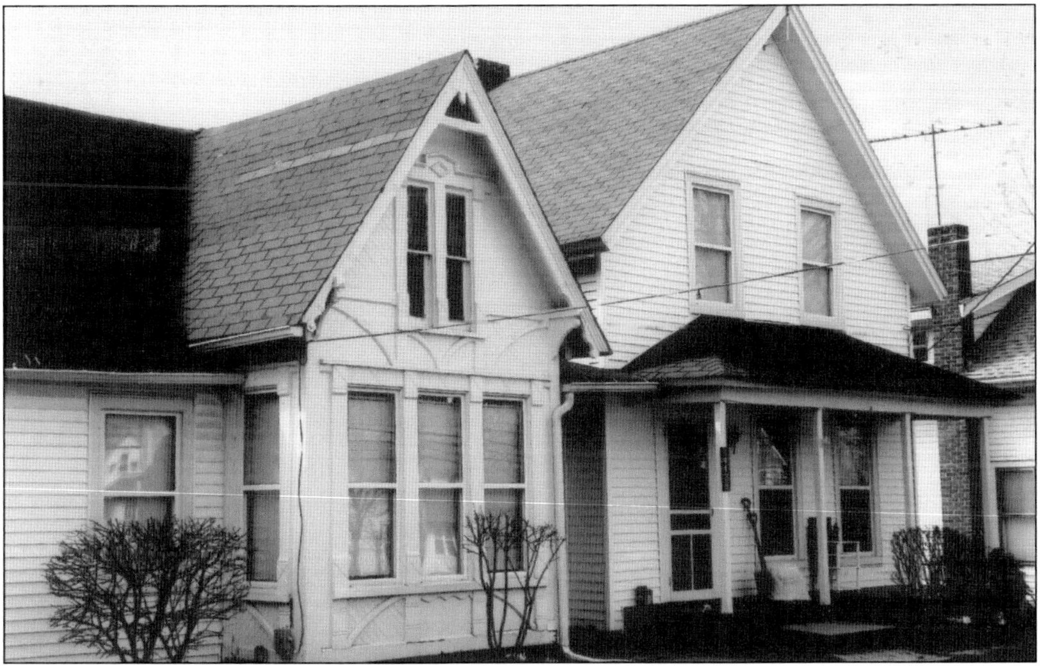

Another unique addition to the Burton Village Historic District is the Cay house, on North Cheshire Street, featuring a projecting gabled section in the middle. The exact date of the home's construction is unknown, but it was built before 1875. Little is known about the original owner except that his name was W. Cay and he was most likely a relative of William Cay, who bought land in Burton in 1833 and passed away in 1846. (Courtesy of Linda Natco on behalf of Little Pond Publishing.)

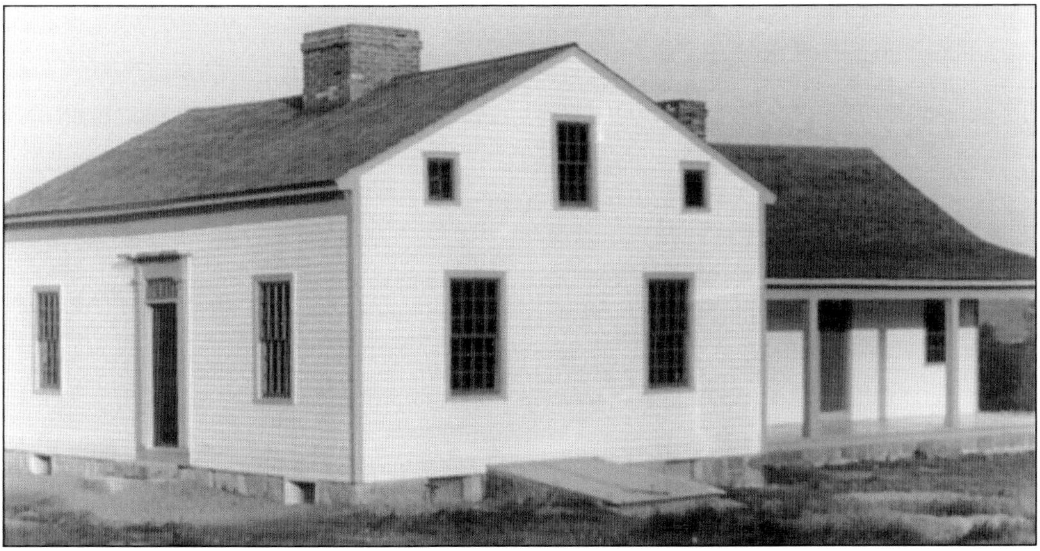

John Cook was born in Cheshire, Connecticut, in 1782. He and his family moved to Burton in 1806 along with the Hitchcocks. He built this home in 1807, making it the first frame house constructed in Burton. Masonic meetings were probably held here in the early 1800s. The Cook house was later moved to the Century Village Museum. (Courtesy of Linda Natco on behalf of Little Pond Publishing.)

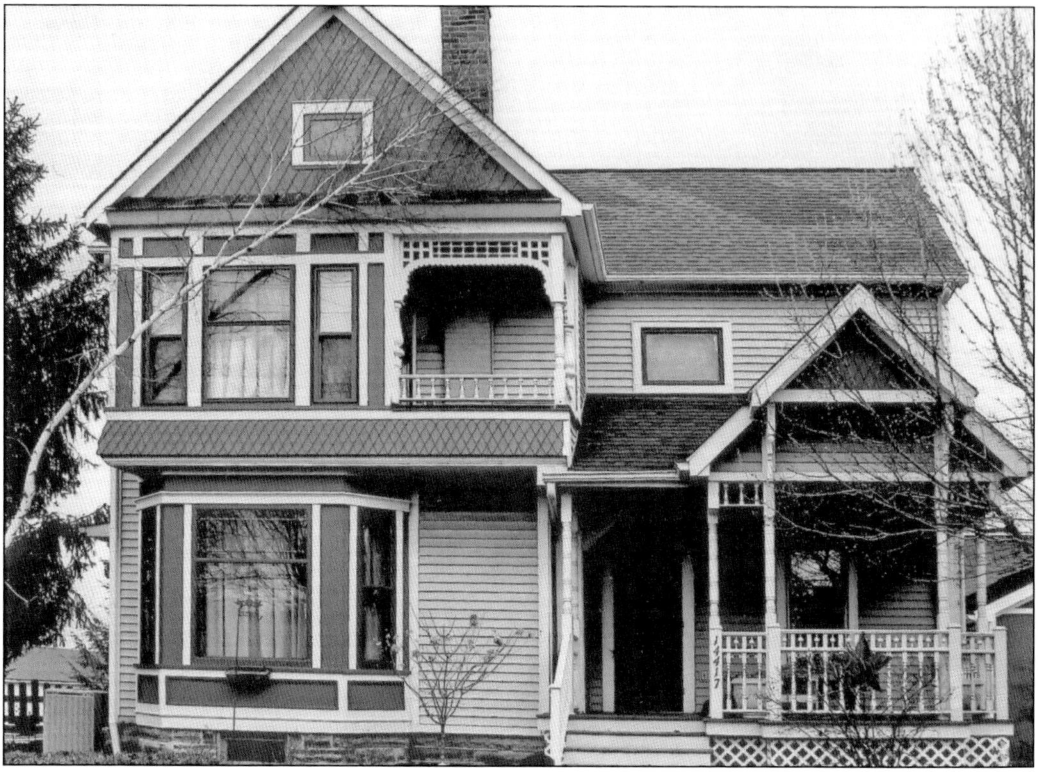

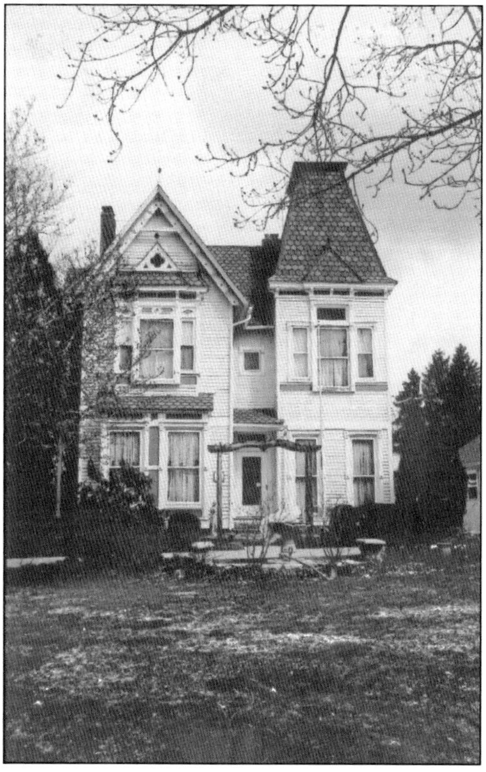

Brothers Charles H. and Arthur Johnson crafted the wildly popular Burton Bobs, sleds which were produced by the Burton Handle Company. Charles was in the lumber business and may have participated in the construction of his house, which was built before 1899. (Courtesy of Linda Natco on behalf of Little Pond Publishing.)

Peter Hitchcock Jr. constructed this house in 1882, relocating from his parents Peter Sr. and Nabby Hitchcock's abode. Hitchcock Sr. was the chief justice of the Ohio Supreme Court, among many other important accomplishments. (Courtesy of Linda Natco on behalf of Little Pond Publishing.)

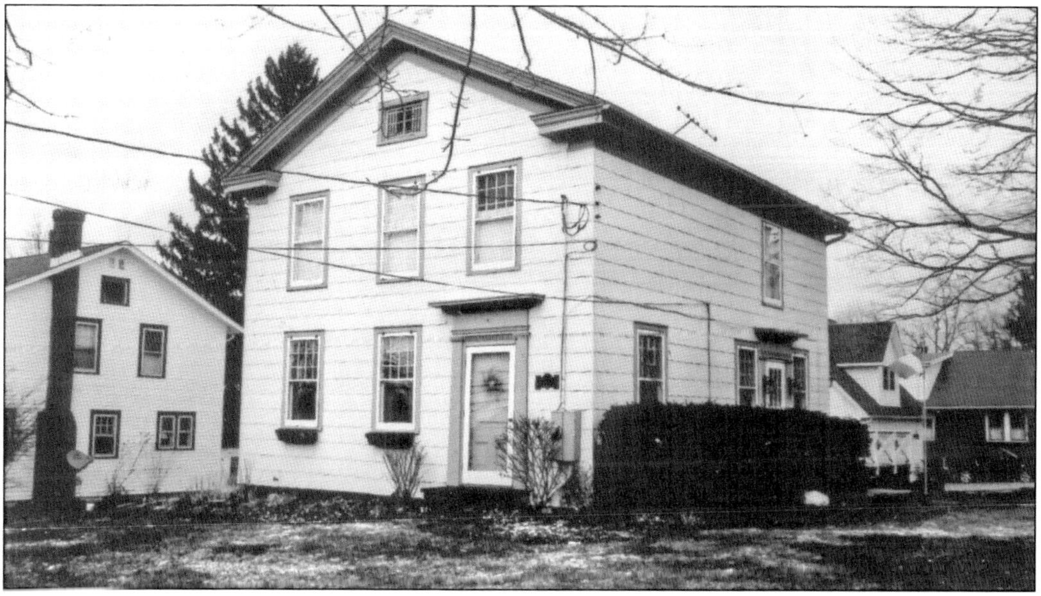

Dr. Sherman Goodwin, son of the respected Dr. Erastus Goodwin, was the proud owner of this Greek Revival house built in 1840. The younger Dr. Goodwin dutifully served as regimental surgeon for the Geauga County Militia, but fell ill, so he moved to the warmer climate of Texas to recuperate. (Courtesy of Linda Natco on behalf of Little Pond Publishing.)

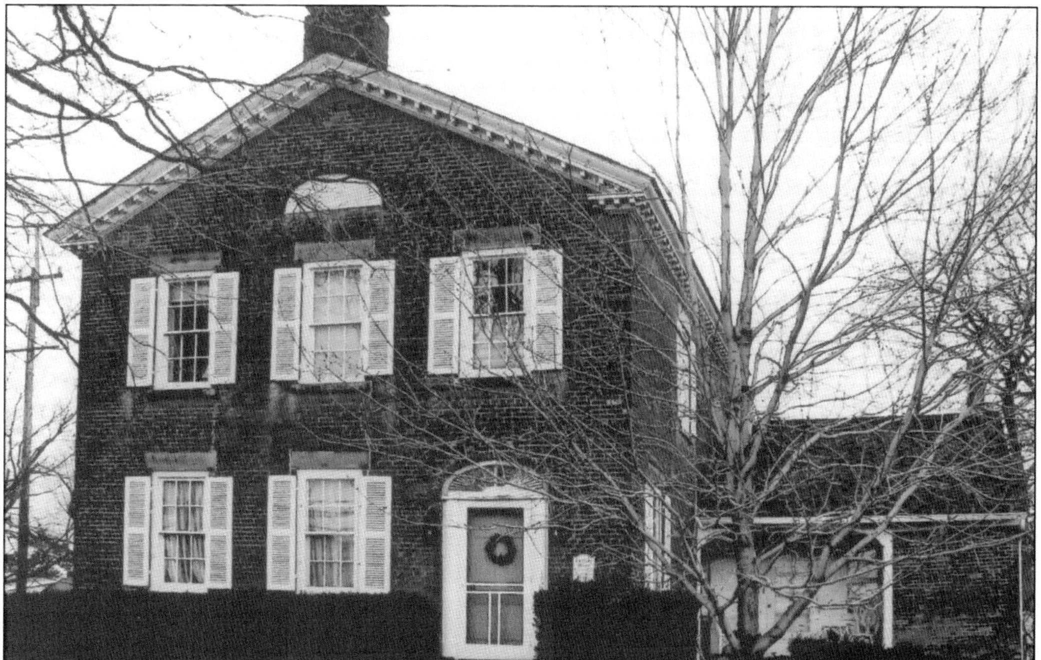

The patriarch of the Burton Goodwins, Dr. Erastus Goodwin, erected this brick house on the corner of North Cheshire Street and what would become Goodwin Street. One of the oldest houses in Burton, the first section was built in 1814, and the other section was added in 1828. In 1875, the house was honored with a listing on the National Register of Historic Places. (Courtesy of Linda Natco on behalf of Little Pond Publishing.)

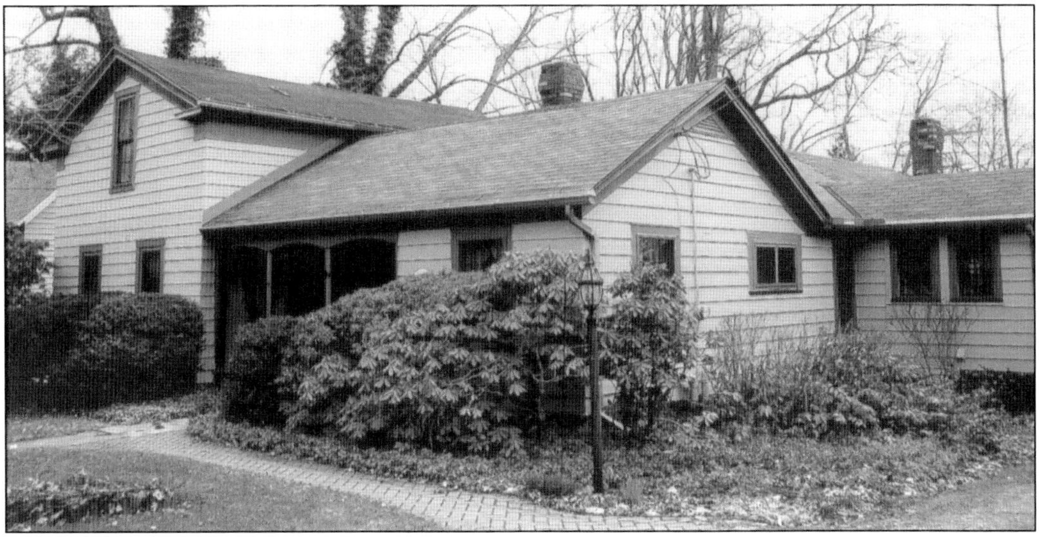

The third Goodwin house belonged to Erastus L. Goodwin Jr., the second son of Dr. Erastus Goodwin. This 1841 house, situated on the edge of his father's estate, is a classic example of the Upright and Wing–style house. (Courtesy of Linda Natco on behalf of Little Pond Publishing.)

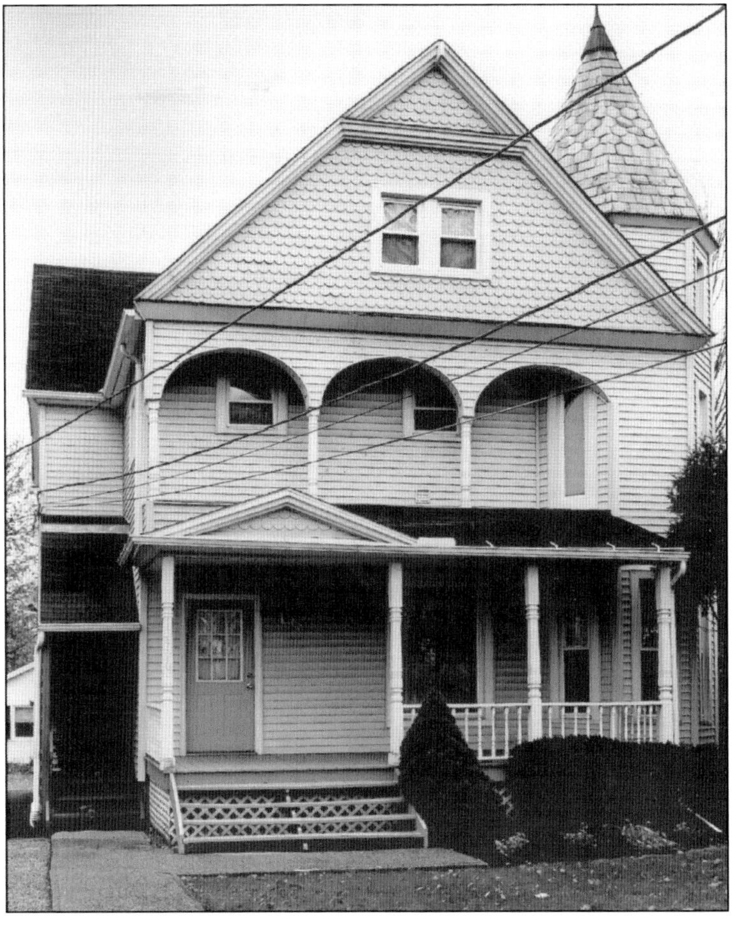

Henry Crittenden, a druggist and grocer, owned a store on the east side of North Cheshire Street. By the 1890s, Crittenden formed H.W. Crittenden and Son, a highly successful pharmacy. (Courtesy of Linda Natco on behalf of Little Pond Publishing.)

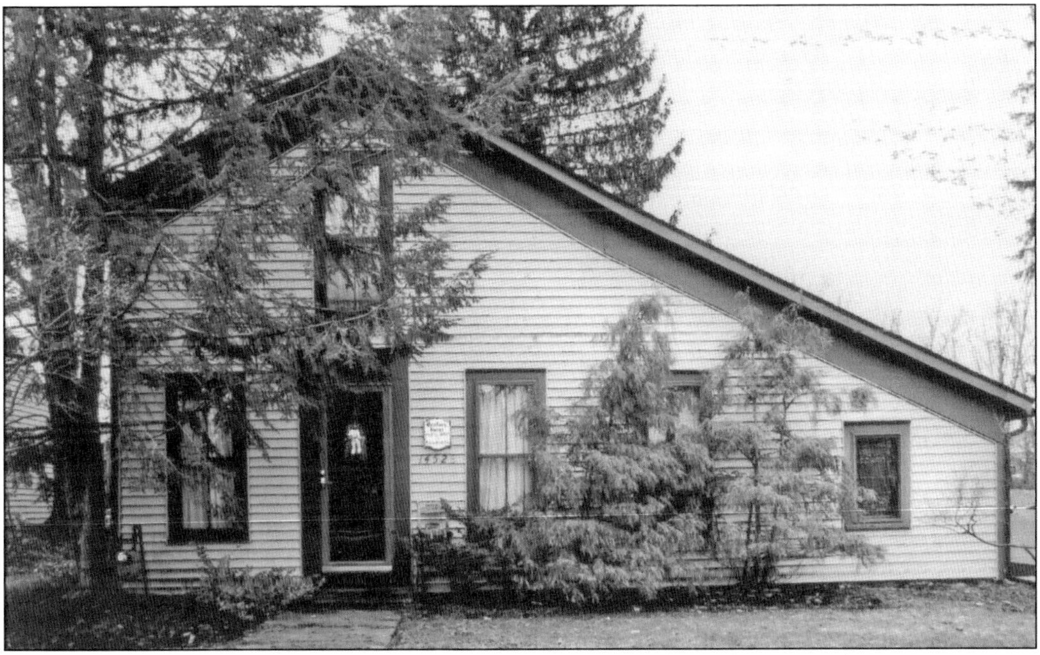

Garry Cramton (often spelled as "Crampton") was affiliated with two houses in the Burton Historic District. Cramton arrived in Burton from Connecticut in 1818, along with his parents and siblings, and owned this 1859 house, as well as multiple lots on Kirtland and Hickox Streets through the middle part of the 20th century. In addition to his landholdings, he also owned and operated a tavern and a grocery store. (Courtesy of Linda Natco on behalf of Little Pond Publishing.)

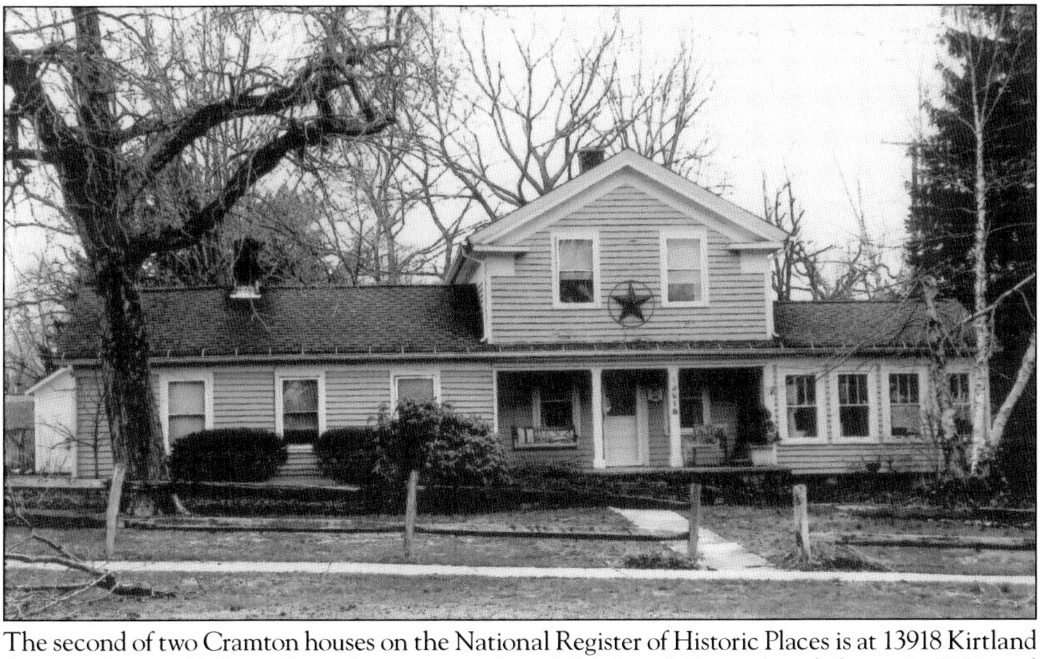

The second of two Cramton houses on the National Register of Historic Places is at 13918 Kirtland Street in Burton Village. Garry Cramton purchased this Greek Revival–style house in 1854, and it remained in the family for several generations. Cramton died in this house at the ripe old age of 90. (Courtesy of Linda Natco on behalf of Little Pond Publishing.)

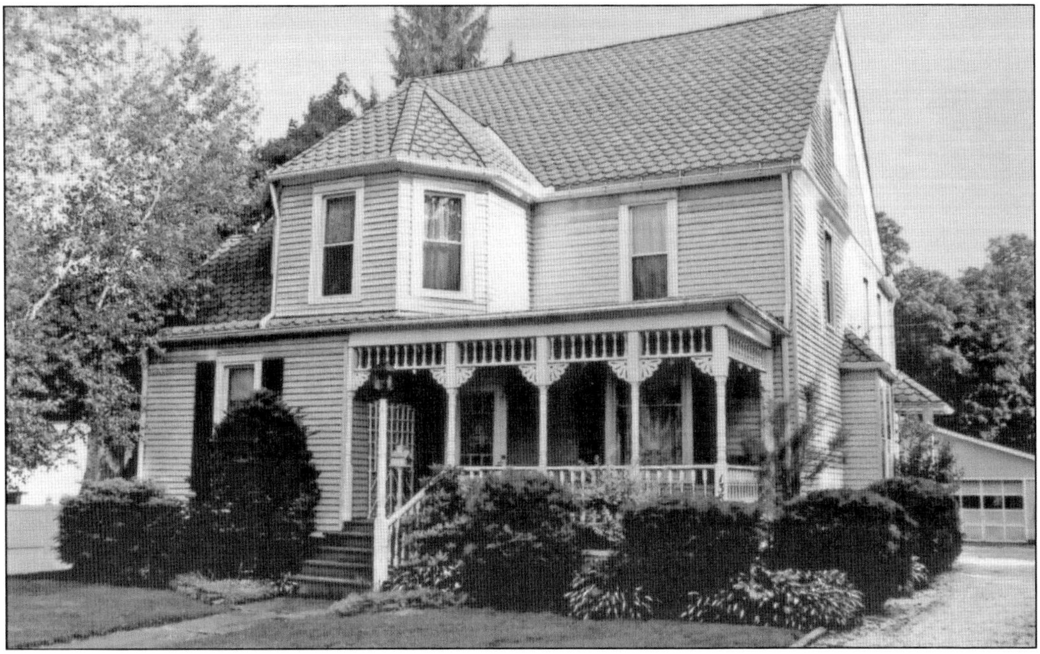

Henry C. Tuttle was elected mayor of Burton in 1899 and proudly served the village for four years. He moved to Burton in 1873 with his uncle Silas Gaylord, the business partner of Edward Griswold. Tuttle was an extremely successful businessman as well, running a couple of prosperous enterprises, most notably Tuttle and Harmon, which dealt in maple sugar and syrup. The Tuttle house in on Kirtland Street. (Courtesy of Linda Natco on behalf of Little Pond Publishing.)

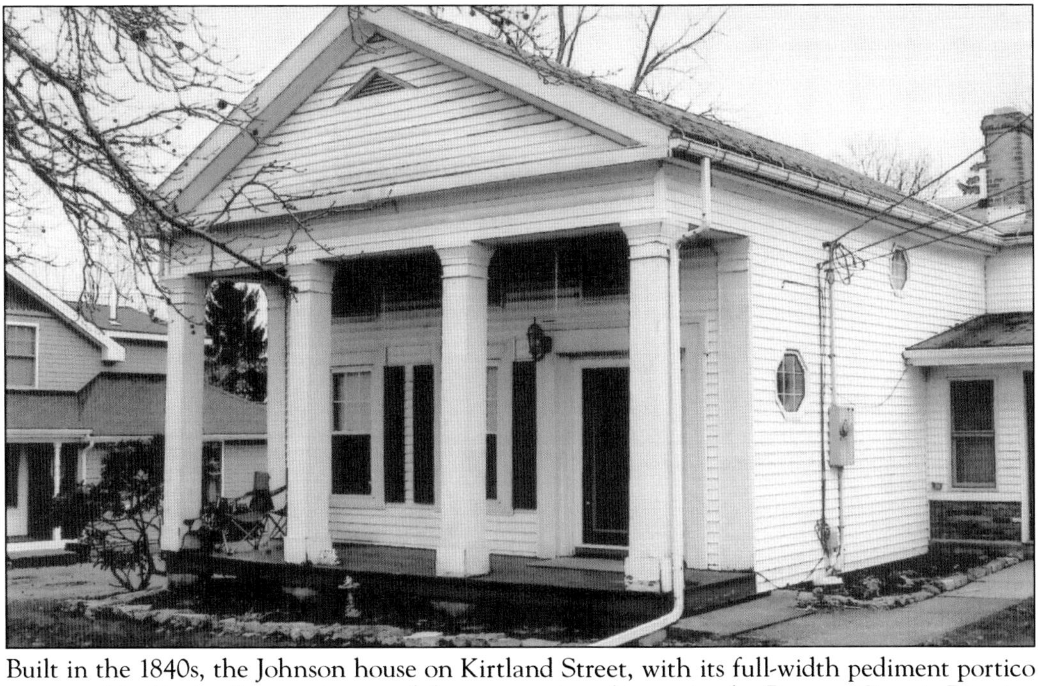

Built in the 1840s, the Johnson house on Kirtland Street, with its full-width pediment portico supported by Doric pilasters, is one of the most unique homes in the Burton Historic District. (Courtesy of Linda Natco on behalf of Little Pond Publishing.)

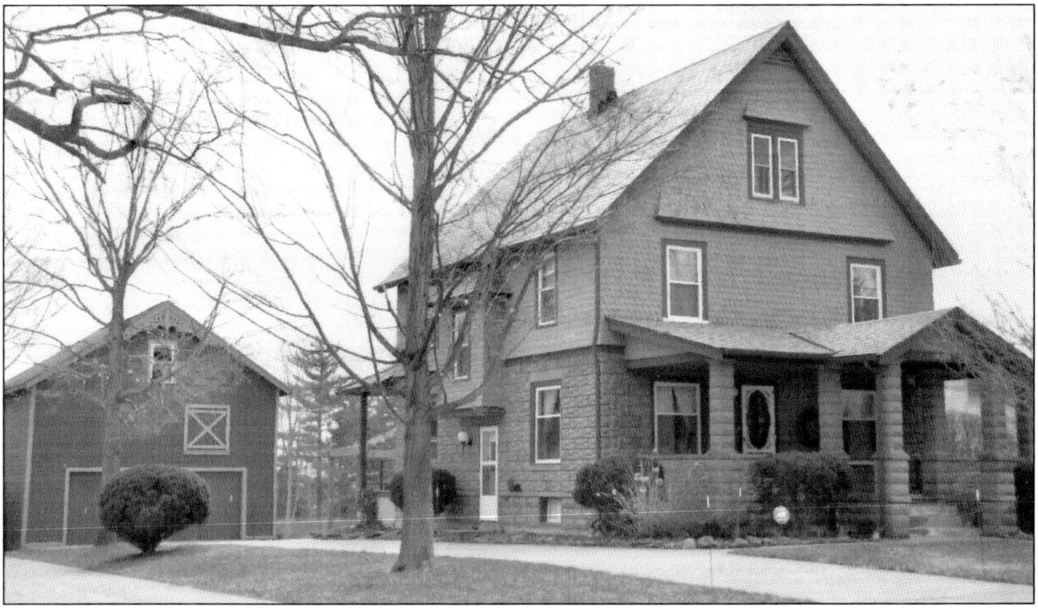

This house, located at 14593 Hickox Street, is an idiosyncratic 2.5-story home, with concrete blocks for the first story and wood shingles completely covering the second story. The unique creation offers a refreshing glimpse of diversity to the Burton landscape. (Courtesy of Linda Natco on behalf of Little Pond Publishing.)

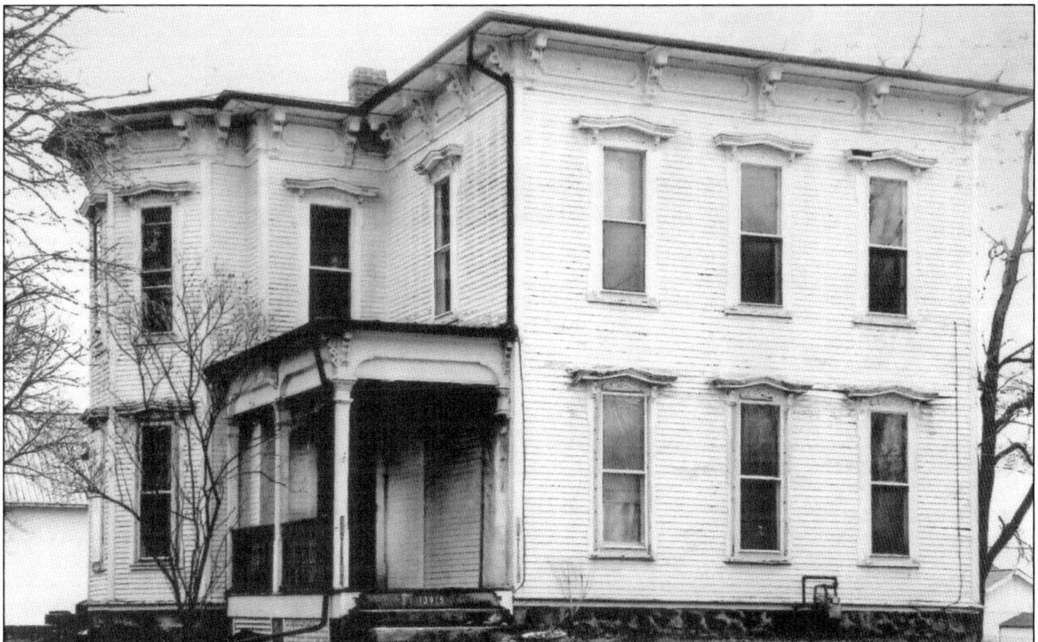

Eleazar Hickox's daughter Marietta and her husband, Samuel Humiston, owned this Italianate-style frame house built in 1868. It is located on the Century Village Museum grounds. The elder Hickox was a prominent and influential member of Burton society and constructed one of the most important buildings in the village: the Hickox Brick. (Courtesy of Linda Natco on behalf of Little Pond Publishing.)

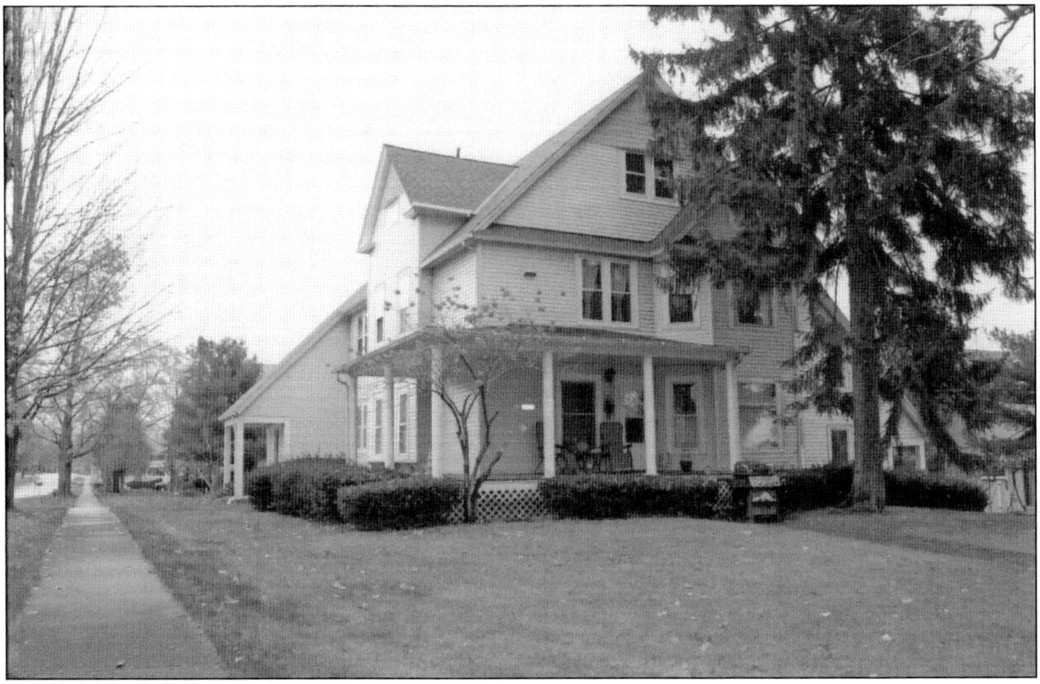

A descendant of John and Easter Ford, C.E. Ford owned this spacious carriage house, built around 1880. The Ford family owned a substantial amount of property in Burton and wielded much influence and financial clout. (Courtesy of Linda Natco on behalf of Little Pond Publishing.)

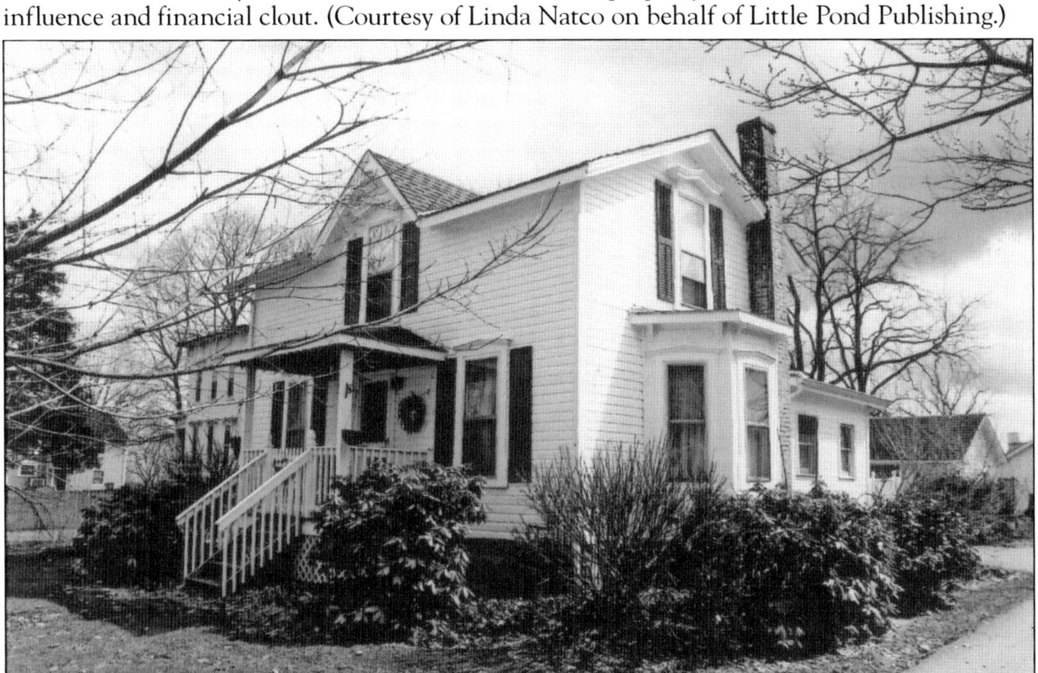

The M.E. Ford house features protruding window lintels, bay windows, and eave brackets associated with the Italianate style, as well as a Gothic-influenced steep front-facing gable bay. (Courtesy of Linda Natco on behalf of Little Pond Publishing.)

Three

The Great Geauga County Fair

It is only fitting that the oldest continuously held county fair in Ohio would reside in the oldest settlement in Geauga County. Opened in 1823, it has not missed a year, even during the Civil War or the world wars. The inaugural fair was held in Chardon with subsequent fairs alternating between Burton and Chardon until the mid-1800s, when it was moved to the fairgrounds in Burton permanently.

The "Great" was added to the name in the mid-1900s to signify its status as the granddaddy of all Ohio county fairs. Every Labor Day weekend, a quarter-million people venture to the fairgrounds in Burton to delight in the various attractions that include more than 12,000 exhibitors and over 2,000 animals. Traditional events, such as cattle shows, mingle with motocross shows and Total Nonstop Action Wrestling (TNA) matches to unite the past with the present. One of the most distinctive attractions of the fair is the Great Geauga County Fair Band, which was formed in 1938 and is the only county fair band in Ohio. The fair also has two historically significant buildings on the grounds: the Domestic Arts Hall, built in 1856 and reconstructed in 1889, and the Flower Hall, erected in 1890. Both structures are listed on the National Register of Historic Places.

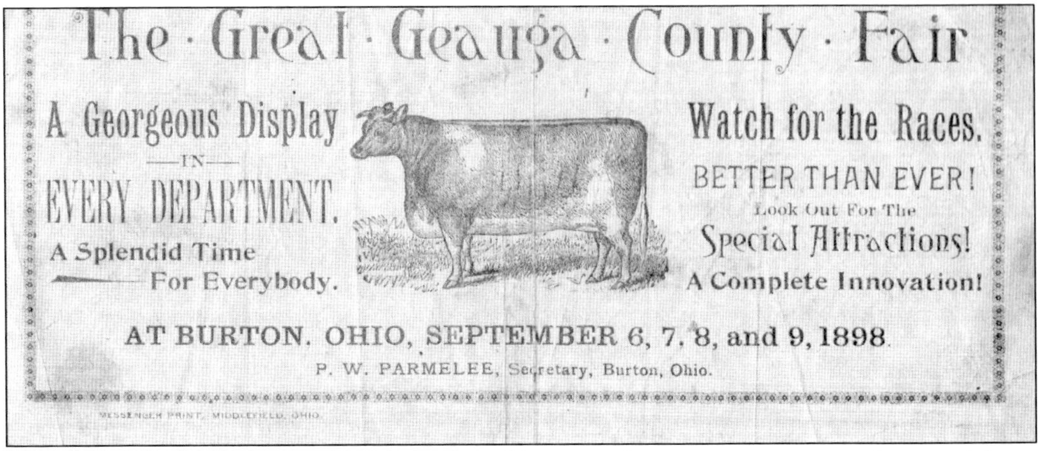

In its infancy, the fair bore only a slight resemblance to the present version, as the initial focus was almost entirely on agriculture and livestock. This 1898 flyer celebrated the 75th anniversary of the fair. (Courtesy of Burton Public Library.)

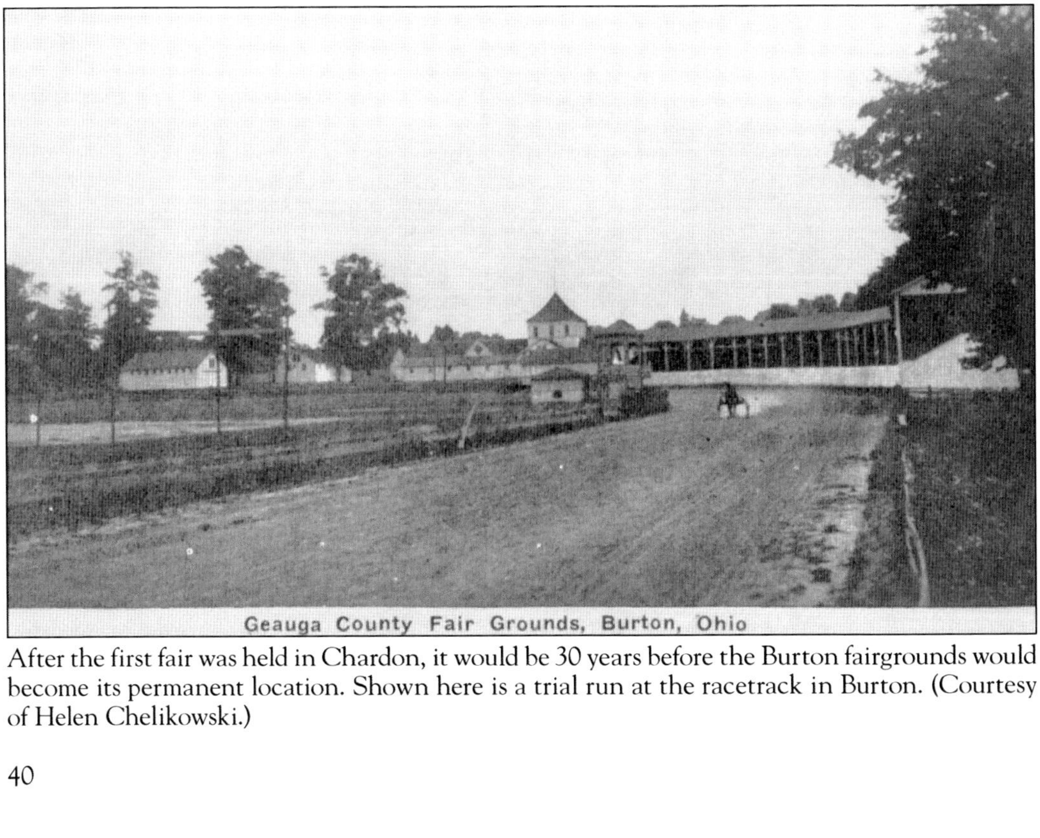

After the first fair was held in Chardon, it would be 30 years before the Burton fairgrounds would become its permanent location. Shown here is a trial run at the racetrack in Burton. (Courtesy of Helen Chelikowski.)

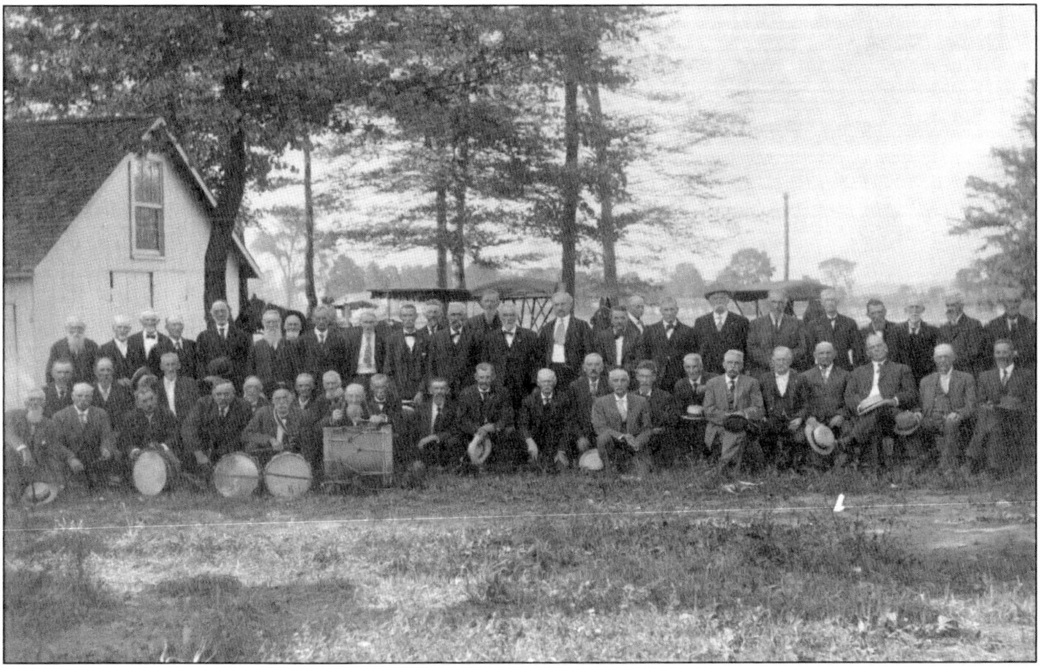

This large group of men poses for a photograph at the Geauga Fairground in 1914. This is possibly the Citizens Band, formed in 1871. The *New York Sun* described the band as "leading citizens, gentlemen of means and musical ability." They were in high demand for a variety of special engagements, including commencements and political rallies. (Courtesy of Geauga County Historical Society.)

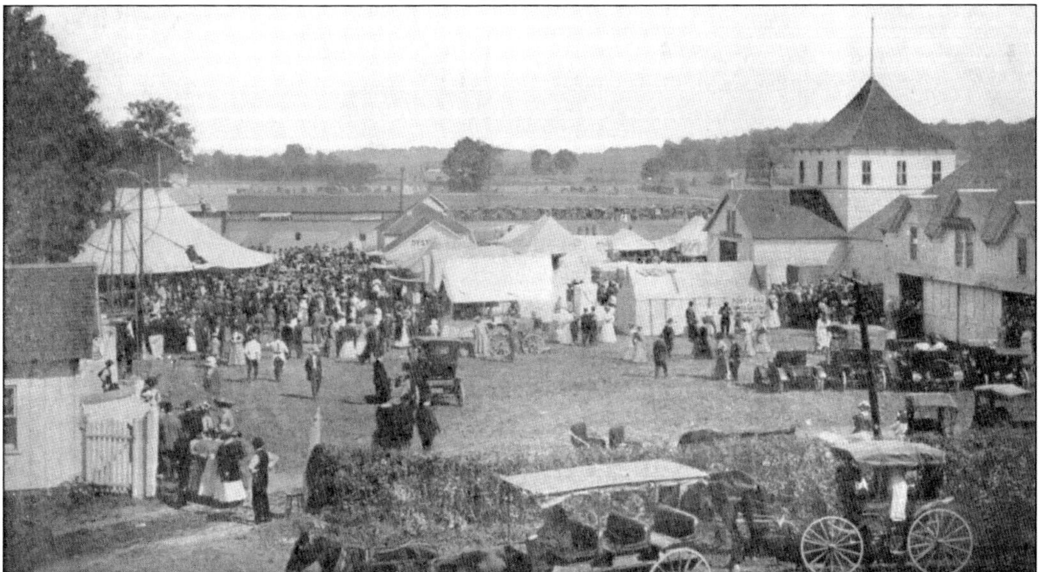

A Glimpse of Burton Fair.

This early-20th-century photograph illustrates the glaring differences from the modern county fair. Dandies in bowler hats abound as horse-drawn carriages chauffeur elegant and erudite citizens to and fro. (Courtesy of Burton Public Library.)

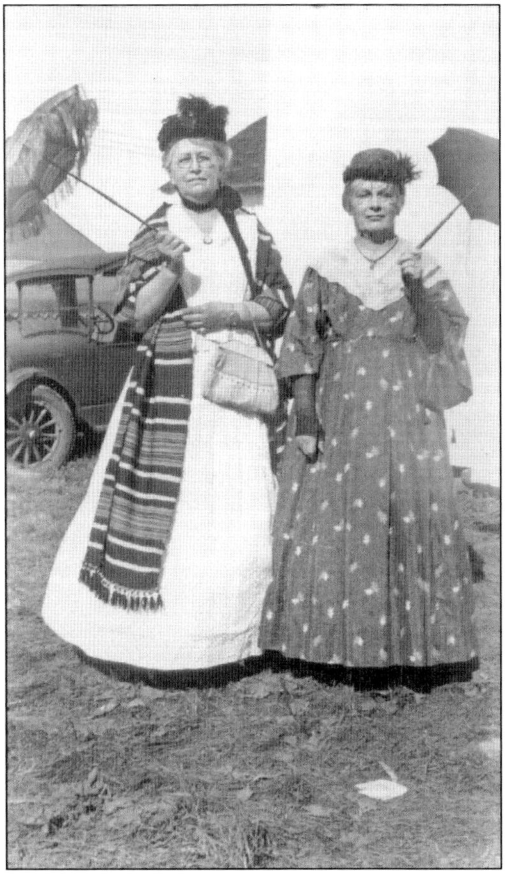

Unbeknownst to committee members and fairgoers, 1923 marked the 100th anniversary of the Geauga County Fair. The committee incorrectly identified 1931 as the fair centennial and commemorated it thusly. The error was later discovered and rectified by the time the 1953 history was published. Here, Laura Doolittle (left) and her sister Lottie Fox pose in dresses and parasols. Fox was the wife of G.B. Fox, a prominent member of Burton society. (Courtesy of Burton Public Library.)

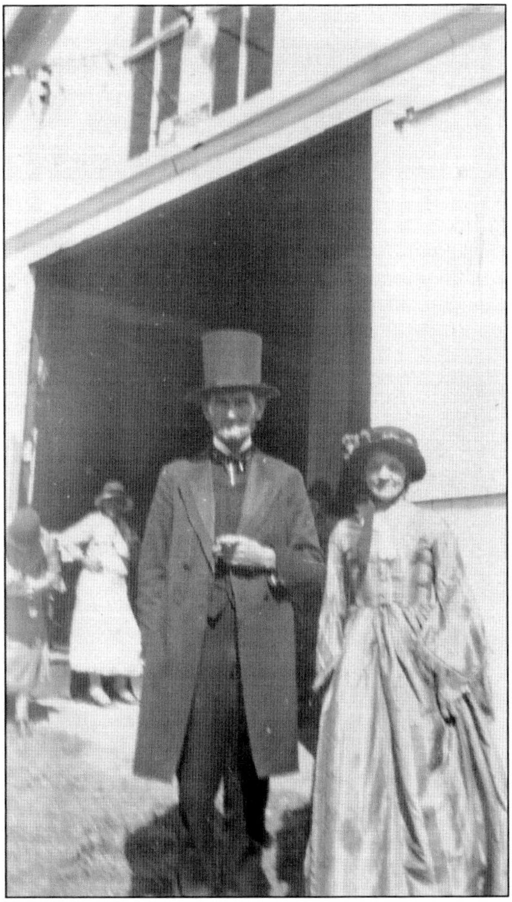

Fred and Mary Talcott, dressed as Pres. Abraham Lincoln and Mary Todd Lincoln, pose at the Geauga County Centennial Fair in 1931. Fred Talcott was a successful businessman in Burton, establishing the popular miniature golf course in Burton Park and owning a supermarket in the Burton business district for many years. (Courtesy of Burton Public Library.)

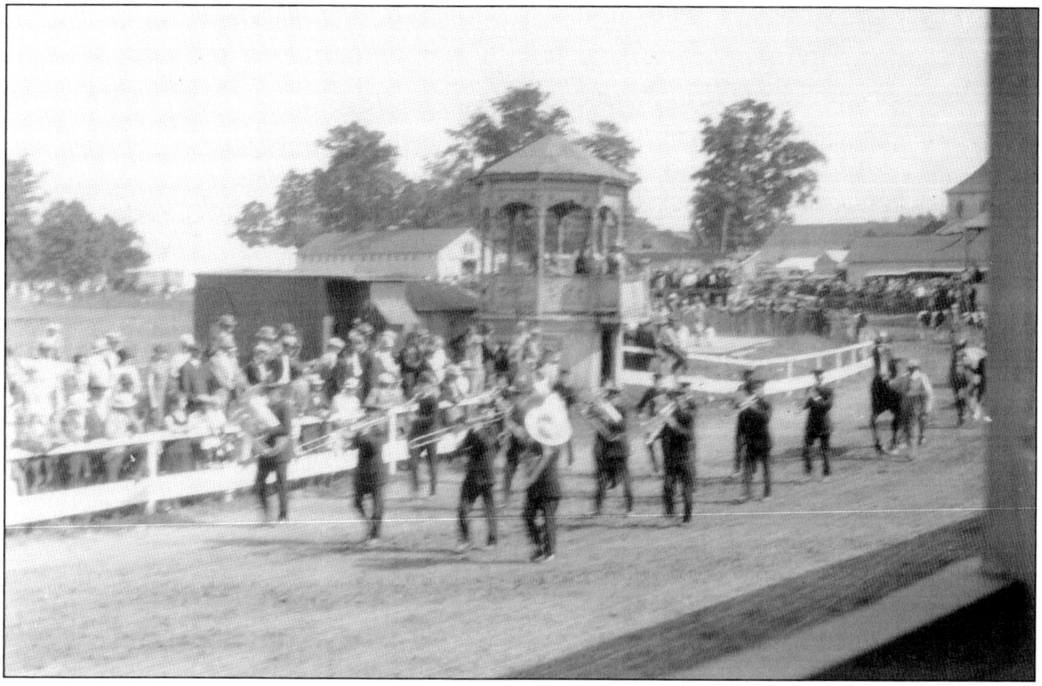

A marching band performs for the approving throng of fairgoers in 1936. Numerous marching bands have played at the fair since its inception, and all have delighted the attendees. (Courtesy of Mary L. Wilson.)

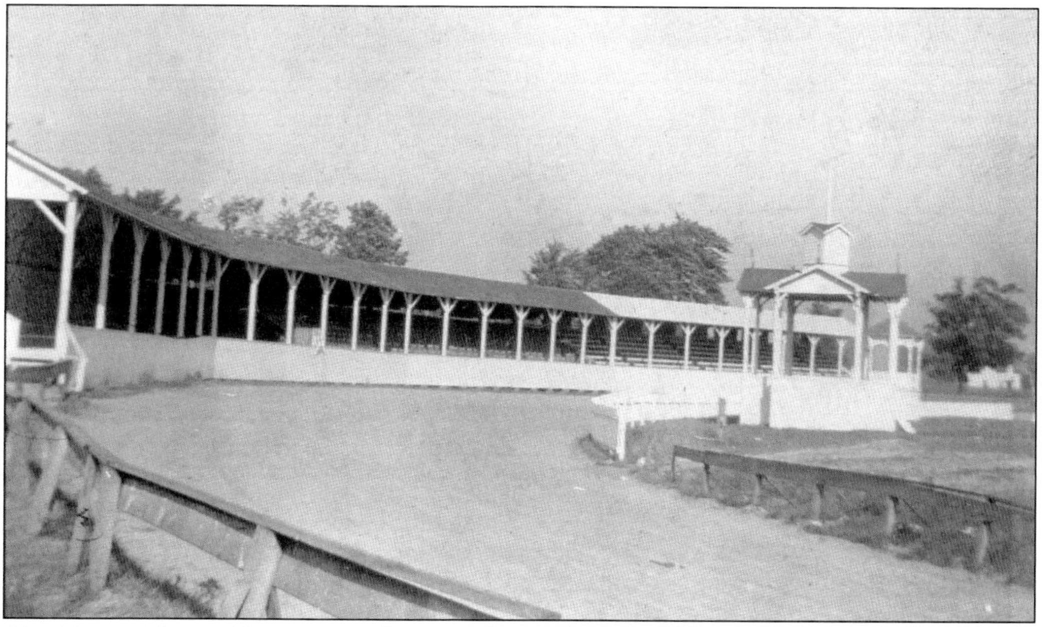

The Geauga County Fair is more than simply marching bands, agricultural exhibits, and fried food; it includes a smorgasbord of other entertaining attractions, such as harness racing. Horse racing has been sanctioned on the fairgrounds for many years, and a multitude of attractions have been added intermittently. Today, the fair offers many modern diversions, including motor sports and even professional wrestling. (Courtesy of Mary L. Wilson.)

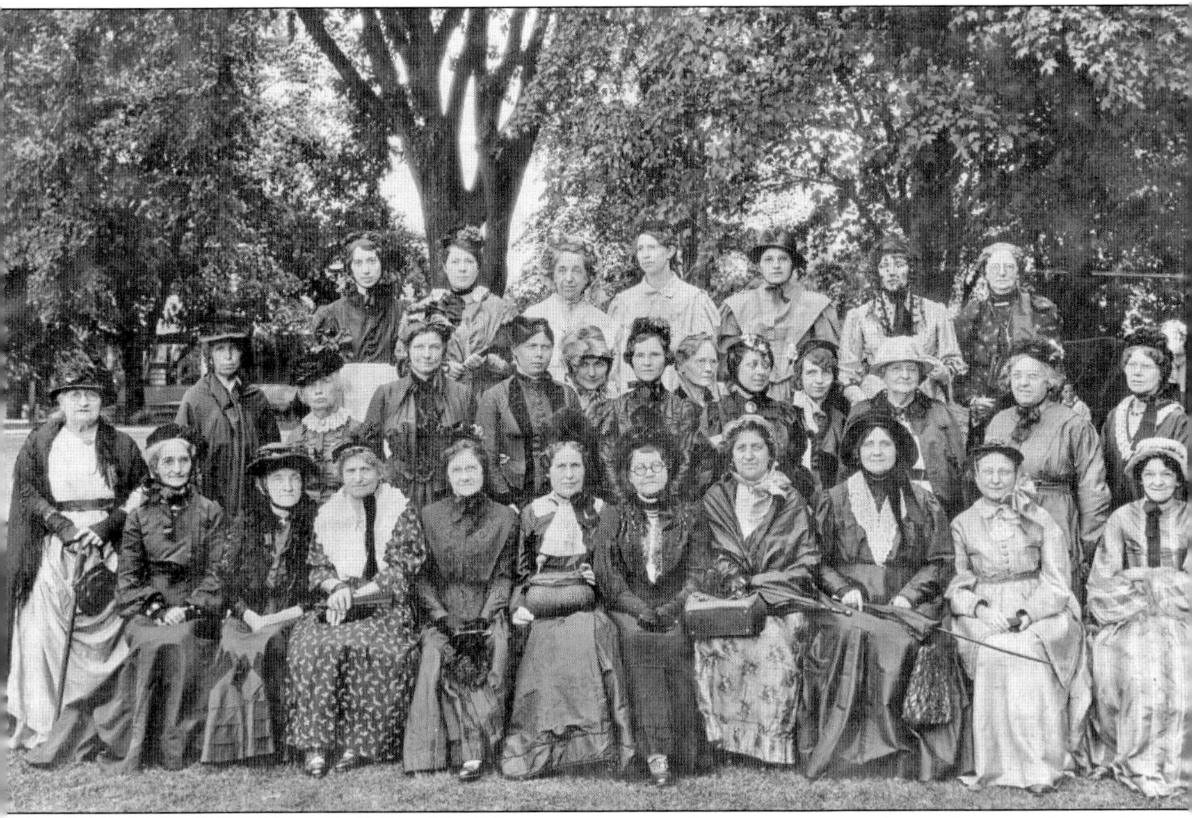

A ladies club takes time out of a pleasant summer afternoon to pose for a photograph on the fairgrounds in 1931. Beginning in the late 1800s, many prominent ladies organizations took root in Burton, including the Clio Club and the Tuesday Club. The women pictured here include Nellie Hickox, Ina Taylor, Nellie Carlton, Viette Norton, Mattie Adams, Abbie Shuart, Mary Goff, Mildred Russell, Carrie Ludlow, Dr. Teed Cramton, Lucy Talcott, Nettie Smith, Bertha Johnson, Marie Cary, Flora Truman, Margaret Thrasher, Lucy Stevens, Mrs. Peter Scholn, Hazel Canfield, Minnie Canfield, Grace Bigelow, Lottie Bittles, Willowie Beales, Gladys Gharky, Fay Owen, and Viola Kennedy. (Courtesy of Geauga County Historical Society.).

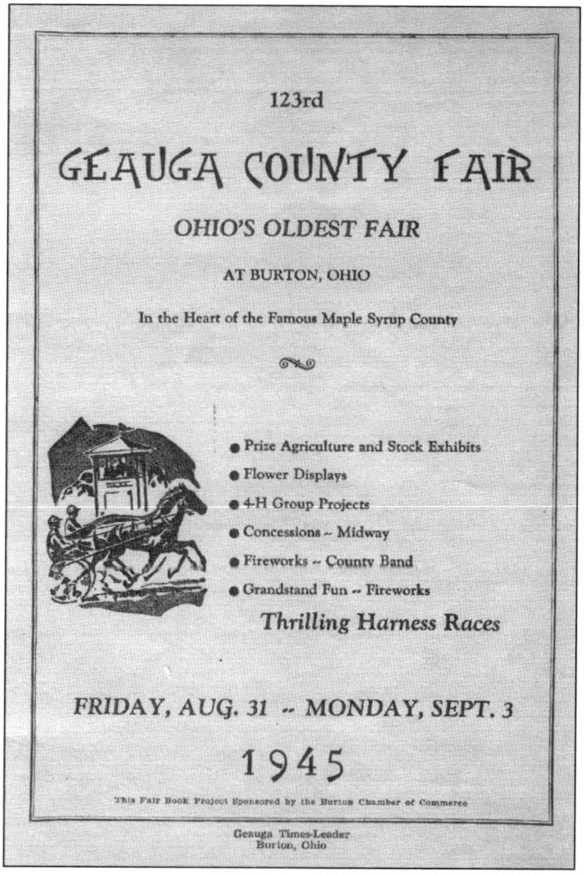

123rd

GEAUGA COUNTY FAIR

OHIO'S OLDEST FAIR

AT BURTON, OHIO

In the Heart of the Famous Maple Syrup County

- Prize Agriculture and Stock Exhibits
- Flower Displays
- 4-H Group Projects
- Concessions -- Midway
- Fireworks -- County Band
- Grandstand Fun -- Fireworks

Thrilling Harness Races

FRIDAY, AUG. 31 -- MONDAY, SEPT. 3

1945

This Fair Book Project Sponsored by the Burton Chamber of Commerce

Geauga Times-Leader
Burton, Ohio

The cover of the program for the 123rd Geauga County Fair in 1945 advertised a variety of exhibits and events, including flower displays, fireworks, and harness races. The townspeople were most likely in a celebratory mood that year since World War II had just ended. (Courtesy of the Burton Public Library.)

The cattle show has been a staple of the Geauga County Fair since the beginning. The state of Ohio was only 20 years old when settlers came together for the first fair, and top prize in the cattle show went to Eleazar Hickox for best bull. His prize was $10, a somewhat handsome sum at the time. Future chief justice of the Ohio Supreme Court Peter Hitchcock gave the public address at the first fair; he was president of the Agricultural Society at the time. (Courtesy of Elizabeth A. Cupp.)

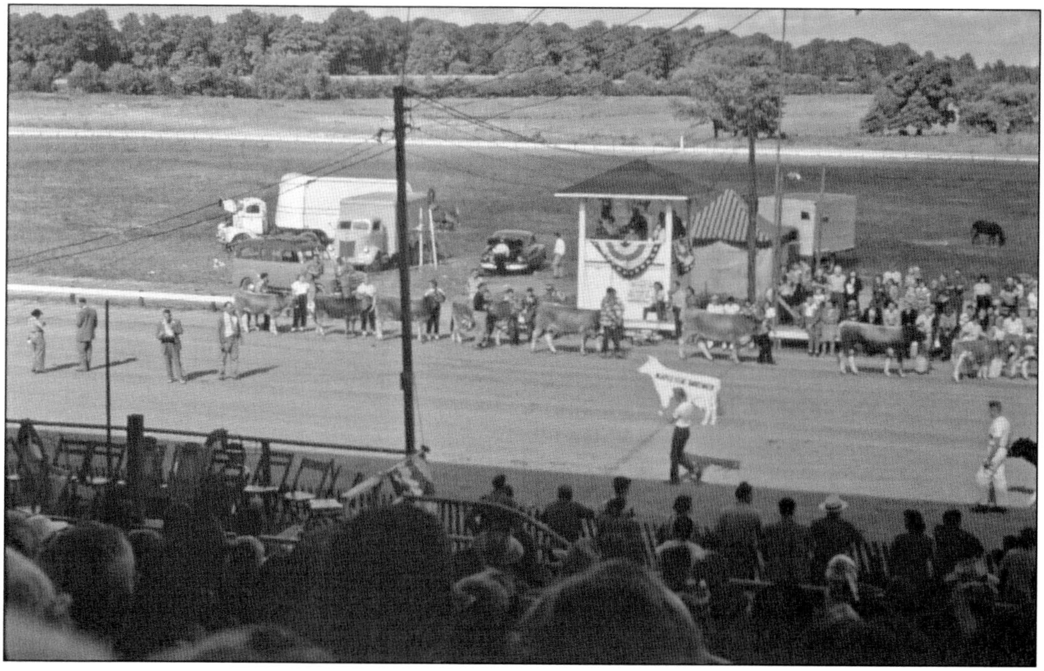

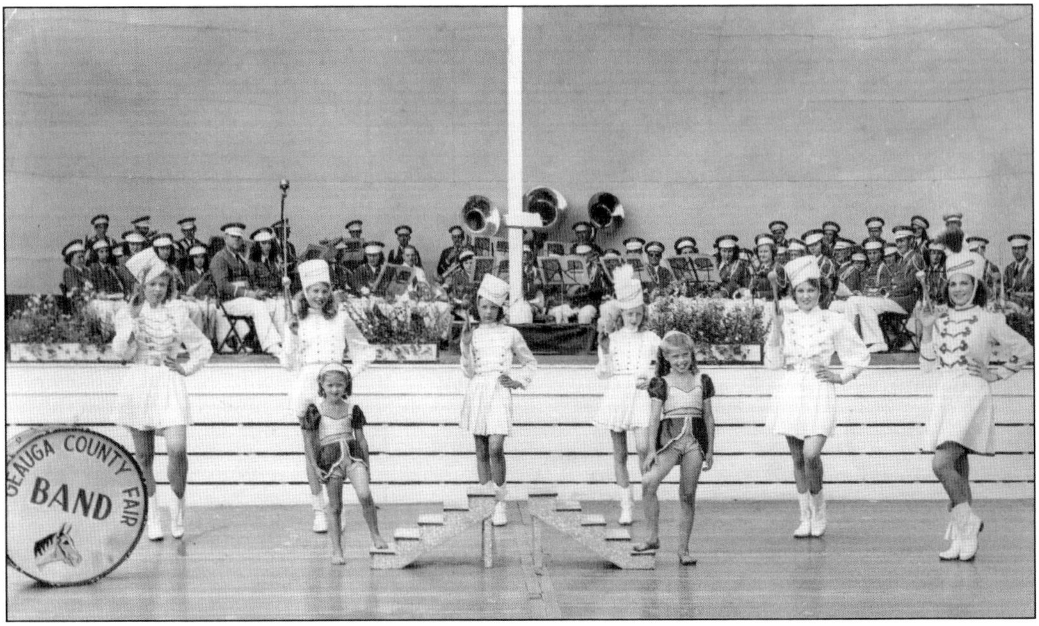

The Great Geauga County Fair Band performs here in 1940. The band, the brainchild of Cliff Rossiter and Azro M. Cheney, was organized in 1938 mainly as a means for high school seniors and other musicians recently out of school to hone their skills. Eventually, the band became much more than that, developing into the fair's official band and playing gigs all across the state, from parades to homecomings. (Courtesy of Burton Public Library.)

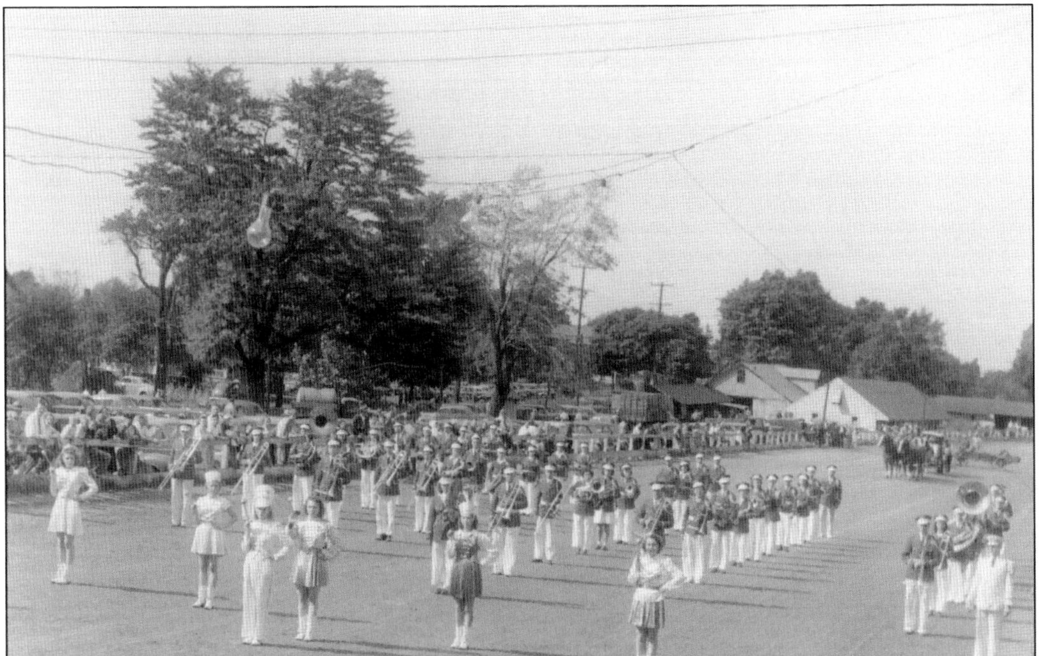

Here, the band performs for an appreciative crowd in 1944. Among the band members shown are Gloria Van Deweel, majorette (front row, second from left) and Mary Jean Humphrey, head majorette (front row, third from left). (Courtesy of Marion L. Howard.)

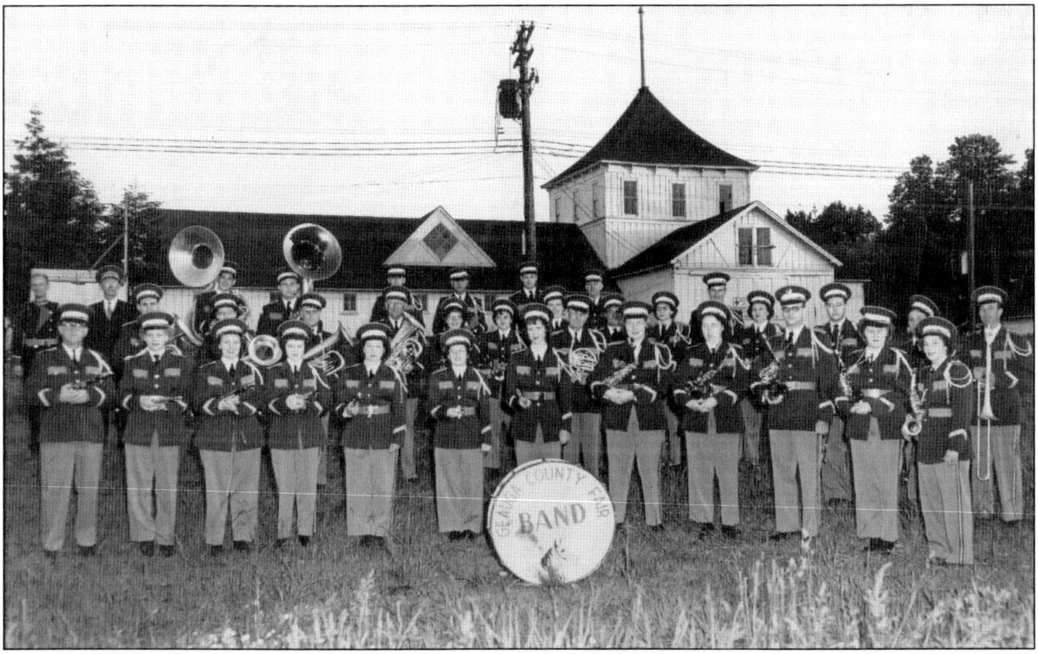

The Great Geauga County Fair Band played for the first time at the 1938 Geauga County Fair and has played there every year since. Through the years, more than 100 members have participated in the band, and in many ways, it has become like one large extended family. Today, the band has about 40 to 50 active members. (Courtesy of Marion L. Howard.)

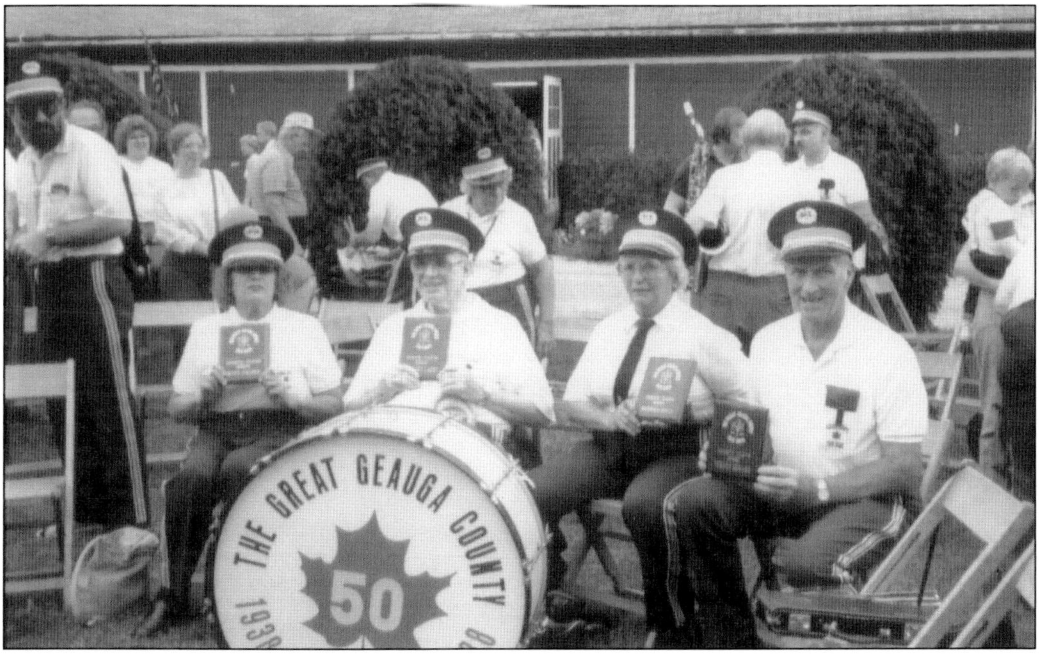

The band celebrated its 50th anniversary in 1988. These four original members of the all-volunteer band—from left to right, Betty Palmer, Dwight Ladd, Barbara Ricca, and Vernon Howard—were awarded plaques in honor of their longevity and loyalty to the band for 50 years. (Courtesy of Marion L. Howard.)

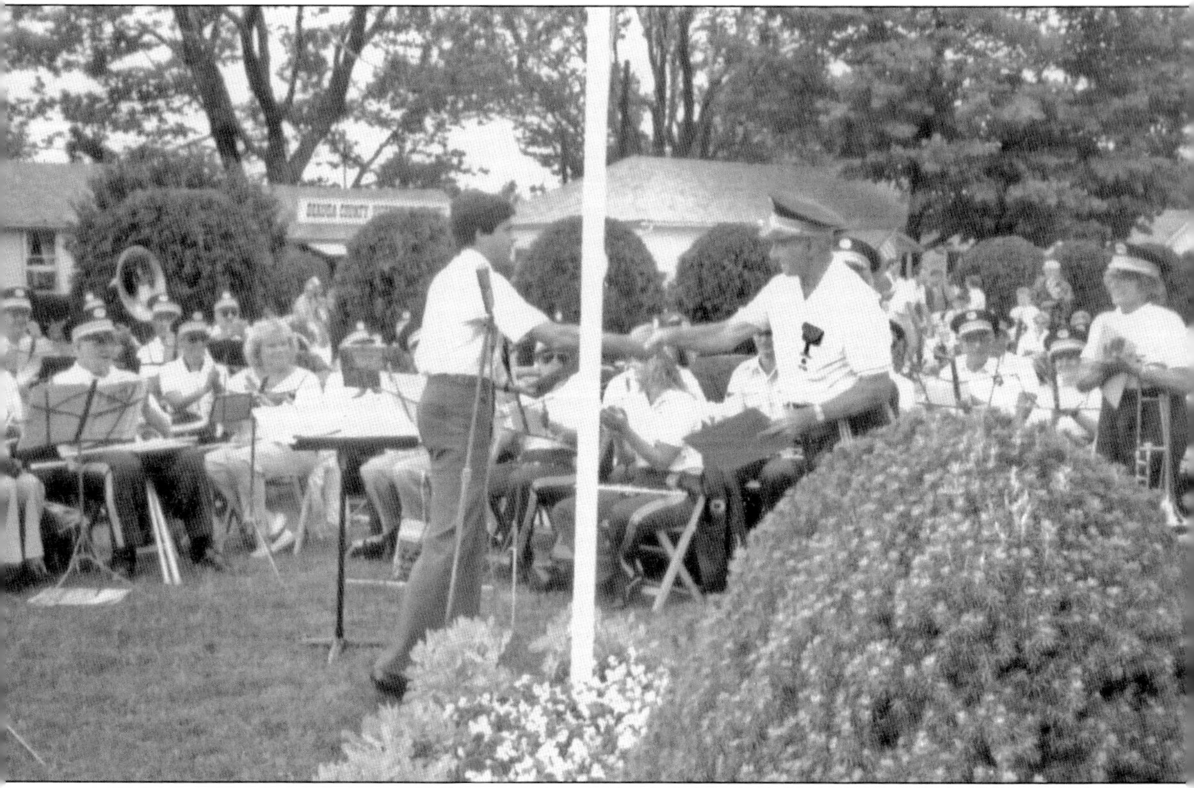

Dennis Eckart (left) congratulates original band member Vernon Howard during a performance commemorating the 50th anniversary of the band. The reputation of the band transcends Burton and even the county line, as illustrated by the acknowledgement given by Eckart, the Cleveland-born former member of the US House of Representatives. Eckart, a congressman from 1981 to 1993, took time out of his busy schedule to attend the 1988 celebration and honor Howard and his bandmates. After his death, the fairgrounds pavilion was renamed the Vernon Howard Pavilion. His wife, Marion, still plays in the band. (Courtesy of Marion L. Howard.)

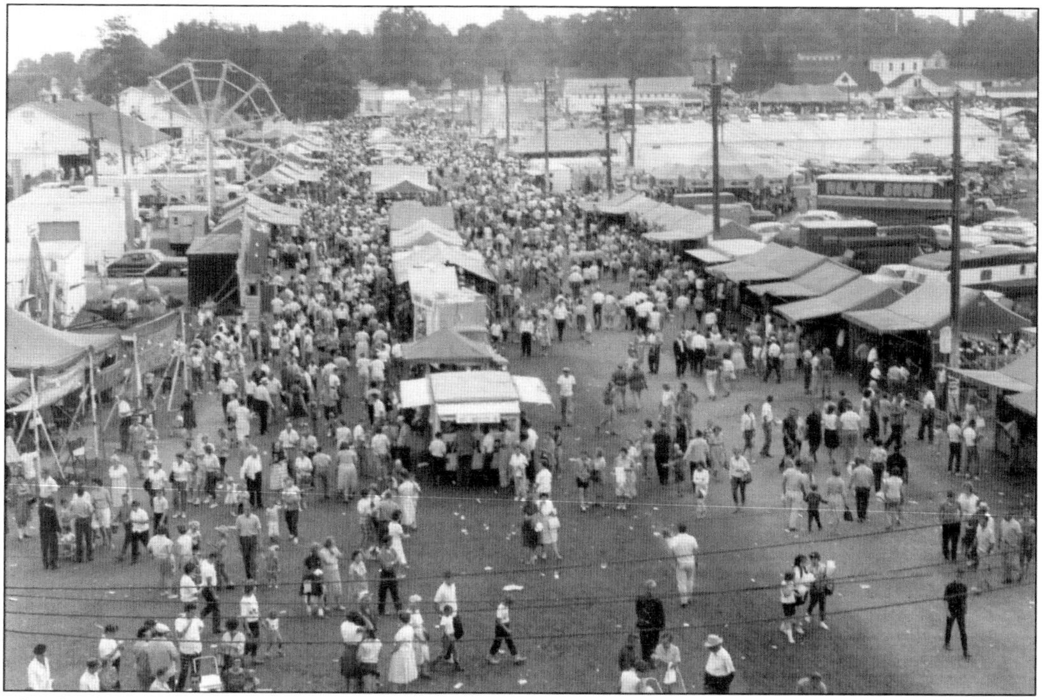

This bird's-eye view of the 1964 fair shows thousands of patrons, a bevy of tents offering exhibits and entertainment, and the Ferris wheel. (Courtesy of Special Collections, Michael Schwartz Library, Cleveland State University.)

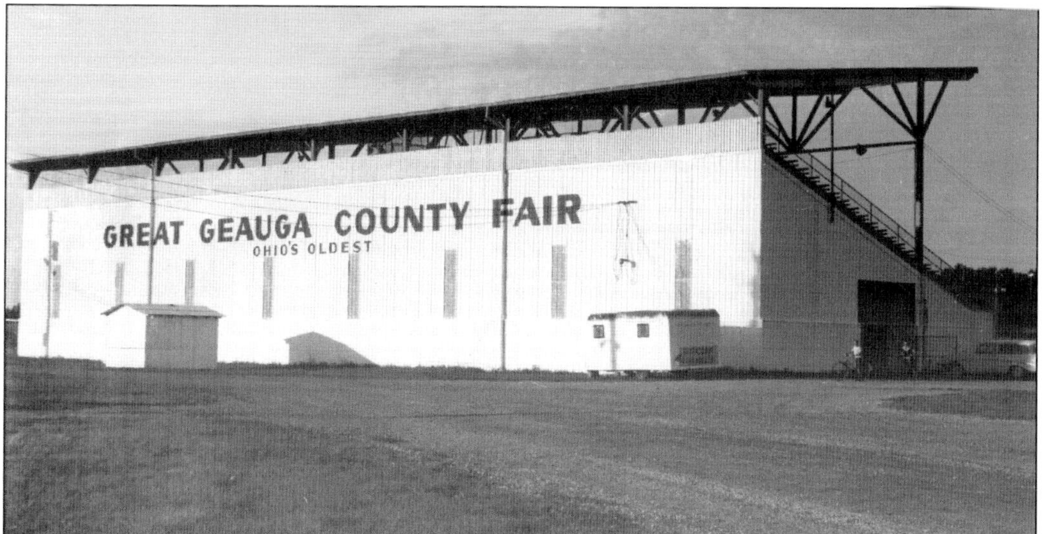

The *Cleveland Press* described a new addition to the fair thusly: "Something new at the fair in Geauga County will be this huge sign painted across the newly enclosed main grandstand. The remodeled stand at the Burton fairgrounds is ready for the opening of the fair on August 30th. Events like the Amish cart races, stock car races and auto thrill and horse shows will be held at the grandstand during the five-day fair, Ohio's oldest. Under the stands, there's a lot more exhibit space." (Courtesy of Special Collections, Michael Schwartz Library, Cleveland State University.)

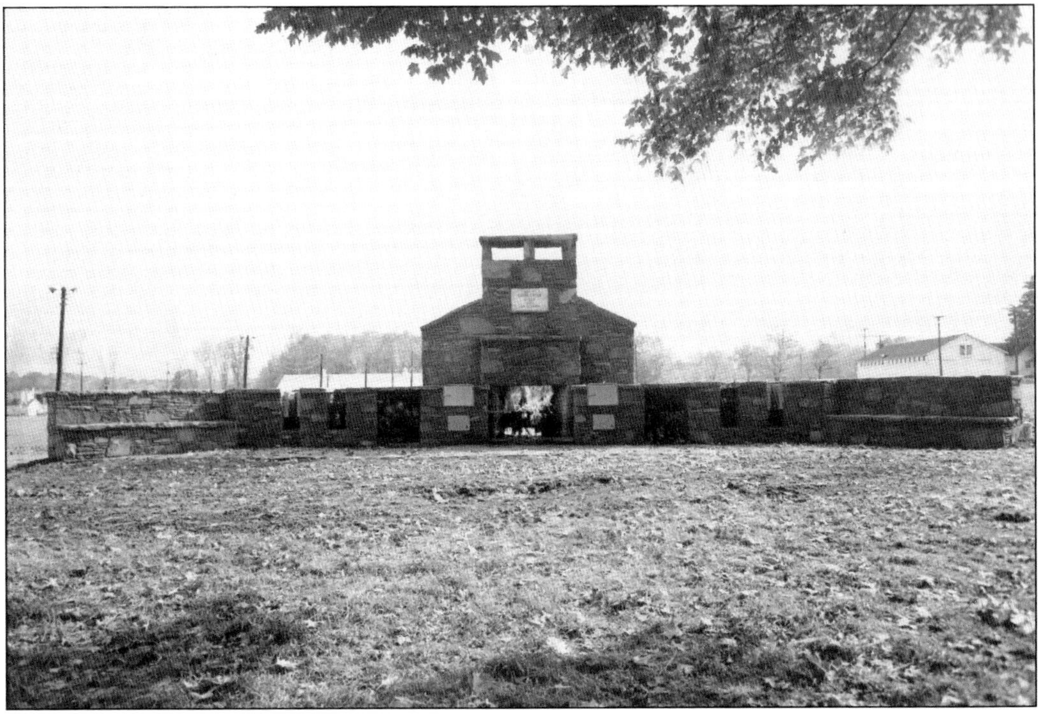

The *Cleveland Press* described the building of the barbeque pit: "The world's largest barbeque pit has been constructed for public use at the Geauga County Fairgrounds in Burton. Stone was furnished by Tom Richmond from his Swine Creek Quarry in Middlefield Township. He hired Julius Shaker, a master mason to put it up, and turned the 54 foot pit over to county commissioners and the fair band." (Courtesy of Special Collections, Michael Schwartz Library, Cleveland State University.)

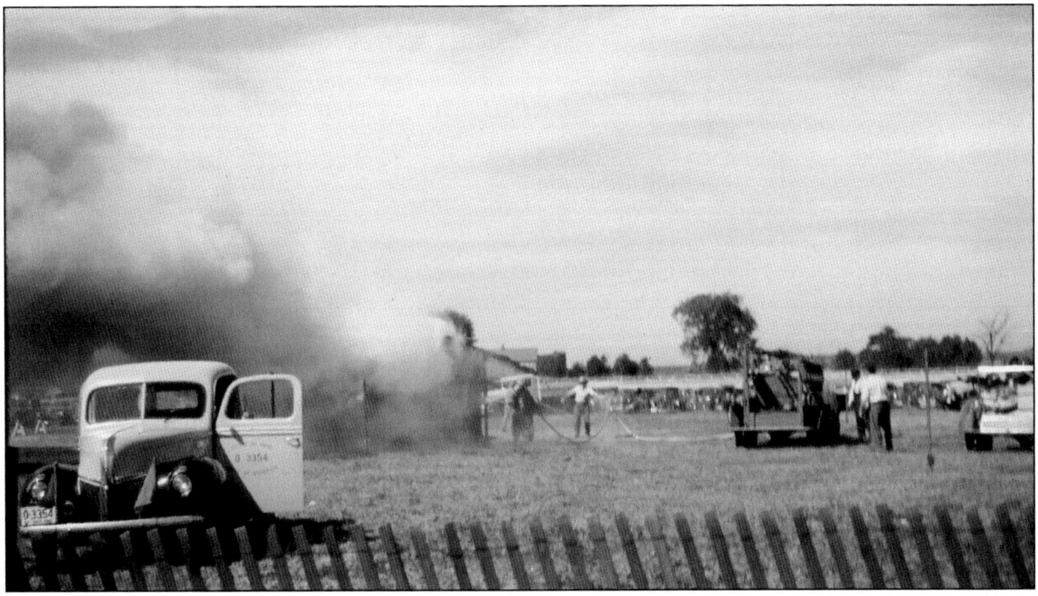

Burton volunteer firefighters put out a fire in an exhibition of bravado and firefighting skills at the fair just after World War II. (Courtesy of Elizabeth A. Cupp.)

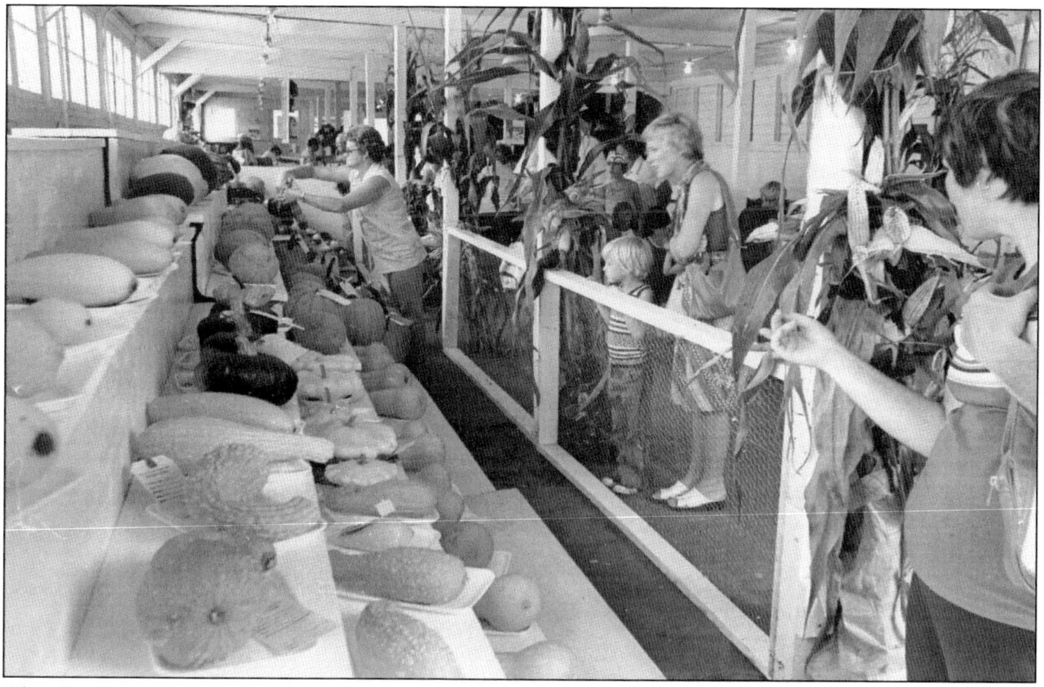

The Geauga County Agricultural and Manufacturing Society came about as a result of a meeting held in Chardon in January 1823. On October 23, 1823, the first fair exhibition by the society was held. Today, the Geauga County Agricultural Society ("Manufacturing" was dropped from the title when it was reorganized in the 1900s) is the oldest existing organization in the county. (Courtesy of Special Collections, Michael Schwartz Library, Cleveland State University.)

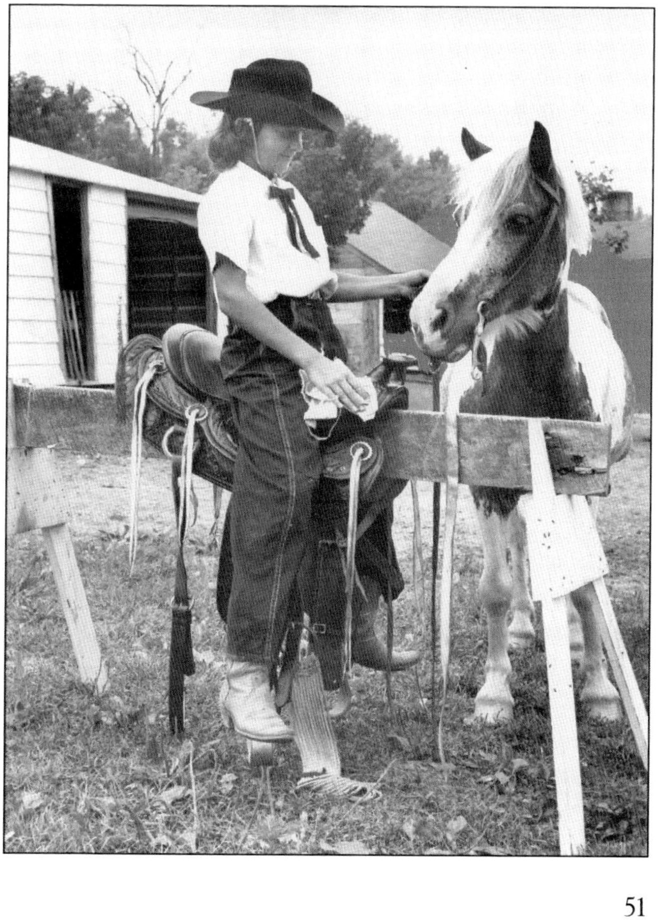

This young girl pets a horse at the 1959 fair. Animal husbandry has always played a major part in the fair, whether as the recipient of a child's affections, a participant in a hotly contested harness race, or the subject of a livestock exhibit. (Courtesy of Special Collections, Michael Schwartz Library, Cleveland State University.)

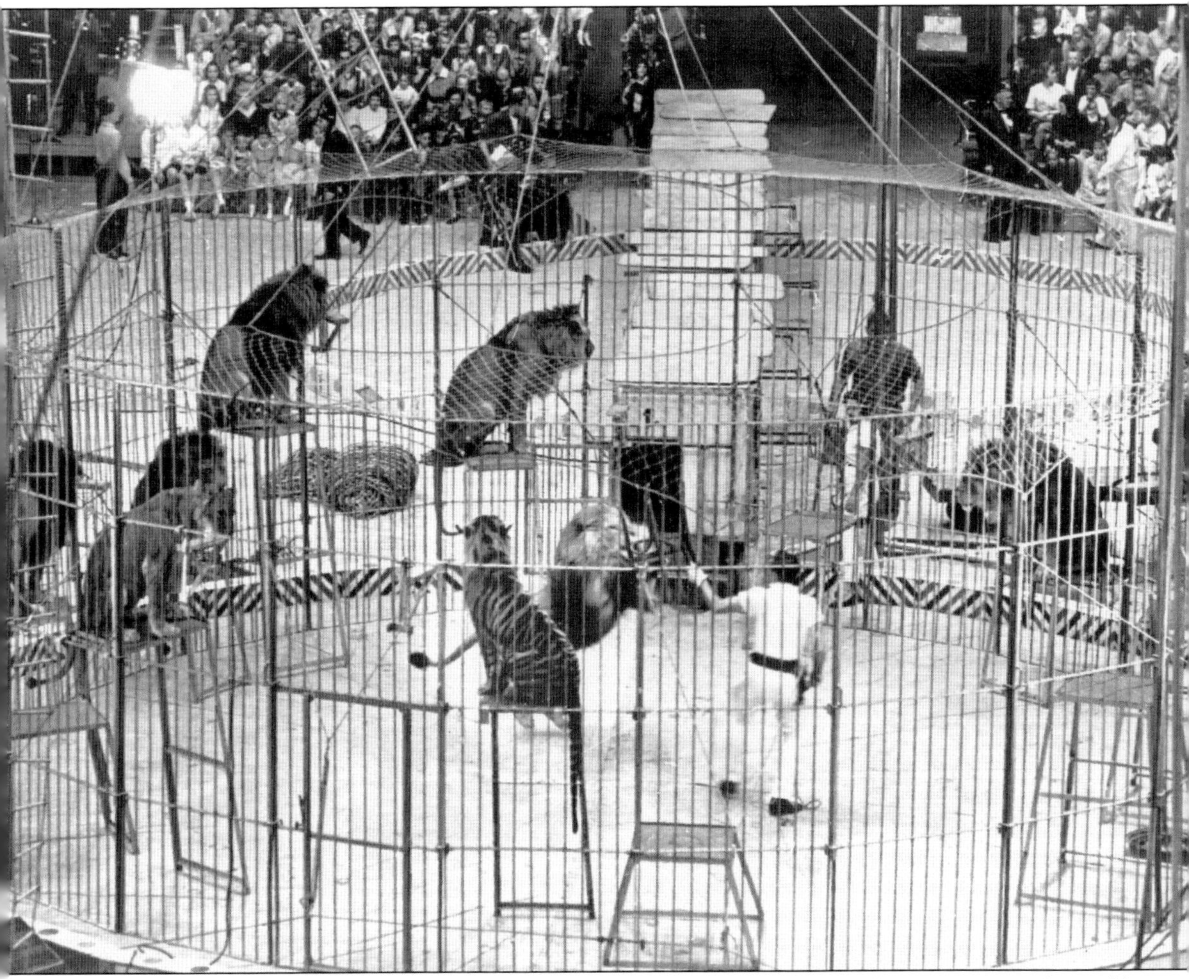

The 1964 Great Geauga County Fair featured an exciting exhibition of lion taming performed by Dave Hoover. A world-renowned lion tamer, Hoover often wore a white jumpsuit and a leather harness with a six-shooter strapped to it. He was notorious for his small wooden chair and leather whip to keep lions and tigers at bay and his fearless abandon to command the ferocious beasts to leap and soar through rings of flames. Hoover was also featured in Errol Morris's critically acclaimed documentary *Fast, Cheap & Out of Control*, which chronicled the obsessiveness, eccentricities, and brilliance of Hoover and three other men: a topiary gardener, a mole rat specialist, and a robot scientist. (Courtesy of Special Collections, Michael Schwartz Library, Cleveland State University.)

Four

Burton Park and Sugar Camp

On October 5, 1803, a deed was drawn up to set aside land for streets and for the establishment of Burton Park. The document was signed by Andrew Hull Jr., Benjamin Doolittle, Samuel Doolittle, Turhand Kirtland, Titus Street, Thomas Umberfield, Amoriah Beard, and Simeon Rose. A proxy was also drawn up for Hull, the Doolittles, and Street. No money exchanged hands; it was simply a gift from a group of men who wanted to see Burton flourish. These early settlers knew their growing village would benefit from having a park at the heart of their community for training, horse and cattle shows, circuses and fairs, and an assortment of other events and gatherings. For over 200 years, Burton Park has been the site for band practices, parades, movie screenings, and so many more activities. The park has been home to the Burton Water Tower in various forms for a number of years, and during the miniature golf craze of the 1920s, it was home to Burton's own miniature golf course.

These days, Burton Park is known for being the home of the Burton Log Cabin Sugar Camp, a working sugarhouse producing maple syrup every spring and making maple candy year-round. It is operated by the Burton Chamber of Commerce, making it the only municipally owned sugar camp in the country. When it opened in the park in March 1931, the *Cleveland Plain-Dealer* labeled it a unique marketing scheme; thousands of visitors came for the cabin's grand opening. The original cabin was patterned after the log cabin in Kentucky where Abraham Lincoln was born, and it was added on to in 1931, 1932, 1954, 1959, and 1962.

More than 200 years after the founders' generous gift, Burton Park is still, geographically and metaphorically, the center of Burton.

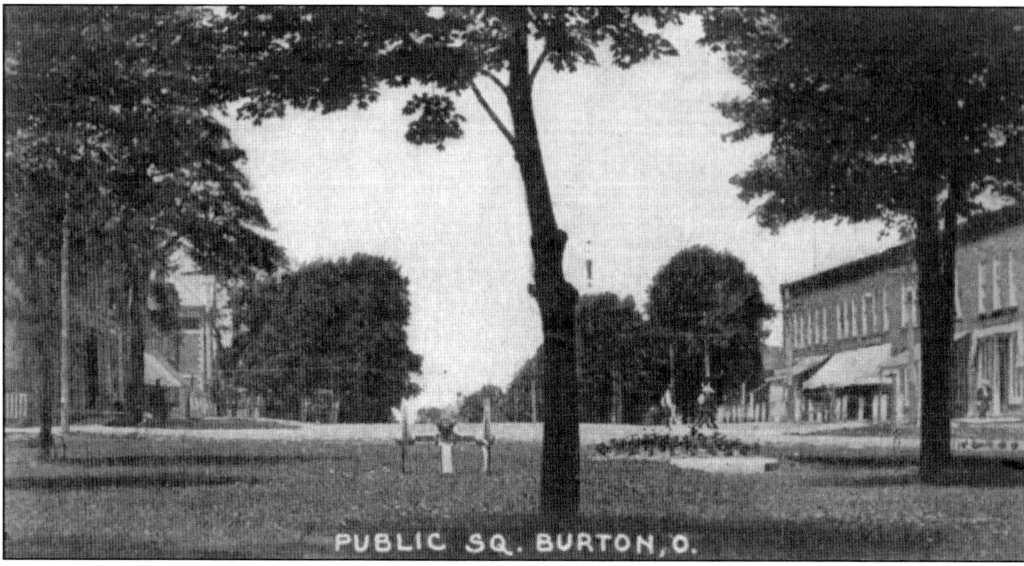

This photograph looks north into the commercial district from the park in 1906. A number of different roads converge into the road circling the park. (Courtesy of Bill Jackson.)

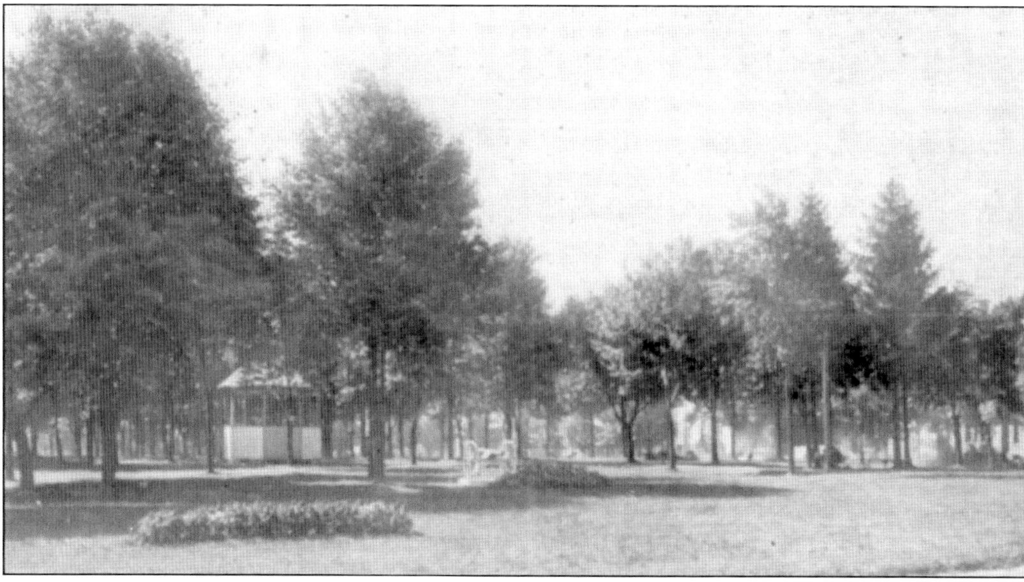

This photograph, also from 1906, shows the park's picnic tables, gazebos, and park benches. Live music was performed on a regular basis, often by the Citizens Band. (Courtesy of Bill Jackson.)

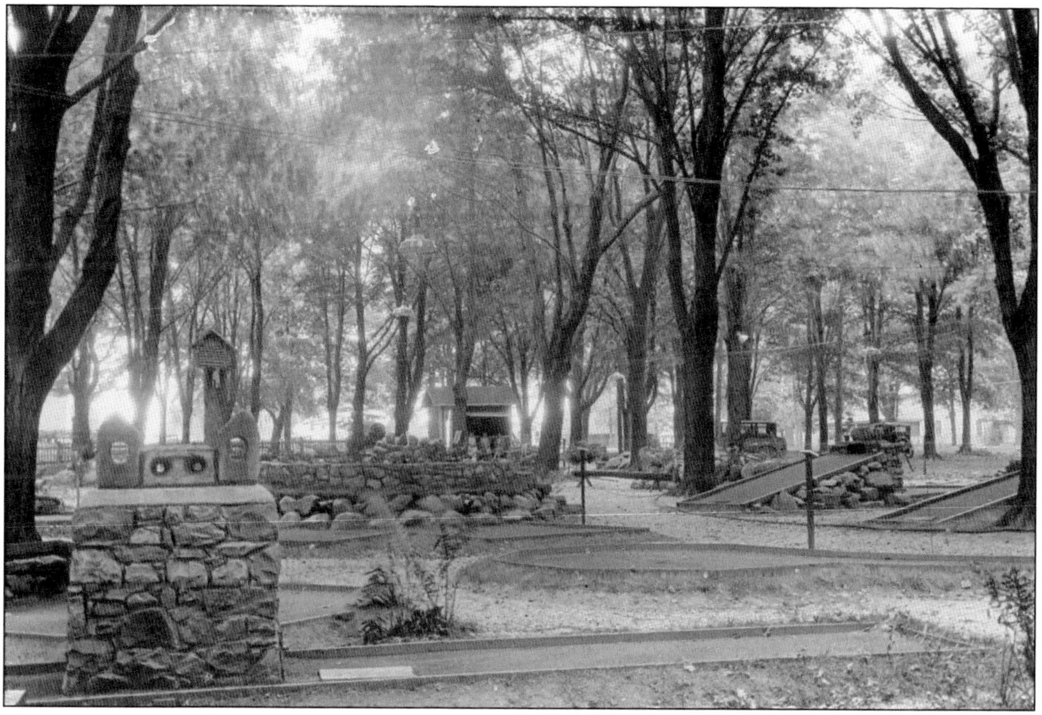

The miniature golf trend started peaking in 1926, and Burton was not going to be left behind. The Talcott family owned the popular putt-putt course in Burton Park, as well as a general store with the slogan, "The Service Store, Treat Yourself to the Best." (Courtesy of Geauga County Historical Society.)

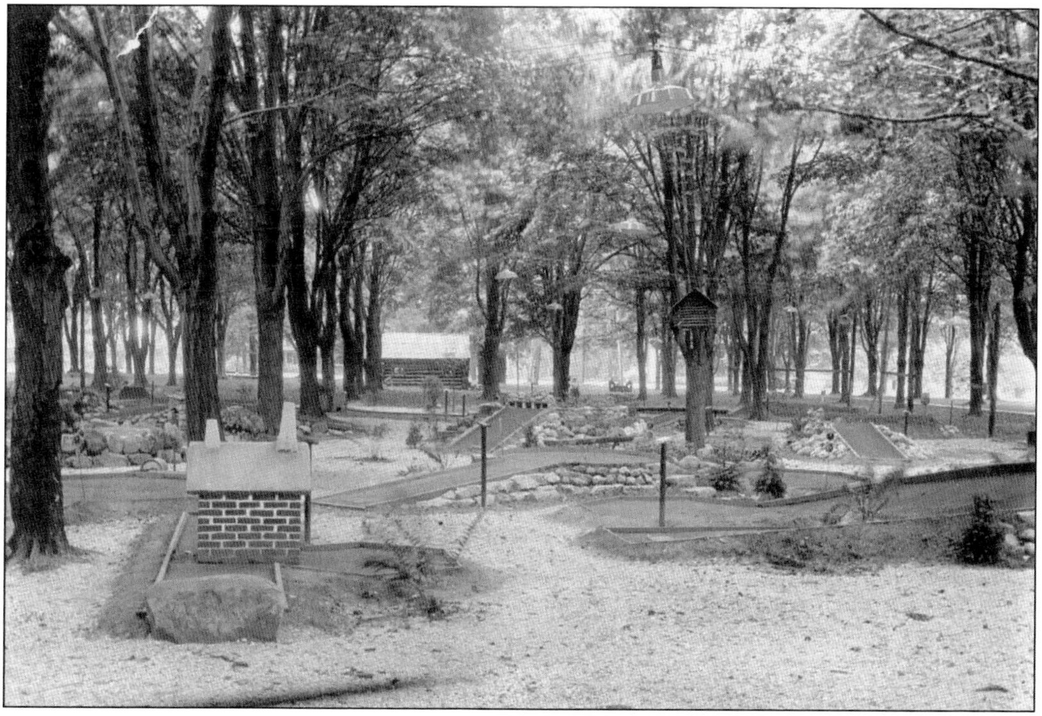

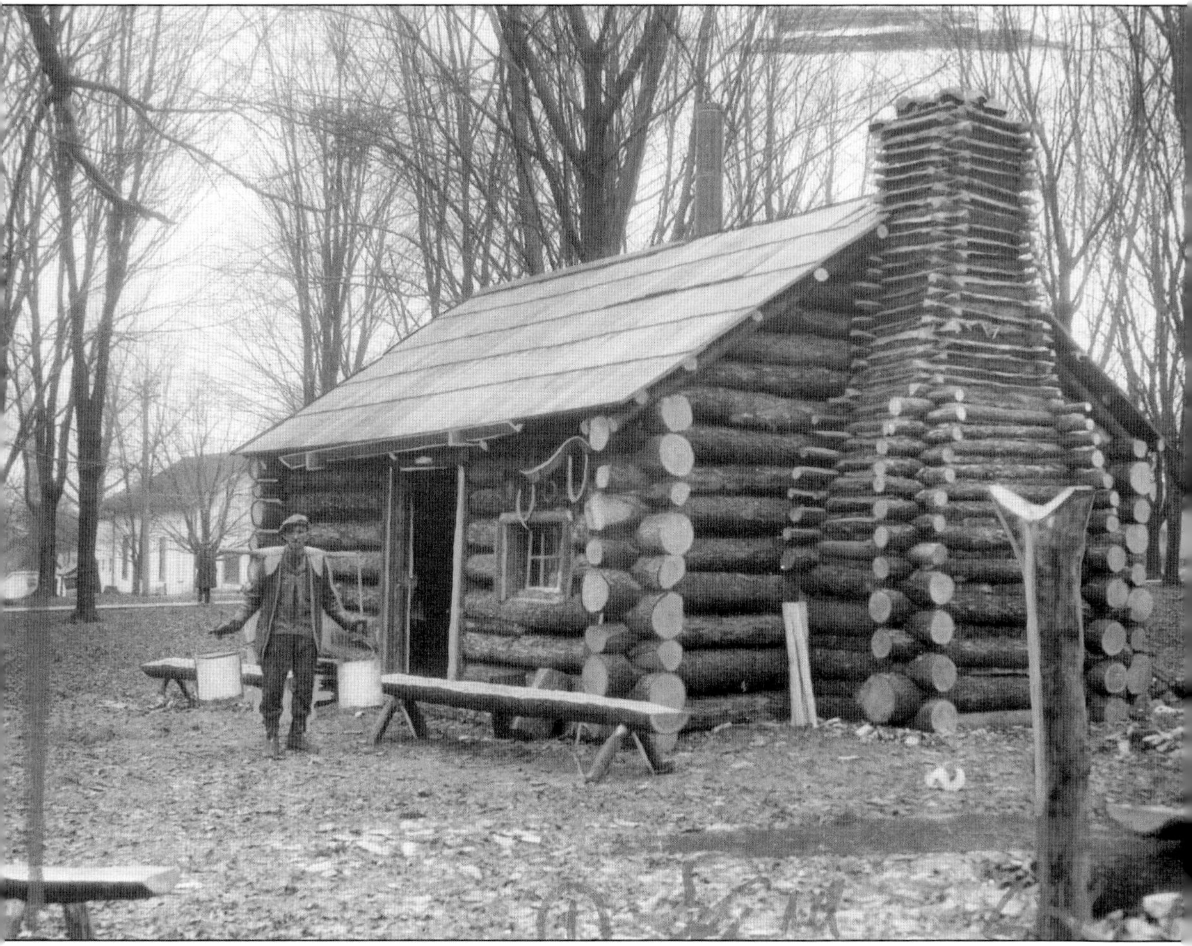

The log cabin is seen here in August 1931, not long after the sugar camp opened. The log cabin was built by the Burton Chamber of Commerce and was (and still is) the only municipally owned sugar camp in the country. The log cabin opened in March 1931 and was so successful, the grand opening drew over 1,000 people. According to most sources, the cabin was added onto later that year and again in 1932. (Courtesy of Special Collections, Michael Schwartz Library, Cleveland State University.)

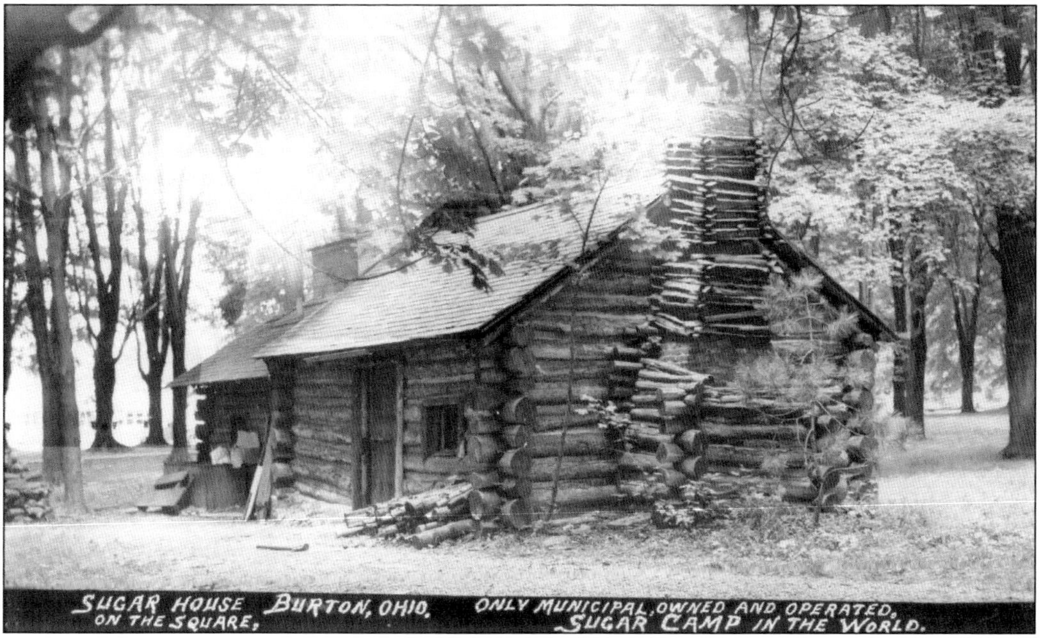

After just half a decade, the demand for maple syrup was already outgrowing the log cabin's ability to produce it, leading to additions like the room on the back end of the cabin, which is easily visible above. It had also become the tourist attraction Burton had hoped for. (Both, courtesy of the Burton Public Library.)

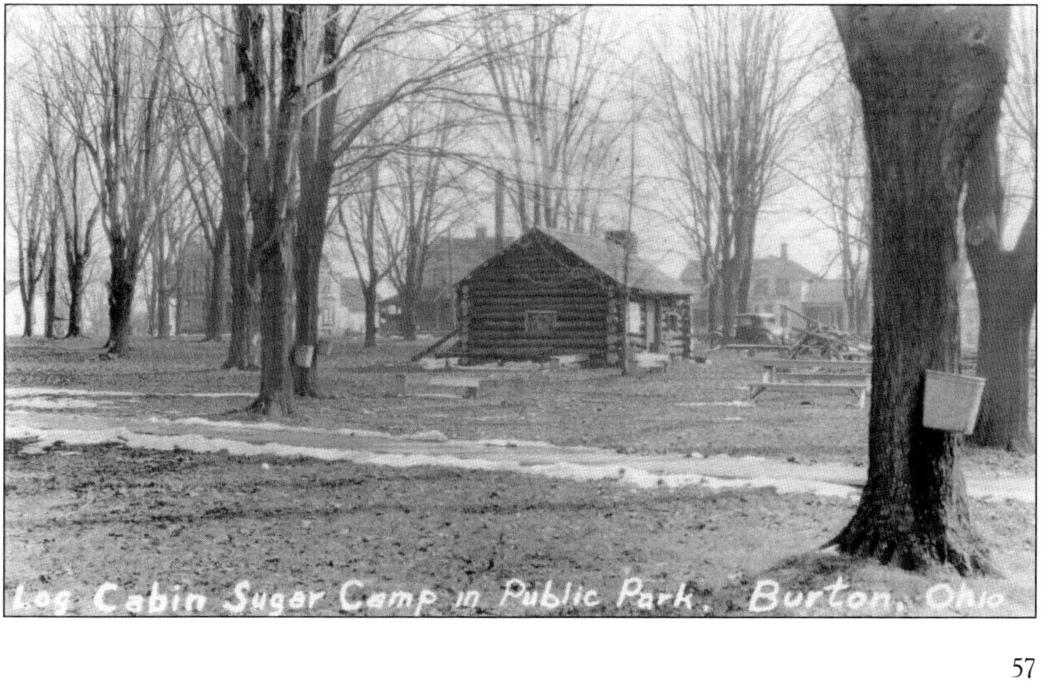

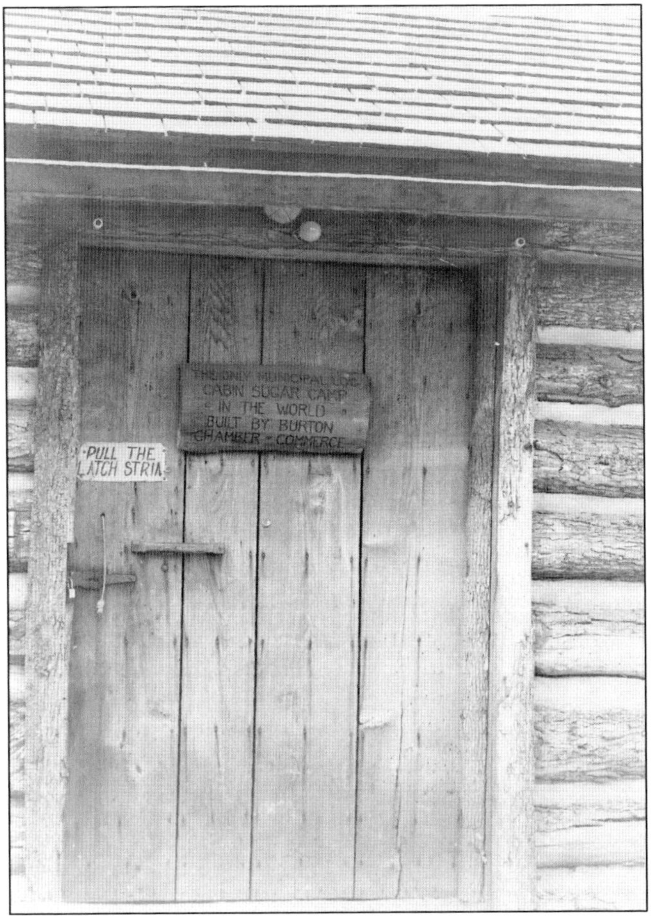

It is a point of pride in Burton that the sugar camp is the only municipally owned sugar camp in the country, as stated on this sign on the cabin door in this 1940 image. (Courtesy of Special Collections, Michael Schwartz Library, Cleveland State University.)

By the time this 1940 photograph was taken, Burton was holding many pancake breakfasts and was well known for its quality maple syrup products, as the town still is today. (Courtesy of Special Collections, Michael Schwartz Library, Cleveland State University.)

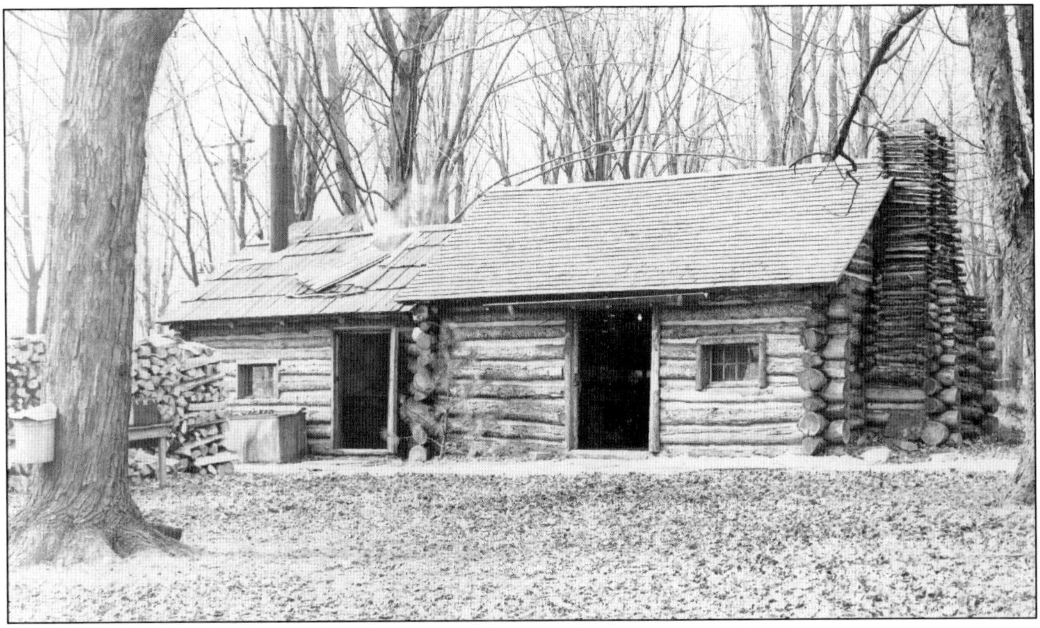

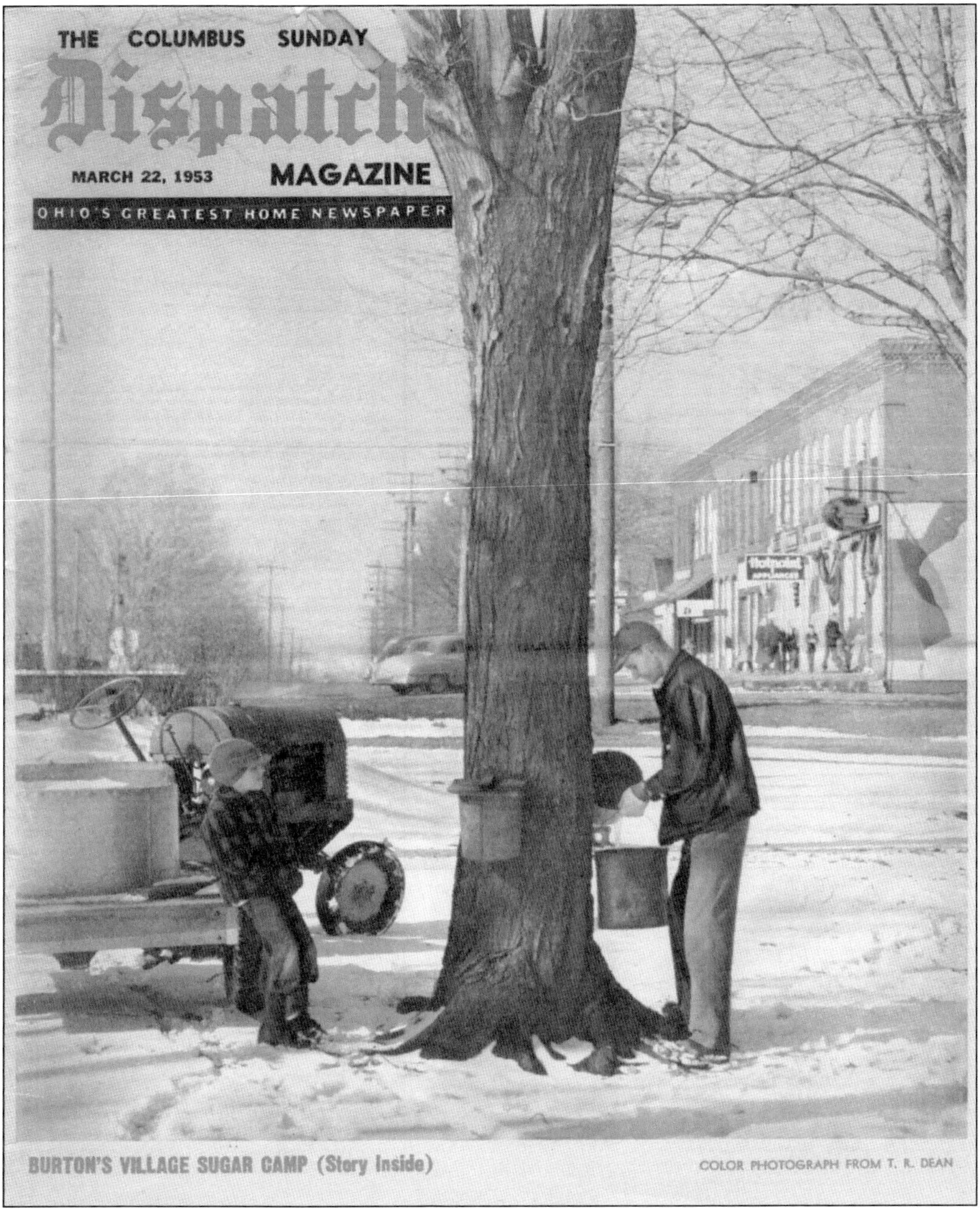

The March 22, 1953, *Columbus Dispatch* Magazine, published on Sundays, featured Burton resident Harlan Potter on the cover. The flattering article described Burton as "Ohio's sweetest town" and contained important facts about Burton and its maple syrup, including details about the Cleveland man who held the record for the most pancakes eaten in one sitting. The inside story also featured pictures of Potter and the sugar camp manager at the time, T.R. Dean, and was very clear about the importance of the cabin to Burton: "When Burton needed money during the Depression folks turned the town's maple trees into profit." (Courtesy of the *Columbus Dispatch*.)

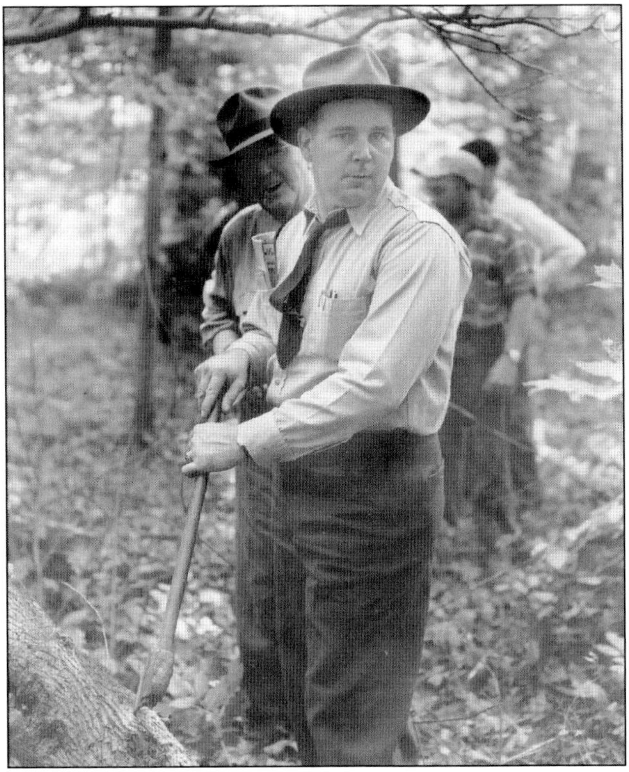

Ture Johnson ran maple sugar production in Burton before going on to join the Ohio Division of Forestry. The New Sugar Maker Award at the Ohio State Fair, given to sugar makers with less than five years of experience, is named for him. (Photograph from the Ture Johnson archives, courtesy of the Johnson family.)

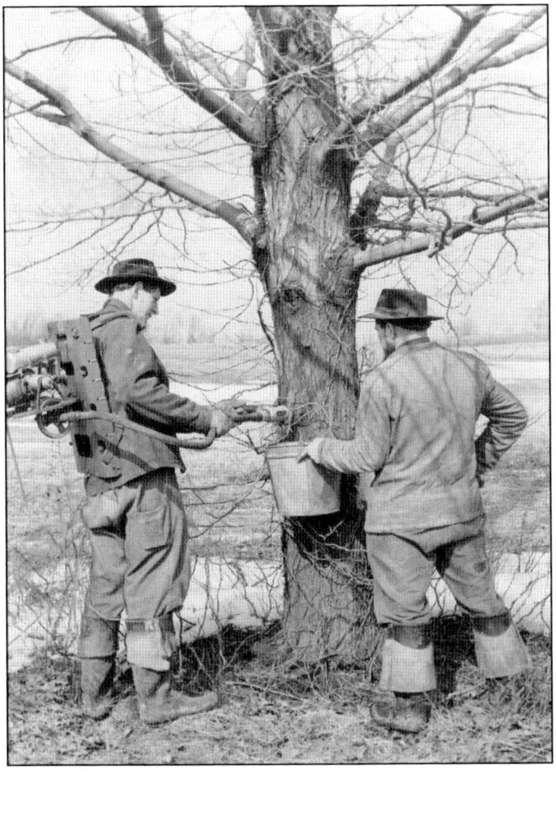

The *Cleveland Press* summed up this scene thusly: "Spring thaws promise a good run of sap for Amish men tapping sugar maples on the 135-acre farm of Donald and Howard McNish. Sap will be converted into syrup and then marketed at the upcoming Geauga County Maple Festival, which begins this weekend. Farmhands here are John Gingerich and Joe Yoder." (Courtesy of Special Collections, Michael Schwartz Library, Cleveland State University.)

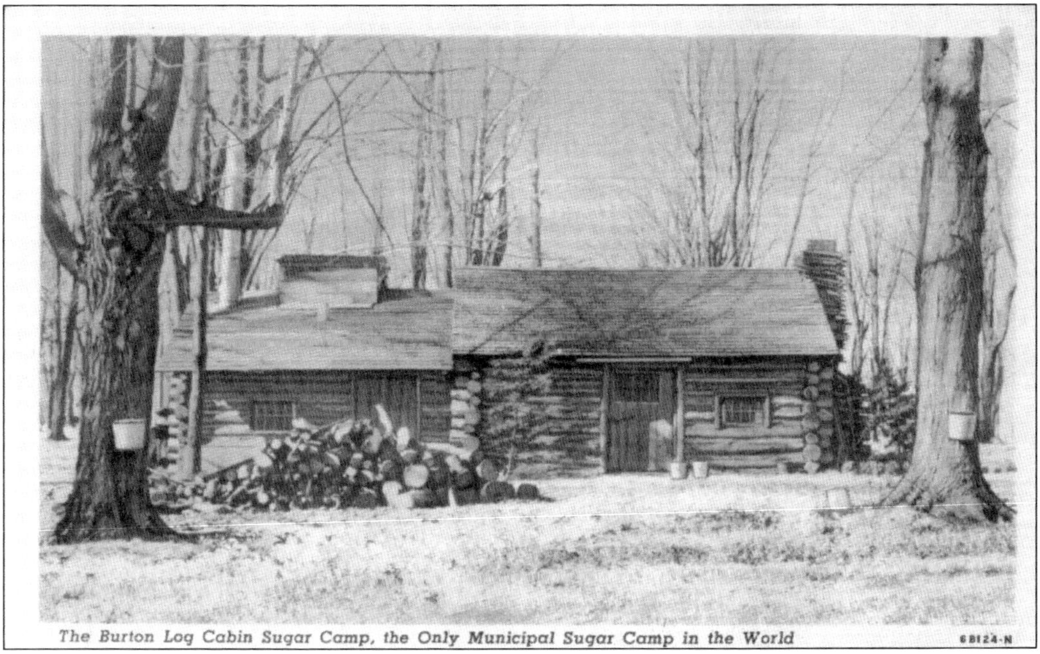

This postcard shows the many additions to the camp. Each March since 1951, Burton has served pancakes to over 20,000 guests. It became so popular, the Burton-Middlefield Rotary Club decided to officially trademark the slogan, "Pancake Town U.S.A." (Courtesy of the Burton Public Library.)

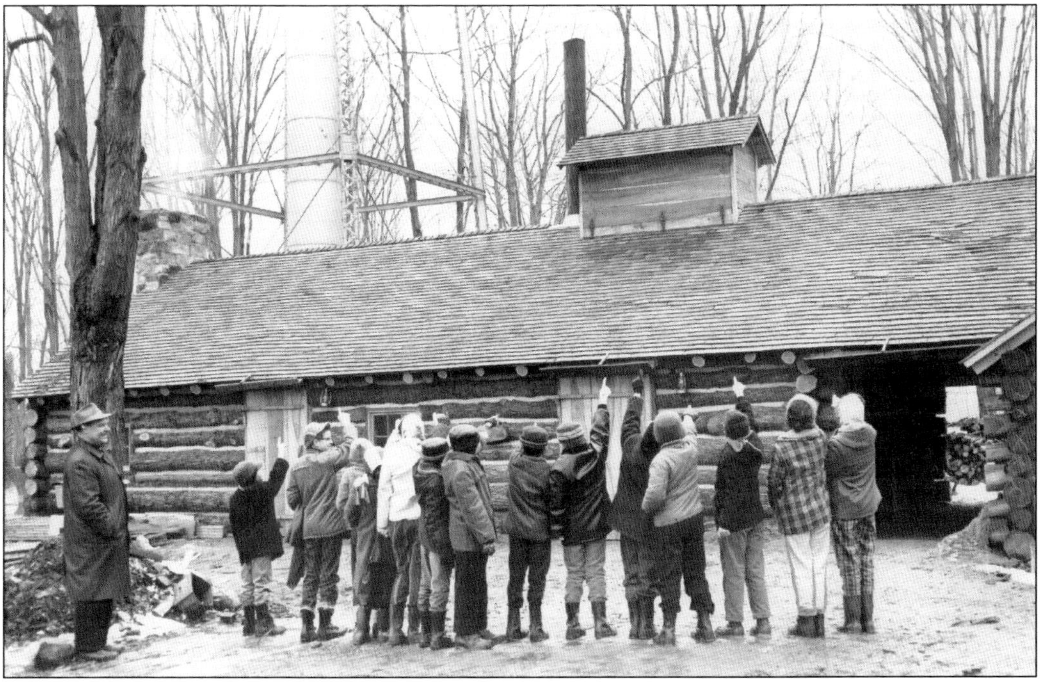

In 1962, children from Youngstown's Woodside School look at the newest addition to the Log Cabin Sugar Camp, the sales room and candy kitchen—the fifth and final addition to the cabin. (Courtesy of Special Collections, Michael Schwartz Library, Cleveland State University.)

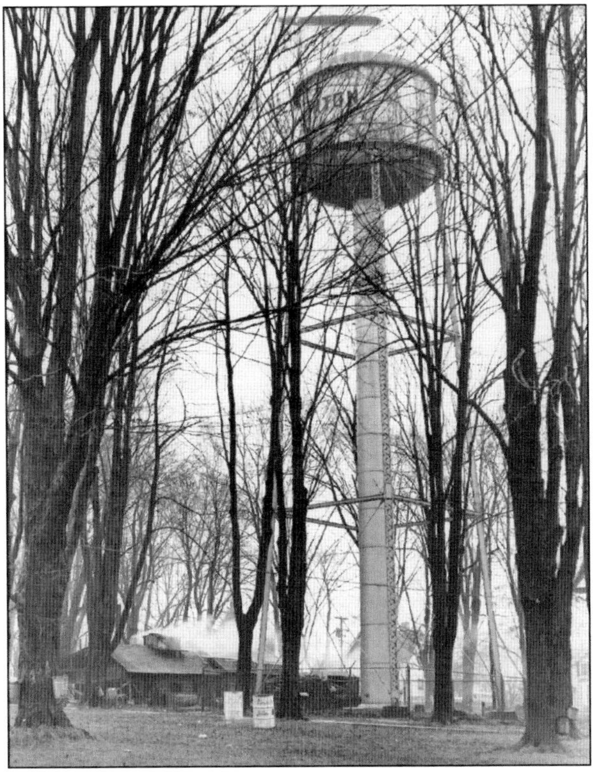

The Burton Water Tower casts a shadow over the cabin. This particular water tower was torn down in the late 1960s and replaced by the current tower, which still stands today. (Courtesy of Special Collections, Michael Schwartz Library, Cleveland State University.)

Children rake leaves in front of the log cabin in the mid-1960s. By this time, it had become a frequent field-trip location that showed youngsters how a sugar camp was operated. (Courtesy of Special Collections, Michael Schwartz Library, Cleveland State University.)

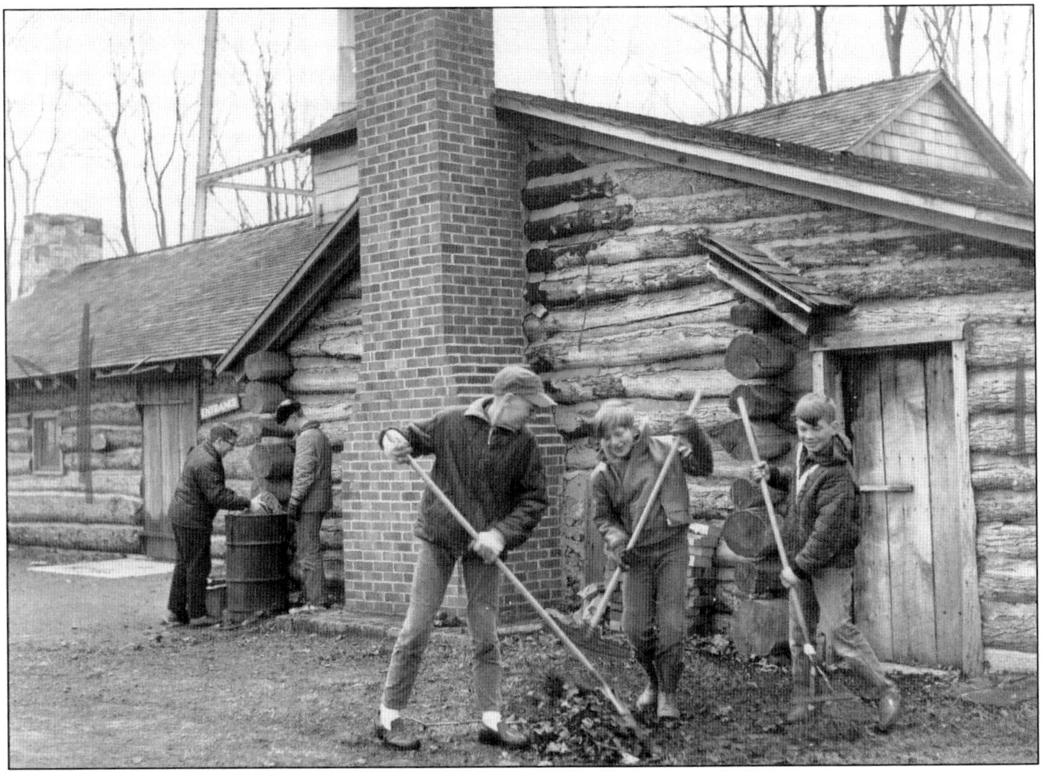

In this 1965 image, George VanDeweel and Ruth Reidl pour boiled maple sap into molds to make maple sugar candy in Burton. The log cabin still makes several different shapes of candy, from teddy bears to seashells. (Courtesy of Special Collections, Michael Schwartz Library, Cleveland State University.)

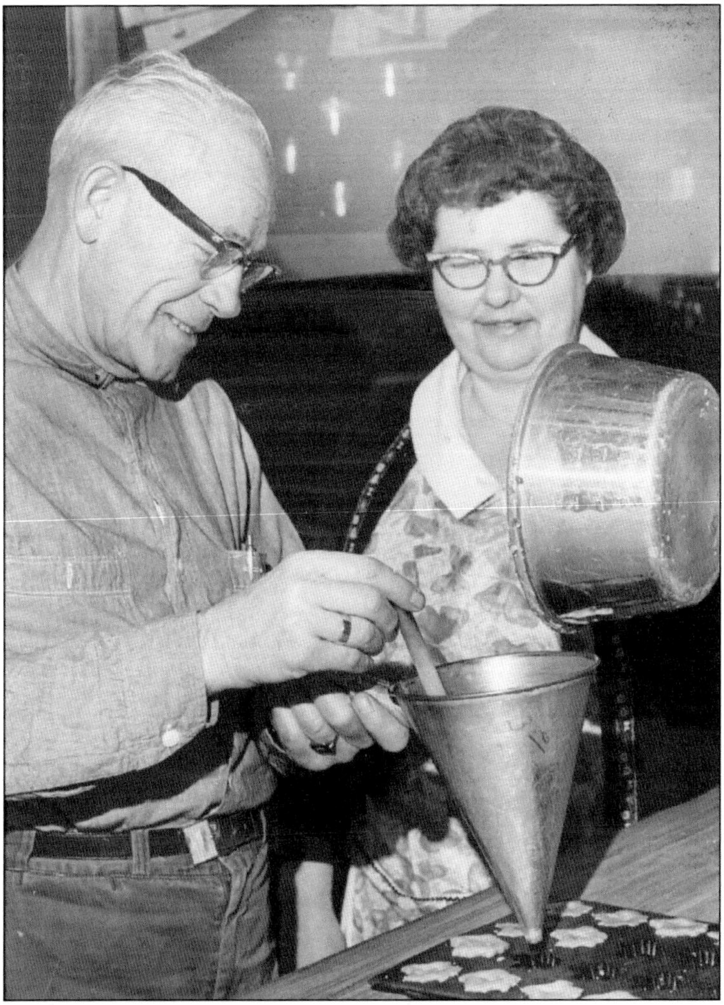

This photograph shows the evaporating station of Geauga Maid, Inc., a maple syrup company owned by Burton business men. It was situated on West Center Street at the current car wash location. (Courtesy of Special Collections, Michael Schwartz Library, Cleveland State University.)

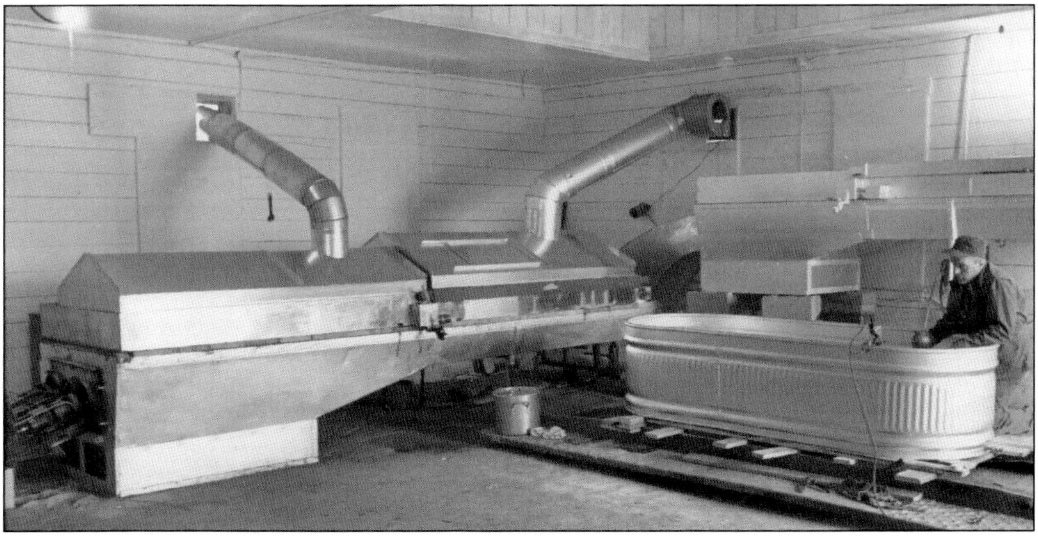

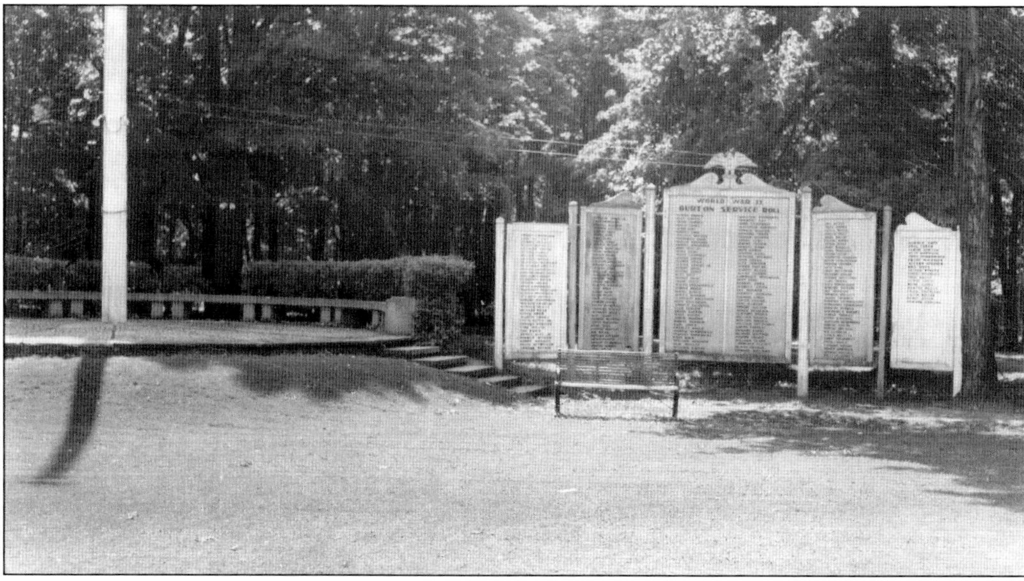

The Burton World War II Service Roll was erected in Burton Park as a dedication to the men and women of Burton who proudly served in World War II. (Courtesy of Elmer Bollinger.)

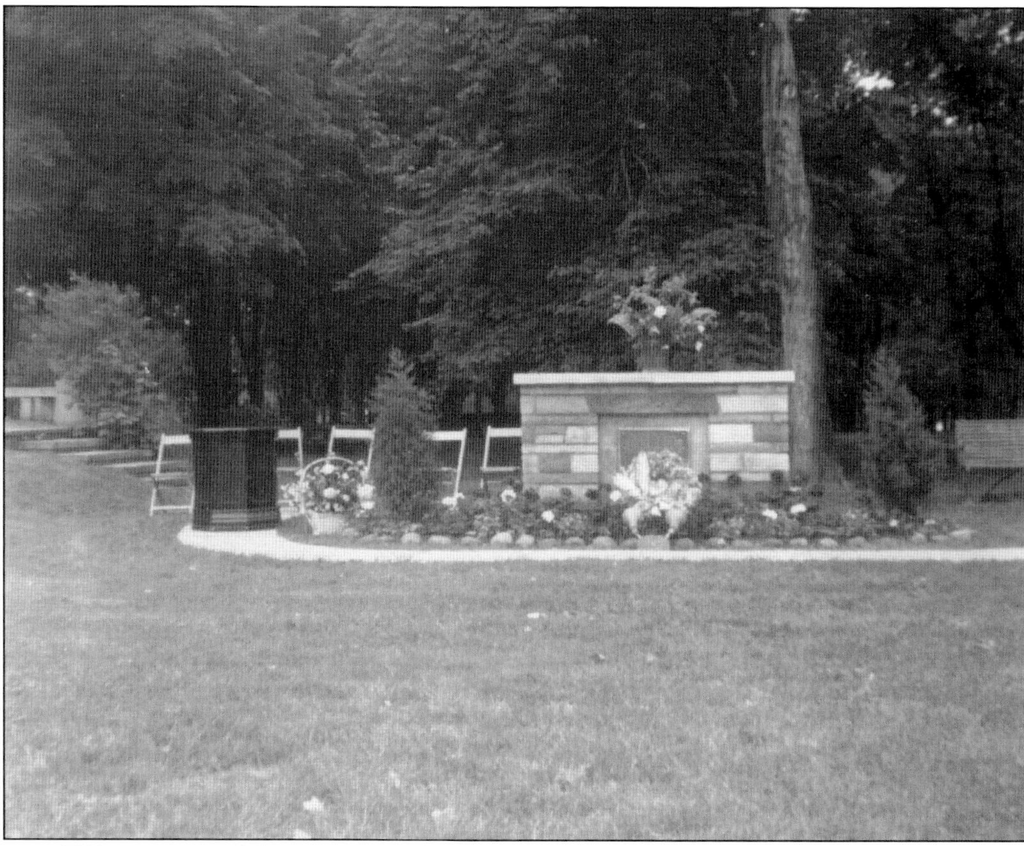

In 1955, Burton erected this monument dedicated to Korean War casualties. Unfortunately, neither this monument nor the World War II Service Roll still stands. (Courtesy of Rosa Herst.)

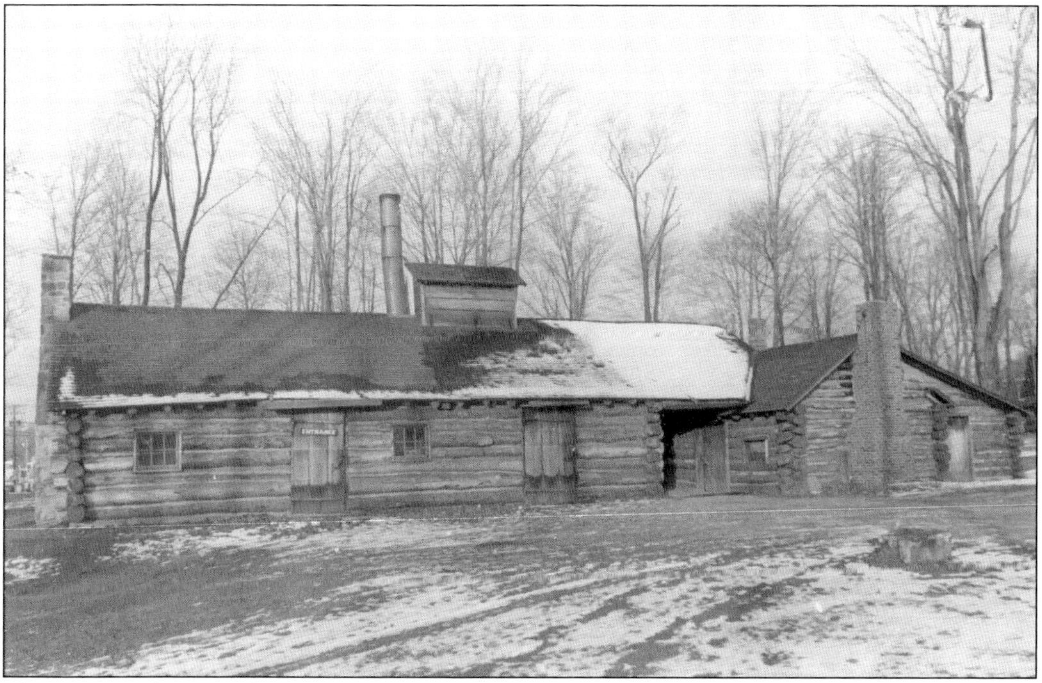

These 1970s photographs illustrate how the log cabin has grown with the times. Currently, there are 39 different products available for order from the sugar camp's website, and every year in February, the camp still holds a tapping ceremony to kick off the maple syrup season and show folks how maple sugar is made. In the photograph below, Theron R. "Deaner" Dean stands at the entrance. (Above, courtesy of Special Collections, Michael Schwartz Library, Cleveland State University; below, Burton Public Library.)

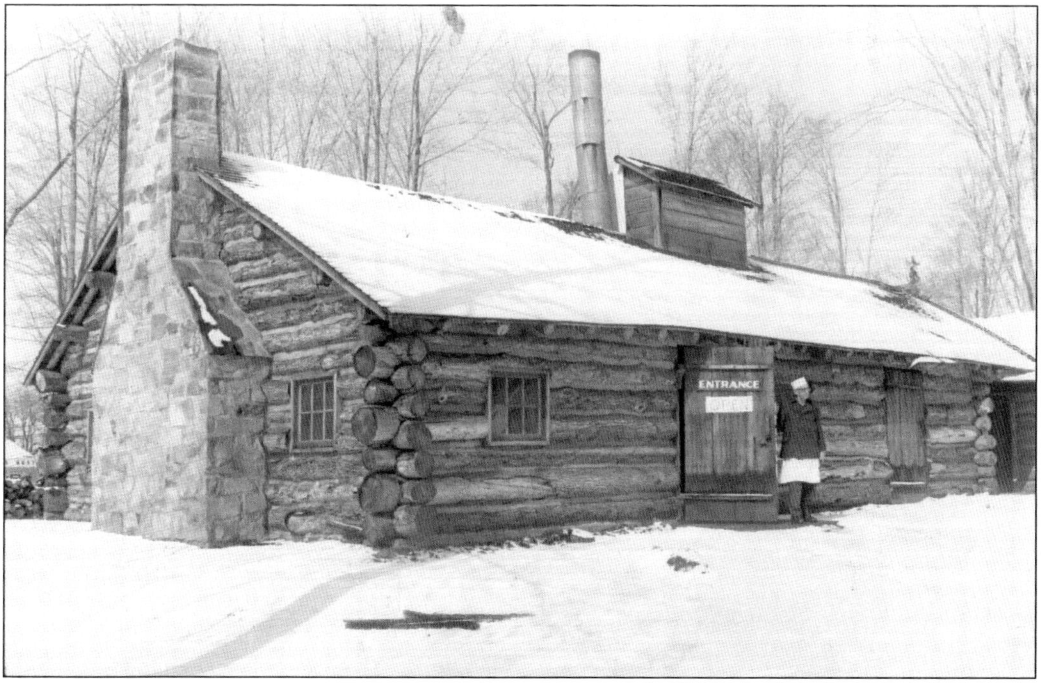

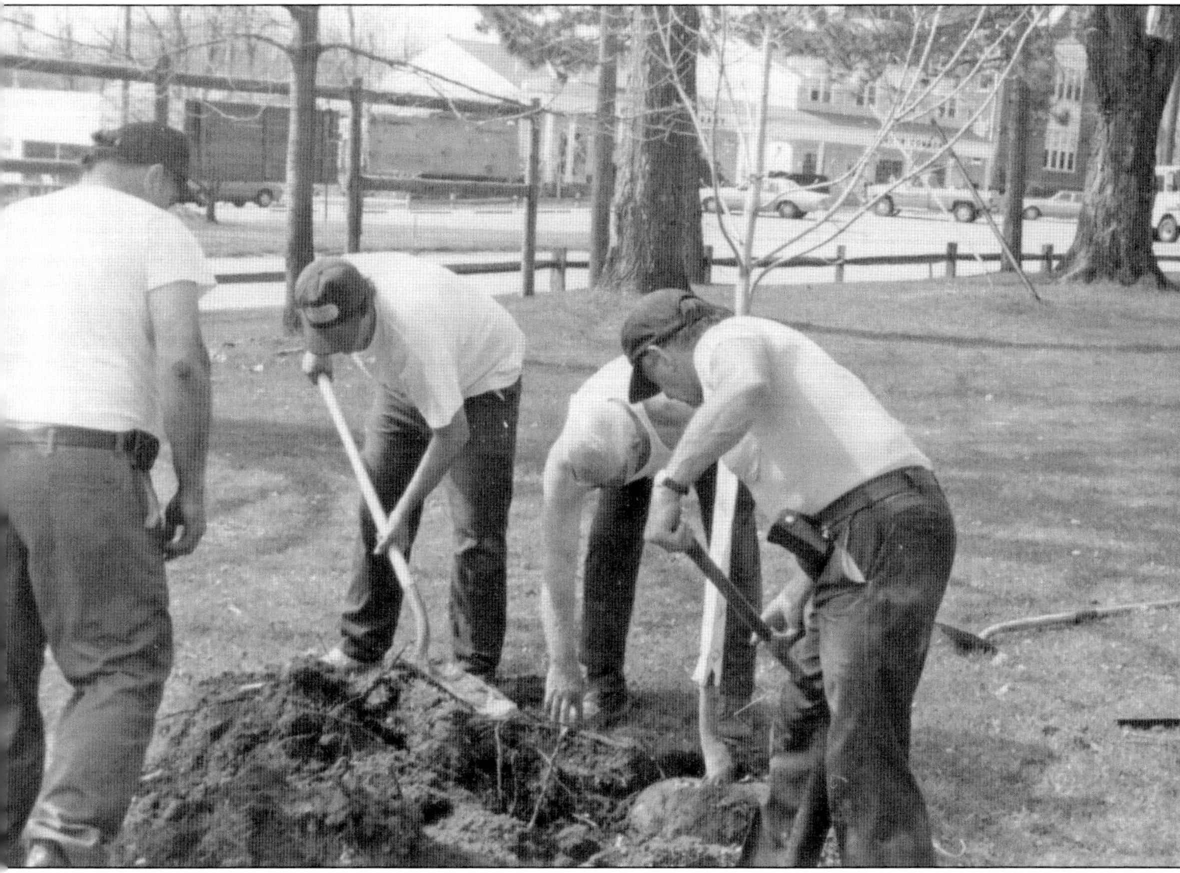

Over the years, a lot of time and effort has been taken to maintain and care for the land deeded to Burton by the founders of the community. Shown here planting more maples in the 1990s are, from left to right, Paul Adams, Paul Eaton, Ture Johnson, and Bob Stack. (Courtesy of Joann J. Hiscox.)

Five

Interesting People and Unique Places

From the first settlers to the present-day custodians of Burton history, countless individuals have been integral in comprising the fabric of this historically significant settlement. Burton's history is filled with intriguing figures such as E.P. Latham, the Civil War veteran who lost both of his arms and the sight in one of his eyes during an overzealous celebration after a victory at the Battle of Cumberland Gap on June 18, 1862. Not one to allow his physical deficiencies hinder his innumerable aspirations, Latham learned to write with a pen between his teeth, was renowned for his remarkable horsemanship, and became a successful cattle buyer; he even served as president of the Geauga Agricultural Society for a time.

This building is endowed with an unusual and interesting history, having served as a town hall, an opera house, a movie theater, and currently as the home of the Burton Fire Department, which had its start in the basement with 17 volunteer firemen and just one truck.

An important event took place on November 23, 1877, when Burton became home to the first telephone line in Ohio. The wires led from the Baltimore & Ohio train depot to the Boughton, Ford & Co. bank, two and a half miles away.

However, no single event may have been more significant than the scandalous 1903 failure of that bank, after which many financially forlorn citizens accused the formerly impervious members of the prestigious Ford family of embezzlement. None of the charges were substantiated, but the collapse inflicted an enormous amount of economic damage on the village.

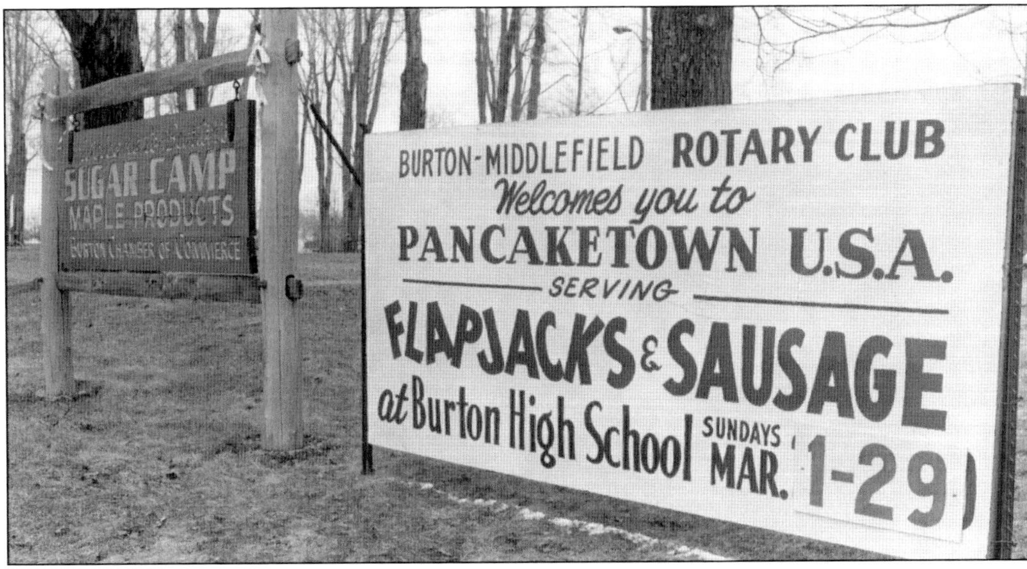

The Burton-Middlefield Rotary Club officially trademarked "Pancake Town U.S.A.," a declaration backed up by an ample supply of delectable pancake breakfasts cooked and consumed at the commencement of each spring. Every March since 1951, more than 20,000 people come from around the state to sample the pancakes served with homemade syrup and sausage courtesy of the Log Cabin Sugar Camp. Overall, approximately 1.5 million pancakes have been served to nearly 450,000 people in Burton. (Courtesy of Special Collections, Michael Schwartz Library, Cleveland State University.)

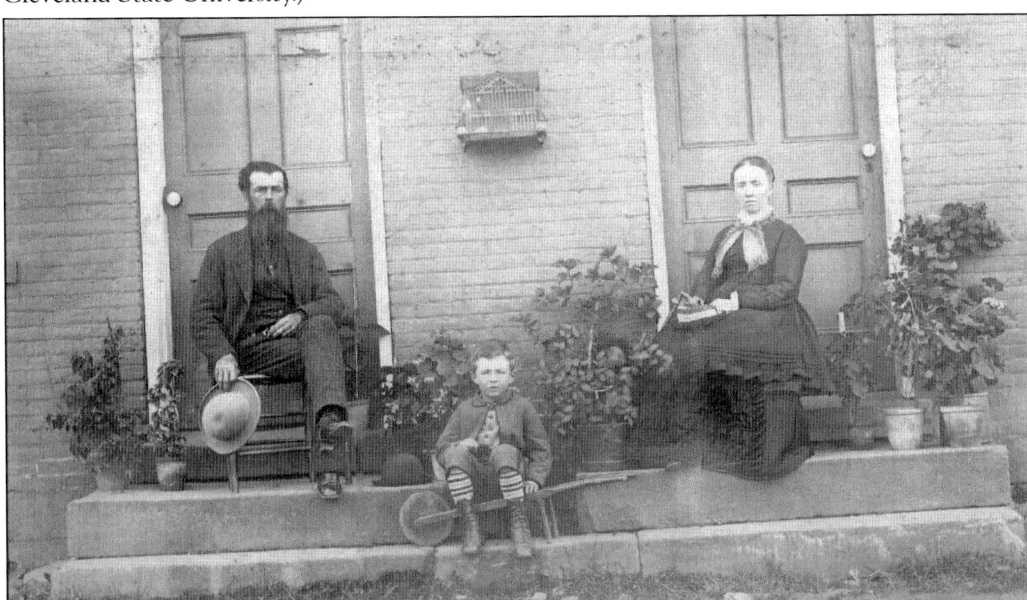

A young Hiram Russell is shown here with his parents. Russell married Mildred Sanford in 1913, and together the couple modernized the Peffers house, which the Russell family had gained ownership of through a previous marriage in 1864. Hiram and Mildred converted the house into a popular lodging and eating establishment called Ye Olde Homestead. (Courtesy of Geauga Historical Society.)

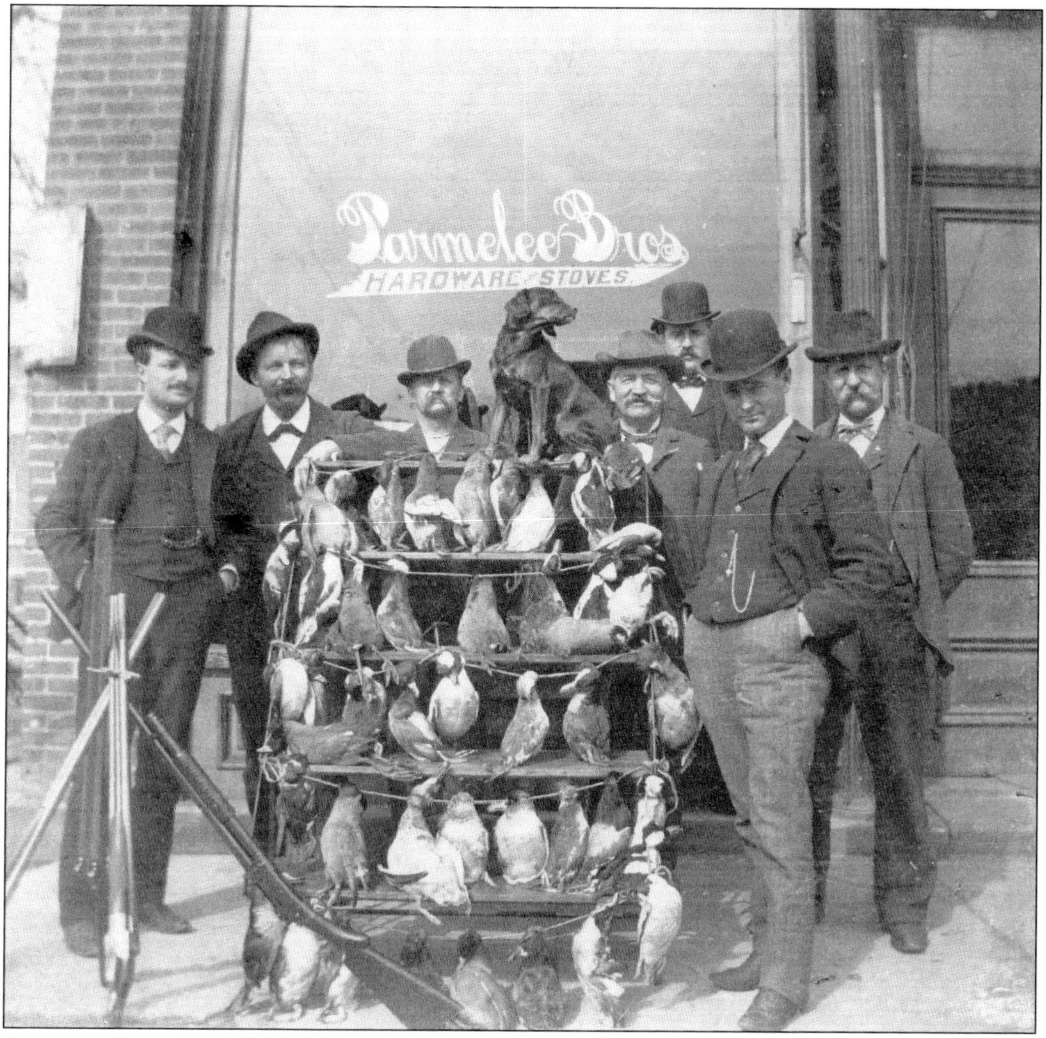

A group of men stands outside of the Parmalee Bros. Hardware store after a triumphant quail hunt on April 15, 1899. Parmalee Bros., established in 1876, featured extensive stocks of hardware, paints, varnishes, window sashes, glass, fence wire, plows, stows, and just about anything else needed for construction, home repairs, or remodeling. For 27 years, it was a lucrative enterprise for brothers Frank and P.W. Parmalee, but the Boughton Bank failure of 1903 devastated their business, as it did to so many other businesses and individuals, and the brothers had to close their doors forever. (Courtesy of Geauga County Historical Society.)

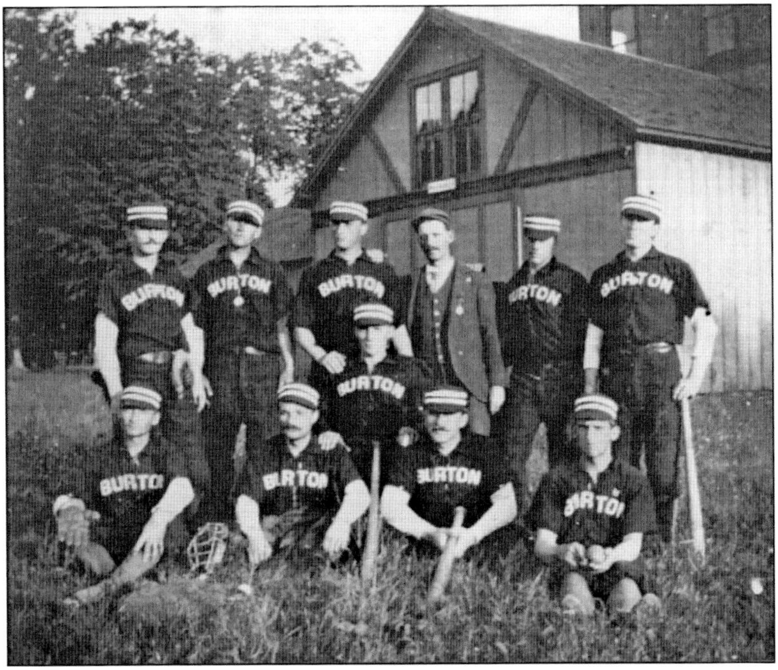

From 1880 through 1897, Burton was renowned for its successful baseball team, when the northeastern Ohio championship belonged to Burton on four different occasions. Their success transcended the borders of Geauga County, as they bested some of the finest semiprofessional squads the Cleveland metropolitan area had to offer. (Courtesy of Geauga County Historical Society.)

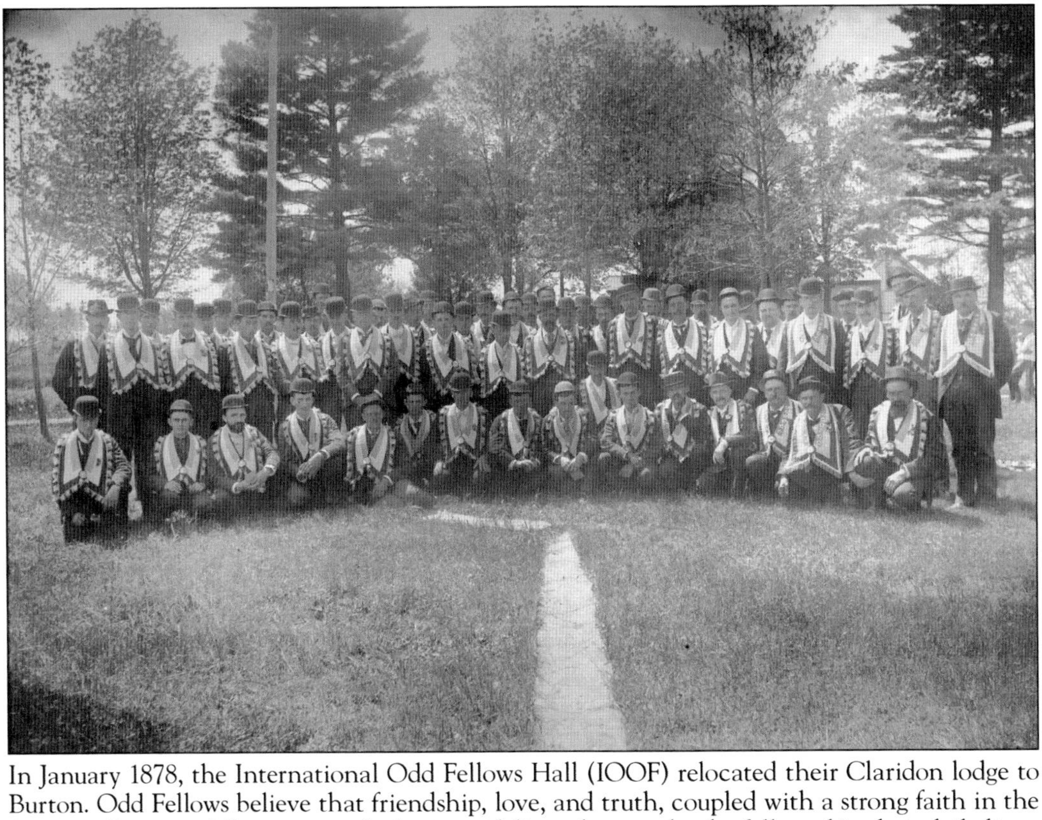

In January 1878, the International Odd Fellows Hall (IOOF) relocated their Claridon lodge to Burton. Odd Fellows believe that friendship, love, and truth, coupled with a strong faith in the Supreme Being and Creator, are the basic guidelines that need to be followed in their daily lives. (Courtesy of Burton Public Library.)

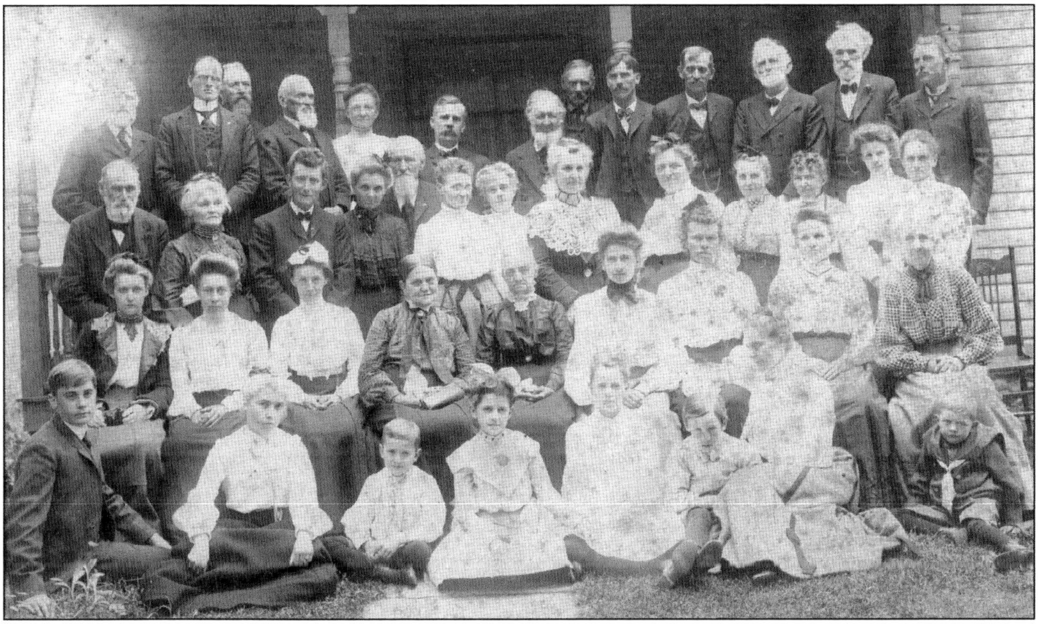

This photograph was taken from a *Geauga Leader* reporter's reunion in the early 1900s. The *Leader* was Burton's first newspaper, with its maiden issue published on December 18, 1874. The *Leader* started as a five-column quarto but expanded its content considerably. J.B. Coffin was the original publisher, and subsequent publishers of note included C.J. Olds and his son Francis. (Courtesy of Geauga County Historical Society.)

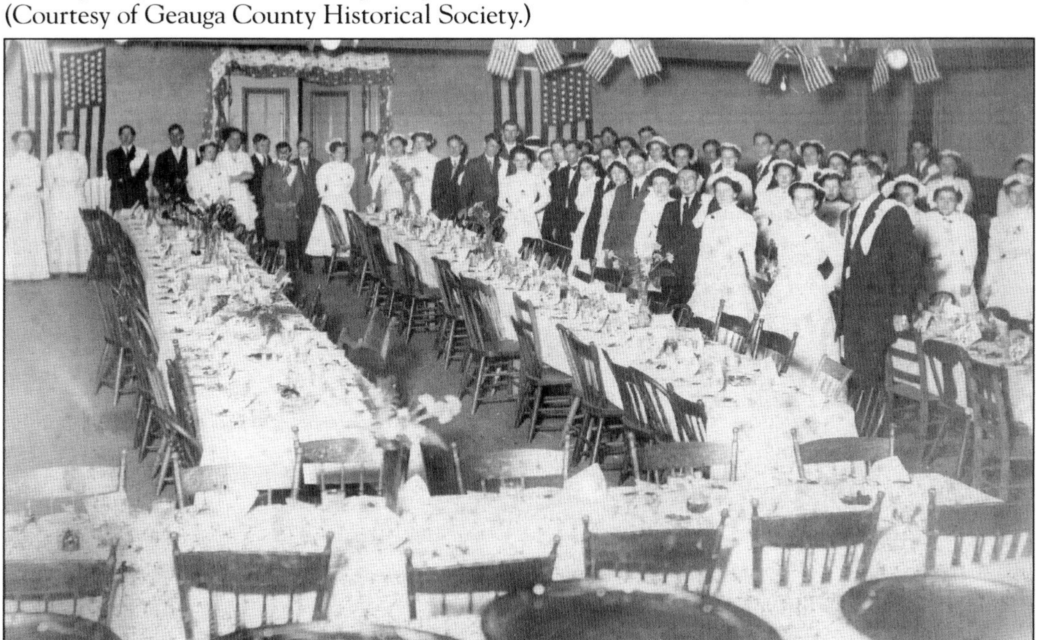

In 1907, the Republican Party held a banquet in Burton, which has long been a party stronghold, hosting a number of major Republican functions. A mere 10 years before this banquet, the Republican Party kicked off its campaign with a rally in support of Sen. Mark Hanna's reelection bid at the fairgrounds; nearly 10,000 enthusiastic devotees attended. (Courtesy of Geauga County Historical Society.)

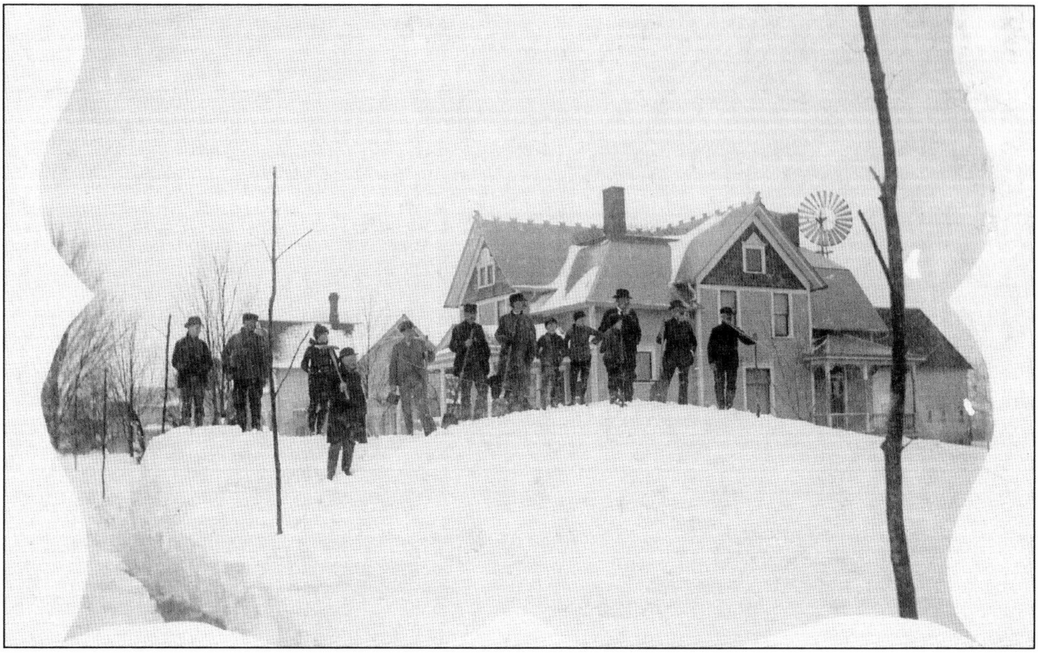

Burton has had its share of treacherous snowstorms, but the blizzards on April 19 and 20 in 1901 were especially harsh. The effect of the low-pressure area was felt over a substantial expanse of land and sea, as an irregular band of precipitation stretched from southern Ontario as far south as Cuba. More than two feet of snow fell in less than 36 hours in many parts of Ohio, disabling much of the northeastern portion of the state, including Burton, for days. (Courtesy of Geauga County Historical Society.)

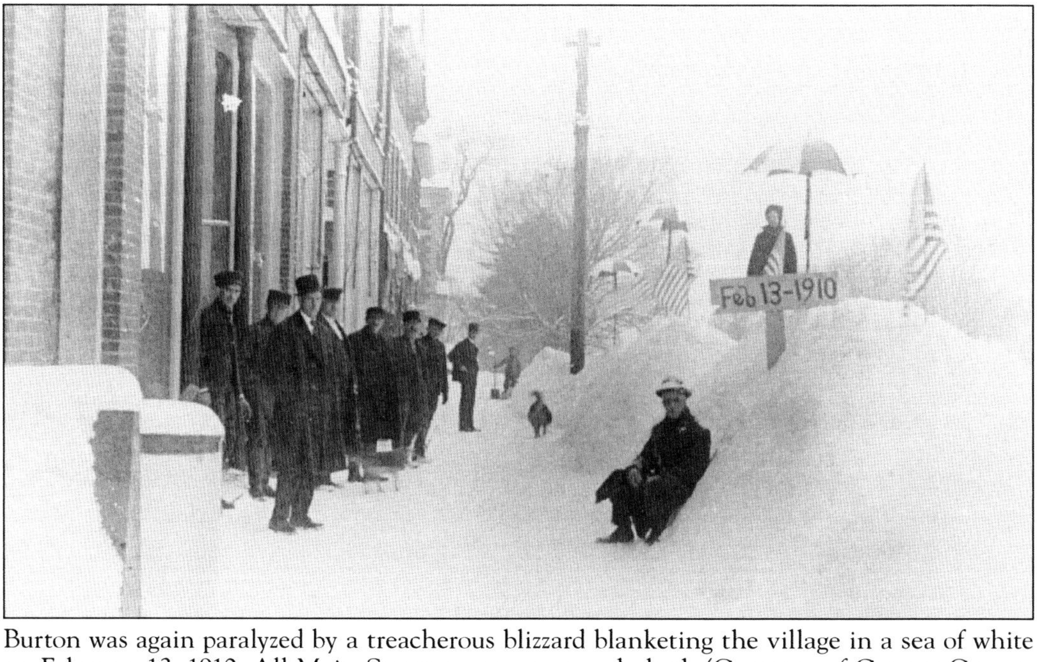

Burton was again paralyzed by a treacherous blizzard blanketing the village in a sea of white on February 13, 1910. All Main Street commerce was halted. (Courtesy of Geauga County Historical Society.)

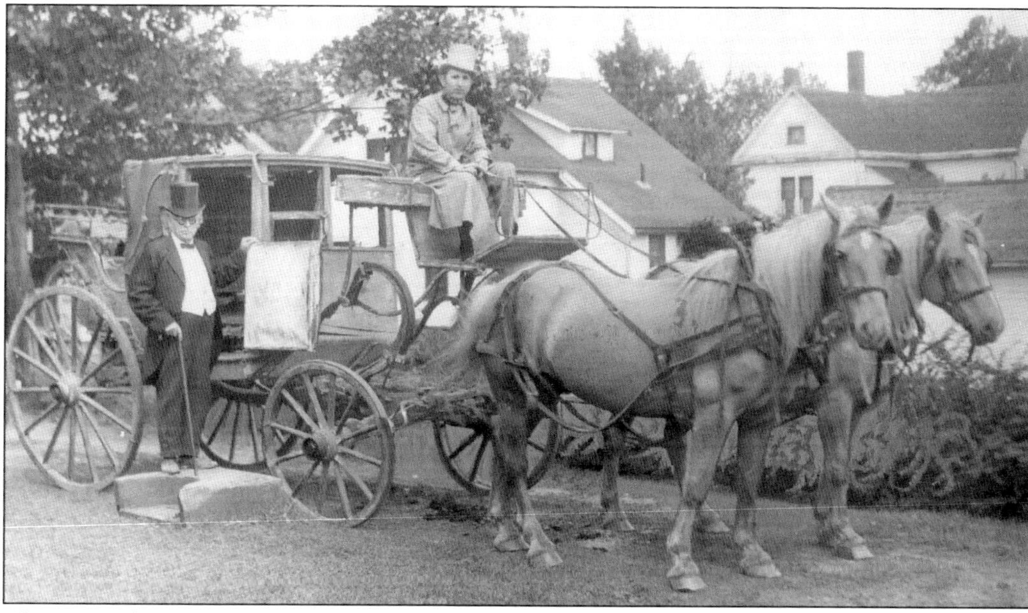

This 1931 photograph, most likely taken at the fairgrounds, shows T.R. Dean (coachman) and N.B. Canfield. The Marquis de Lafayette, the French aristocrat and military officer who honorably served as a major general for the Continental Army under George Washington during the American Revolution, allegedly rode in this coach while visiting America in 1787. (Courtesy of Special Collections, Michael Schwartz Library, Cleveland State University.)

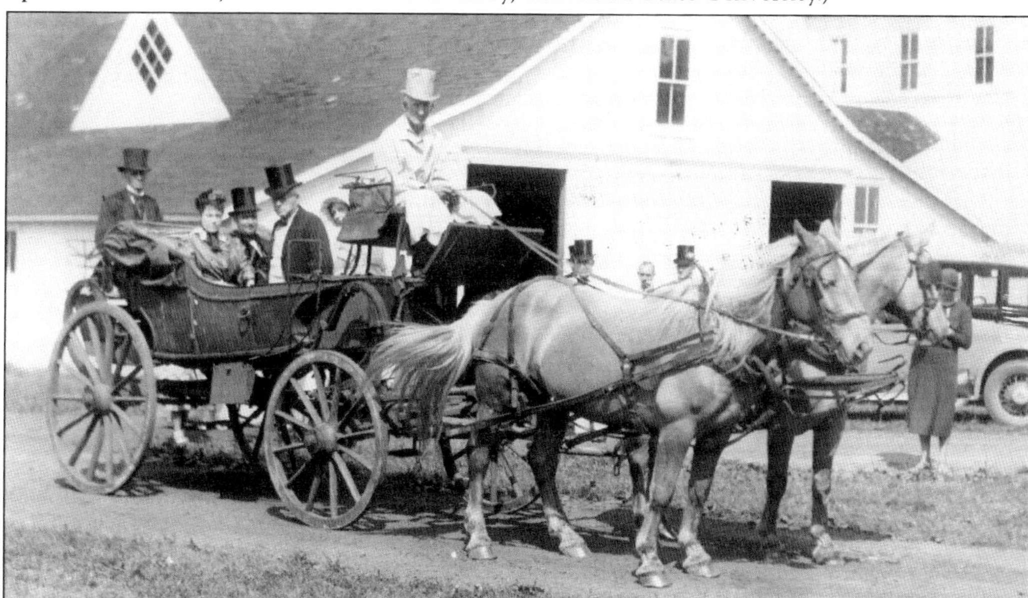

This coach, allegedly owned by Edward III of England at one time, is seen utilized by prominent Burton citizens on August 8, 1931. Coachman Perry Crosley provides a carriage ride for N.B. Canfield and Helen Coats (seated backward), R.L. Coats (rear), Lowell Masters, and B.J. Shanower (facing front), who was mayor of Burton, president of the Geauga County Historical Society, and president of the Geauga County School Board for more than 20 years. (Courtesy of Special Collections, Michael Schwartz Library, Cleveland State University.)

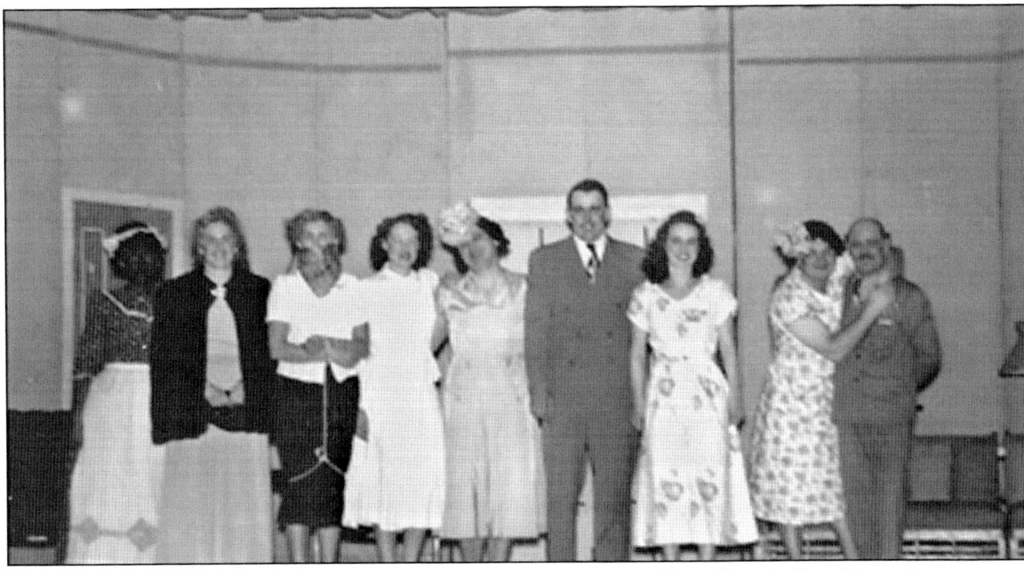

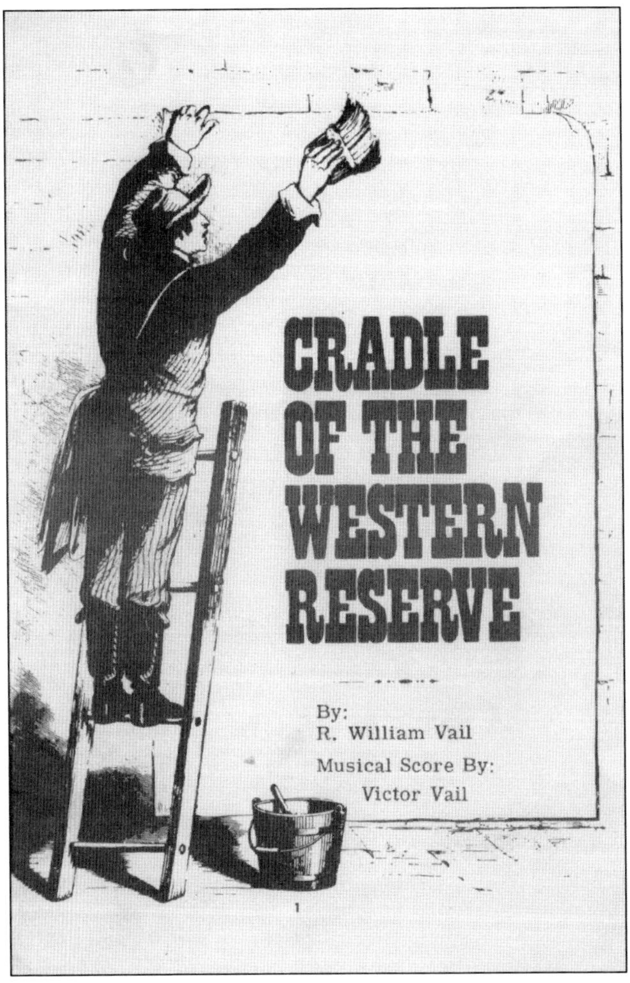

Your Face Is Familiar, a farce in three acts, was presented by the Women's Auxiliary and the Burton Volunteer Fire Department on Monday, March 26, 1951, at the Burton School Auditorium. Seen here from left to right, Addie Farmwald, Kay Russell, Jeanette Burnett, Barbara Goff, Wendell Hansel, Karl Goff, Patricia Williams, George Williams, and Carl Harms made up the entire cast. (Courtesy of Burton Public Library.)

In 1973, *Cradle of the Western Reserve*, written and directed by R. William Vail, was performed specifically to commemorate the 175th anniversary of Burton. The author's son Victor composed the music for the production, and his wife, Martha, played Hope, the female lead. (Courtesy of Burton Public Library.)

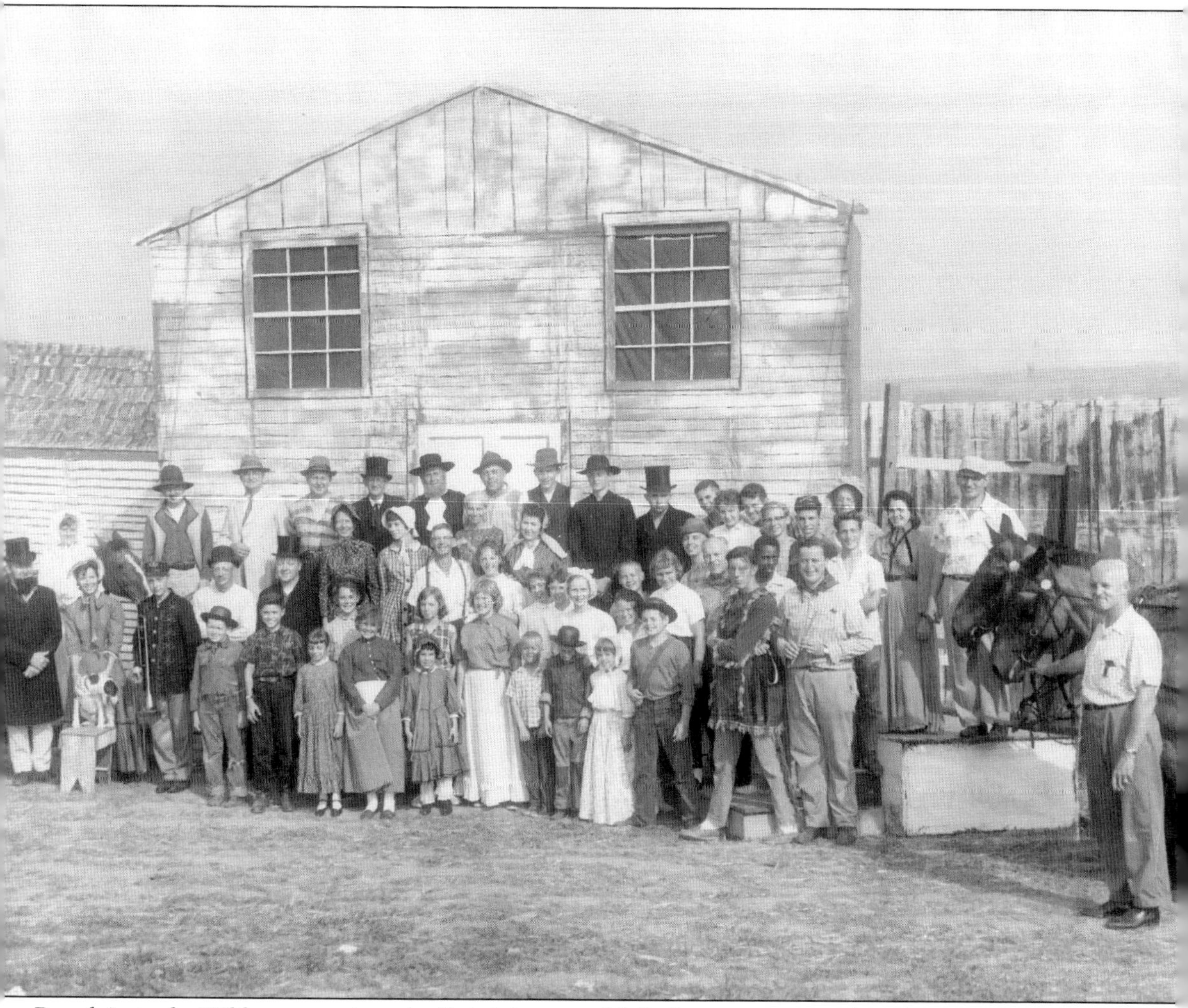

Broad Ax in the Wilderness, written by E.A. Moore and P.G. Contius, was produced in 1960 by the American Heritage Theatre Association, a local organization that put on a different play every year pertaining to the Western Reserve. This photograph includes, in no particular order, Bob Schwind, Jackie Schwind, Betsy Samuel, Raymond Stone, Glenn Evans, Clyde Russell, Elmer Pierce, Ture Johnson, Lois Hann, Hugh Locke, Linda Rice, Harry Reynolds, Gordon Hann, Keith Evans, Mahel Cook, Sandy Ford, Helen Roy, Rob Roy, Kenneth Miller (in top hat), Harmond Richardson, Frank Merritt, a Mr. Arnold, Shirley MacMillen, Jerry Gentile, Mary Dee Foft, Donna Burnett, Dick Locke, Stephanie Mann, M. Schwind, Bitsy Ludlow, Susan Ludlow, Sally Ludlow, J. Margaret Samuel, Robin Schwind, Shari Walters, Jerry Dines, a Mr. Furbee, Carl Weln, Dicky Mann, Tom Ludlow, Janet Wells, Tommy Ford, John Dingman, Tony the horse, Pupper the dog, and Jake Miller's team. (Courtesy of Jacqueline Samuel.)

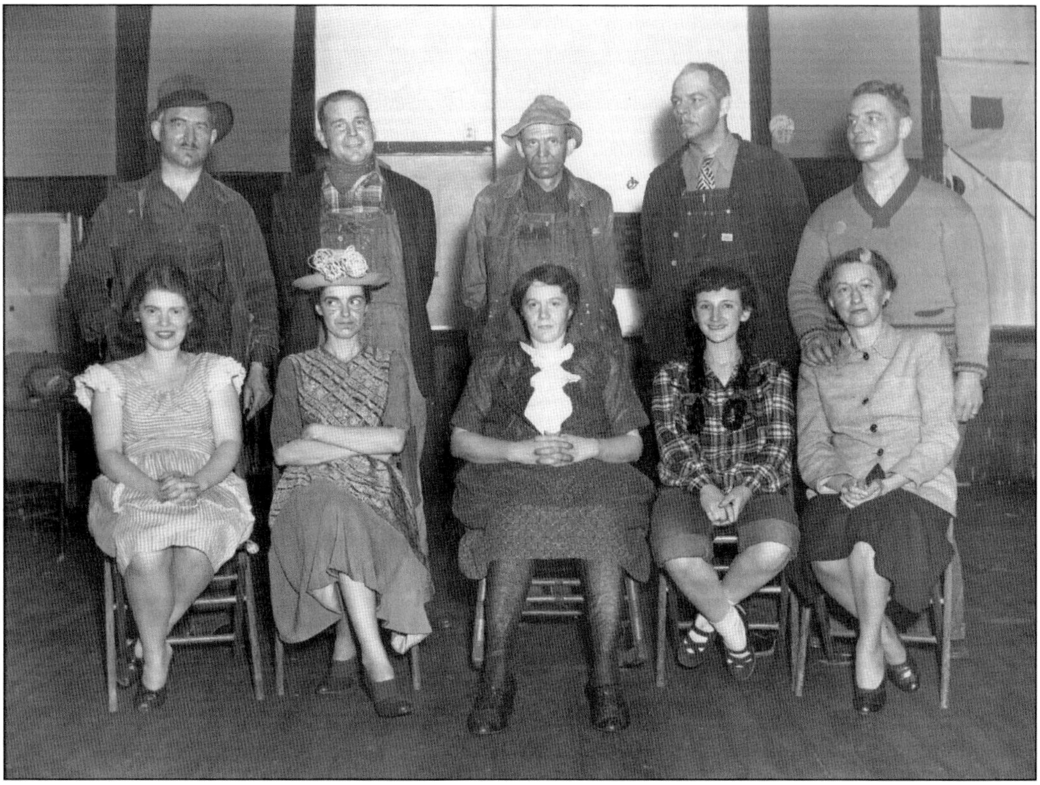

The Mr. & Mrs. Club was a Burton Village drama club that staged plays in the mid-1900s. In 1948, Dorothy Russell directed this production of *Apple of His Eye*, featuring, from left to right, (first row) Sally Hornhorst, Dorothy Barthold, Ethel Rowland, Katie Stuart, and Ethel Dingman; (second row) Glenn Maben, Ture Johnson, Frank Samuel, Bruce Scott, and county agent Charles A. Haas. (Courtesy of Geauga County Historical Society.)

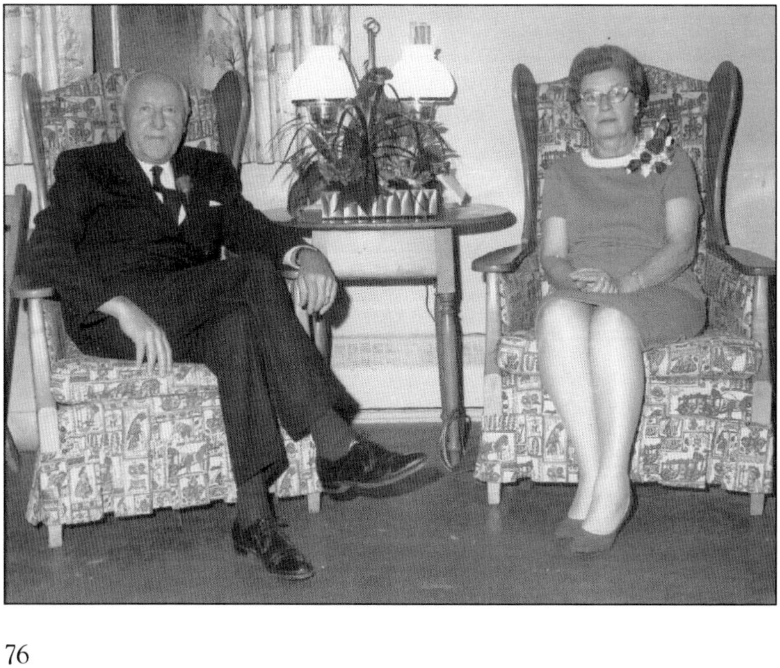

Dr. William Albert Reed and his wife, Lois Darsie Reed, pose for this 1978 photograph. Dr. Reed was the trusted town physician for many years. His house, located on the east side of the park, was built by Edward Griswold and Silas Gaylord, the duo responsible for the construction of several historic homes in the village. (Courtesy of Elizabeth A. Cupp.)

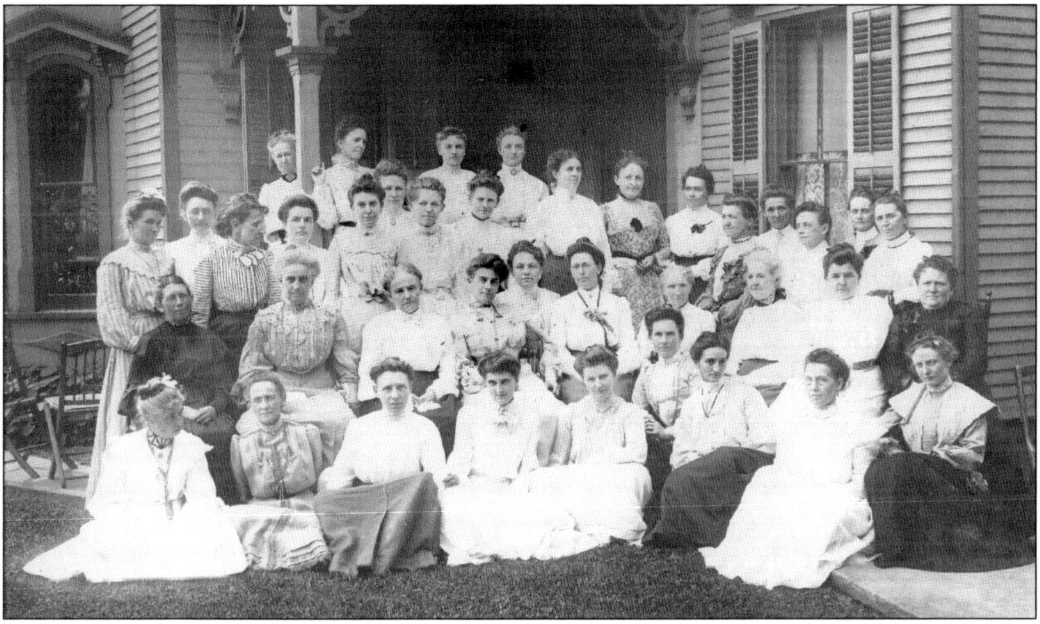

The two most prominent ladies' literary clubs in Burton are the Tuesday Club, formed in 1895 at the home of Corrine Ford, and the Clio Club, named after the goddess of poetry and history, formed three years later. Both of these esteemed groups met to read and discuss literature, as well as donate to needy causes. They came together for this photograph in 1904. (Courtesy of Geauga County Historical Society.)

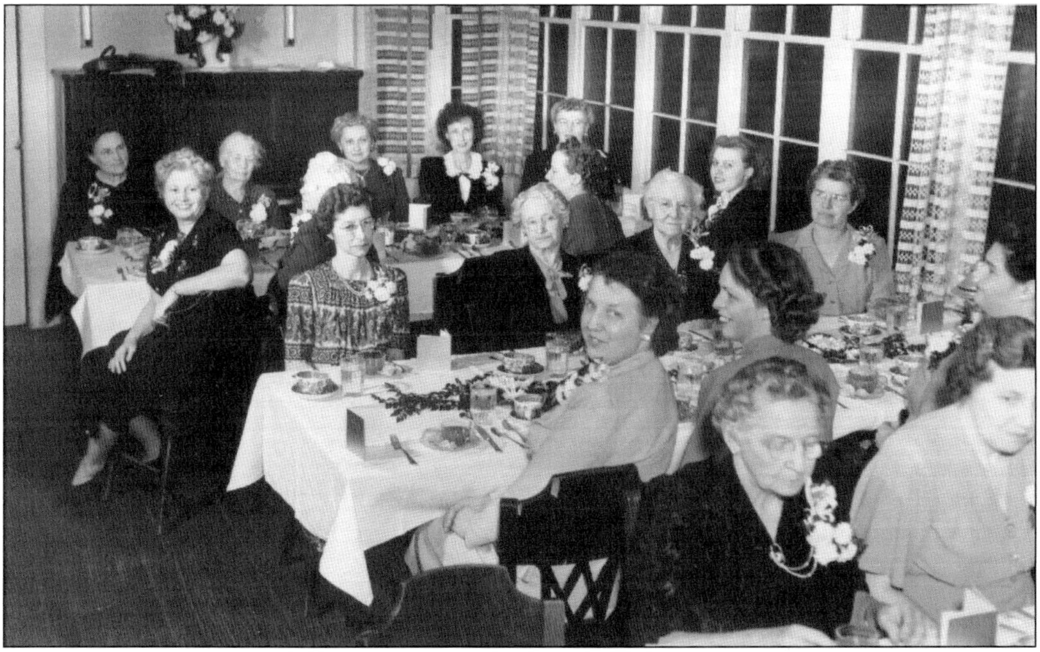

Members of the Clio Club included, in no order, Grace Brown, Bertha Johnson, Helen Laughlin, Donna Dean, Faye Owen, Pauline Hedlund, Elizabeth Nye, Marjorie Ludlow, Marjorie Wells, Lois Smith, Rose Strang, Vern Richards, Alta Linton, Katherine Maben, Helen Neill, Mildred Blair, Grace Petersen, and Nellie Petersen. (Courtesy of Mary L. Wilson.)

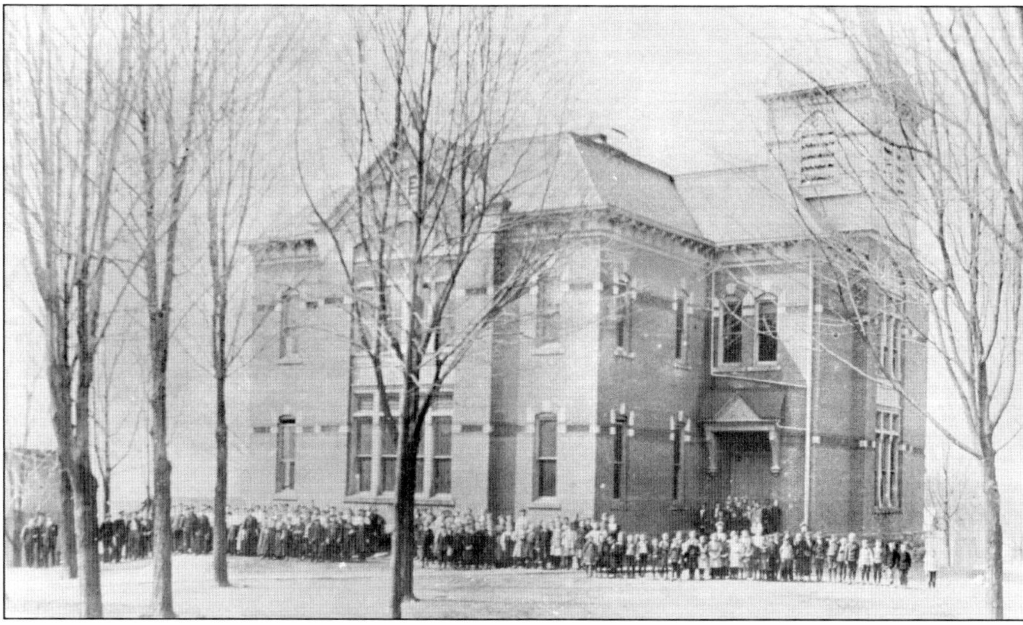

The Burton Public Library originally opened on January 19, 1910, with a yearly membership fee of $1. The library was relocated on numerous occasions, but in 1937, it found its permanent home in what had formerly been the second high school. (Courtesy of Geauga County Historical Society.)

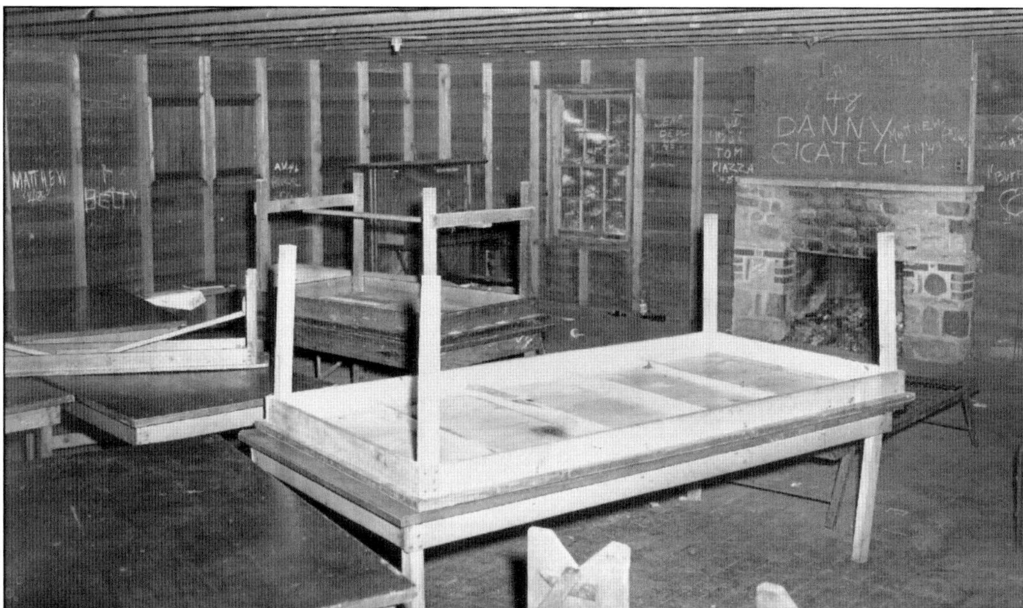

For a brief time approximately 50 years ago, Alta House had a camp in Burton. Founded in 1895 by John D. Rockefeller, the Alta House Social Settlement began as an organization offering support for Italian immigrants in the Mayfield-Murray Hill area of Cleveland, better known today as Little Italy. Children from that area came to Burton for summer camp. Alta House Camp was located on Hotchkiss Road. A small amount of information was recorded regarding the settlement's Burton camp. (Courtesy of Special Collections, Michael Schwartz Library, Cleveland State University.)

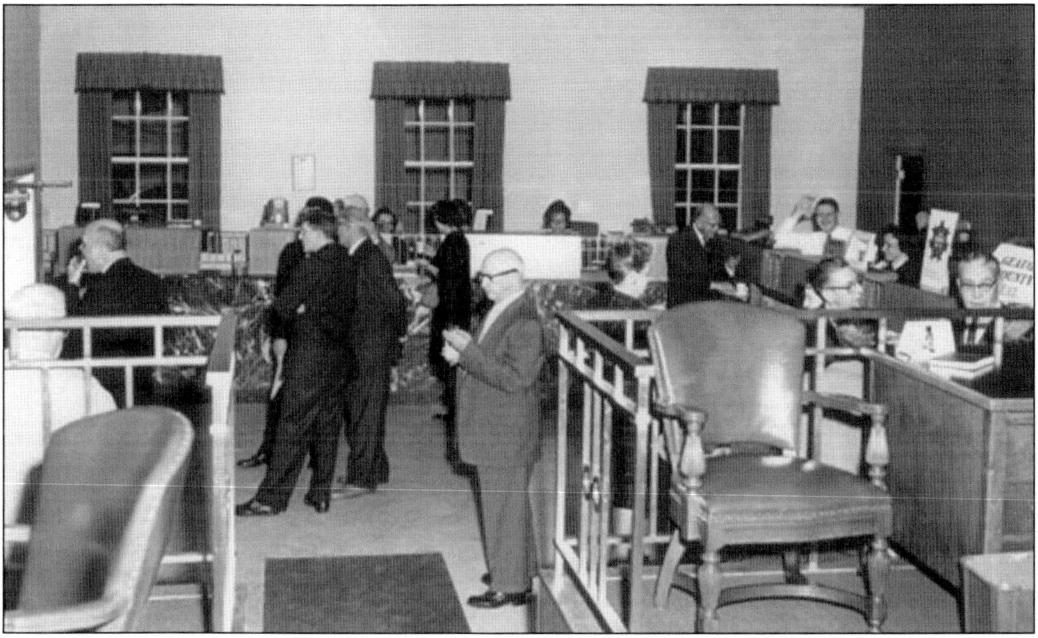

Bank employees and patrons interact at the First National Bank of Burton in 1963. The bank opened in 1902, just months prior to the collapse of the Boughton, Ford & Co. bank in January 1903. Boughton's collapse allowed First National Bank to become the dominant financial institution in Burton. (Courtesy of Elmer Bollinger and Rosa Herst.)

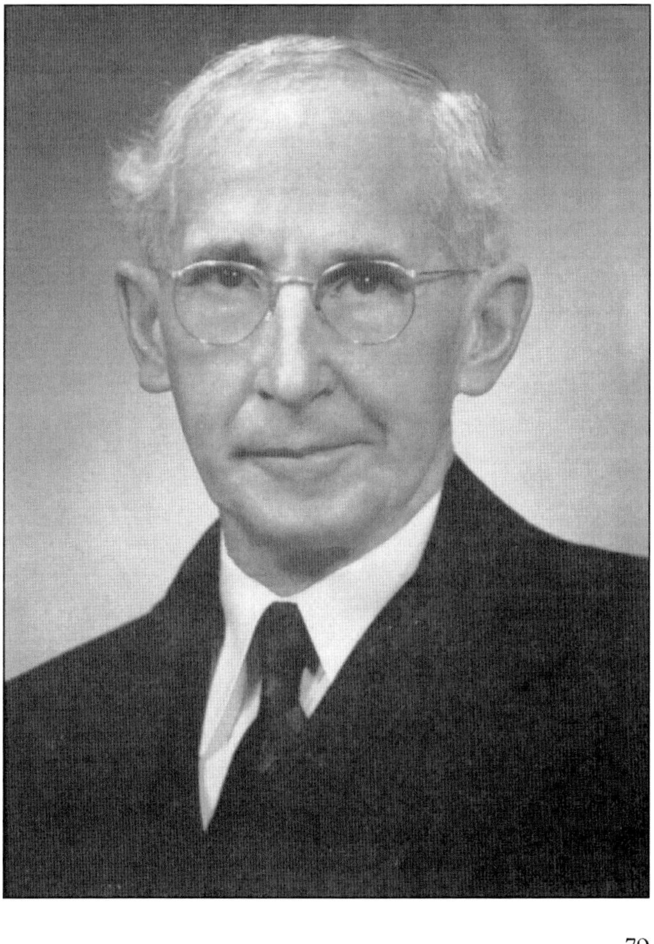

G.B. Fox was a prominent figure in Burton, serving as village treasurer for 34 years from 1915 to 1949, directing the sales of bonds during World War II, and acting as president of the First National Bank of Burton. Through his job at the bank, first as a cashier and then in his lengthy tenure as president, from 1911 until his retirement in 1957, and his position on the bank's board of directors, he was known and respected in the village. (Courtesy of Elmer Bollinger And Rosa Herst.)

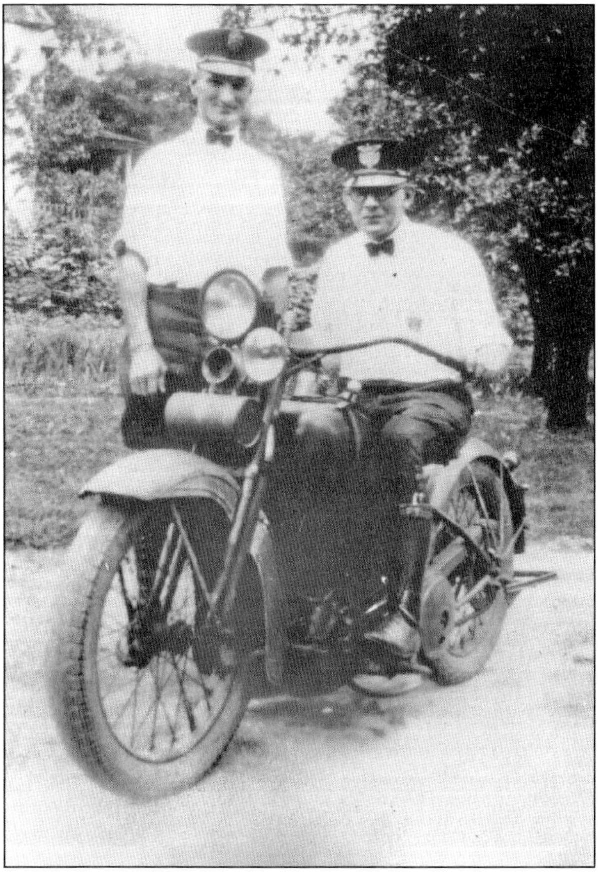

Venerable Burton residents Ray Linton (left) and Laverne Petersen were police constables. Linton went on to become the first fire chief of the Burton Volunteer Fire Department, serving from 1926 through 1930. (Courtesy of Mary L. Wilson.)

On January 14, 1926, a small group of men led by chairman G.E. Olson called for the organization of the Burton Volunteer Fire Department. The firemen served not only their hometown, but also Troy, Claridon, Newbury, and Auburn. Kurt Vonnegut once described volunteer firefighters as "the only examples of enthusiastic unselfishness to be seen in this land." Burton and its neighbors are blessed to have been bestowed with these volunteer firefighters who have served with enthusiastic unselfishness since 1926. Even though this fire was in Chardon, it exemplifies the scene at that time. (Courtesy of Special Collections, Michael Schwartz Library, Cleveland State University.)

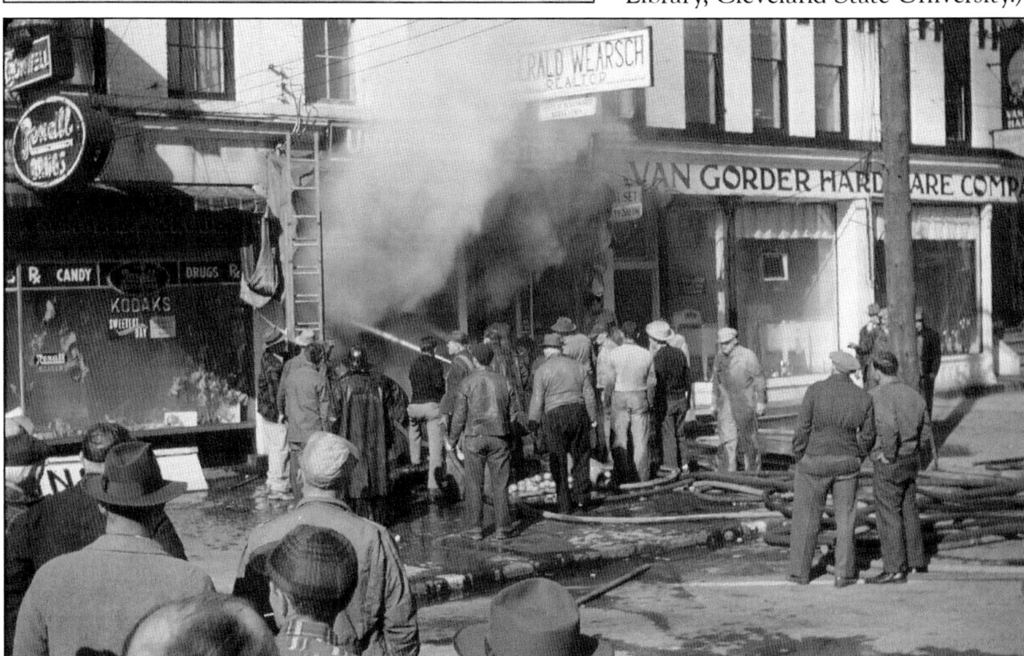

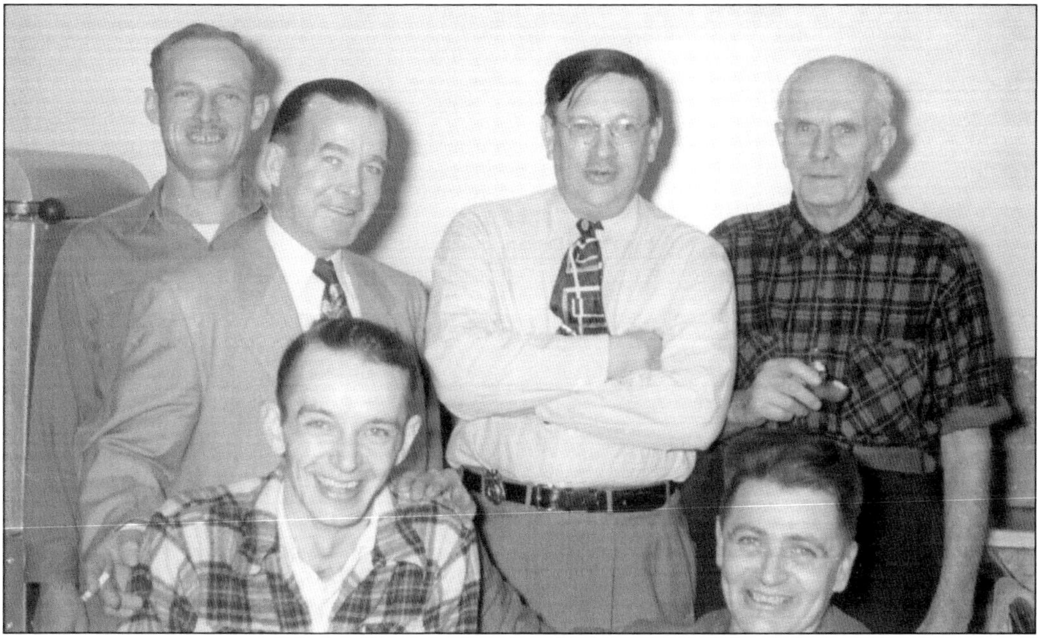

A party was thrown for the opening of the Burton firehouse in Old Town Hall in 1957. From left to right are Bill Owen, Walter Osborn, Clyde Russell, Frank Brown, Harry Bolander, and Oliver Smith. (Courtesy of Geauga County Historical Society.)

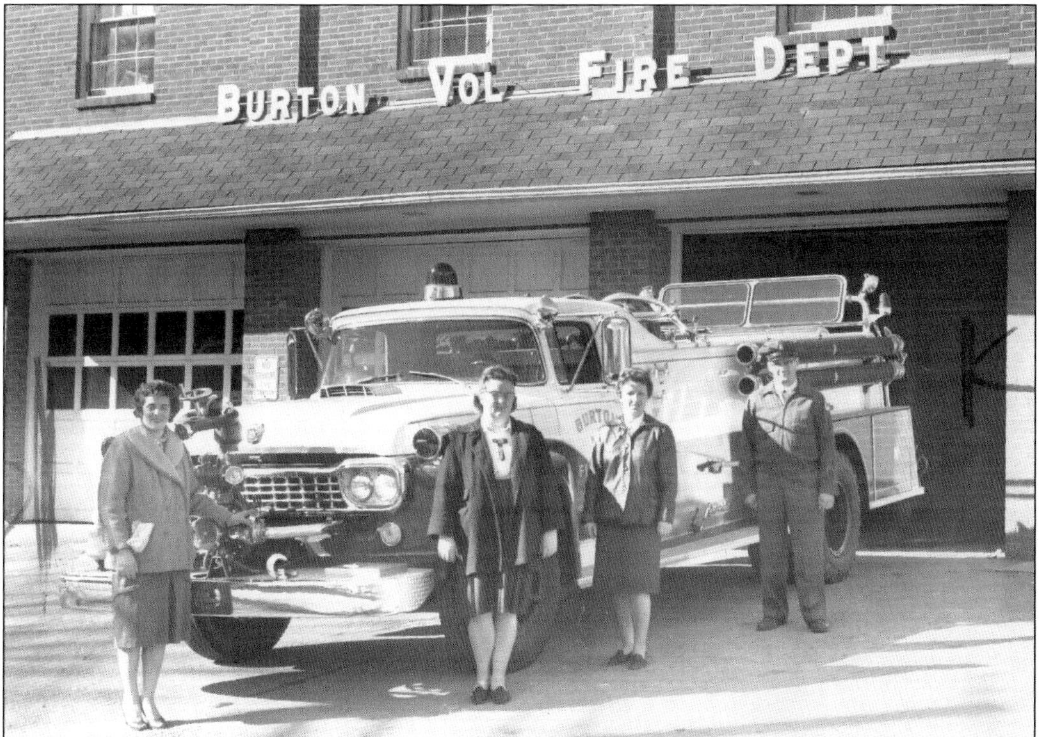

From left to right, Kay Russell, Pat Malensek, Ann Vickeroy, and assistant fire chief Frank Malensek stand in front of the Burton Volunteer Fire Department in 1961. (Courtesy of Joseph E. Cole.)

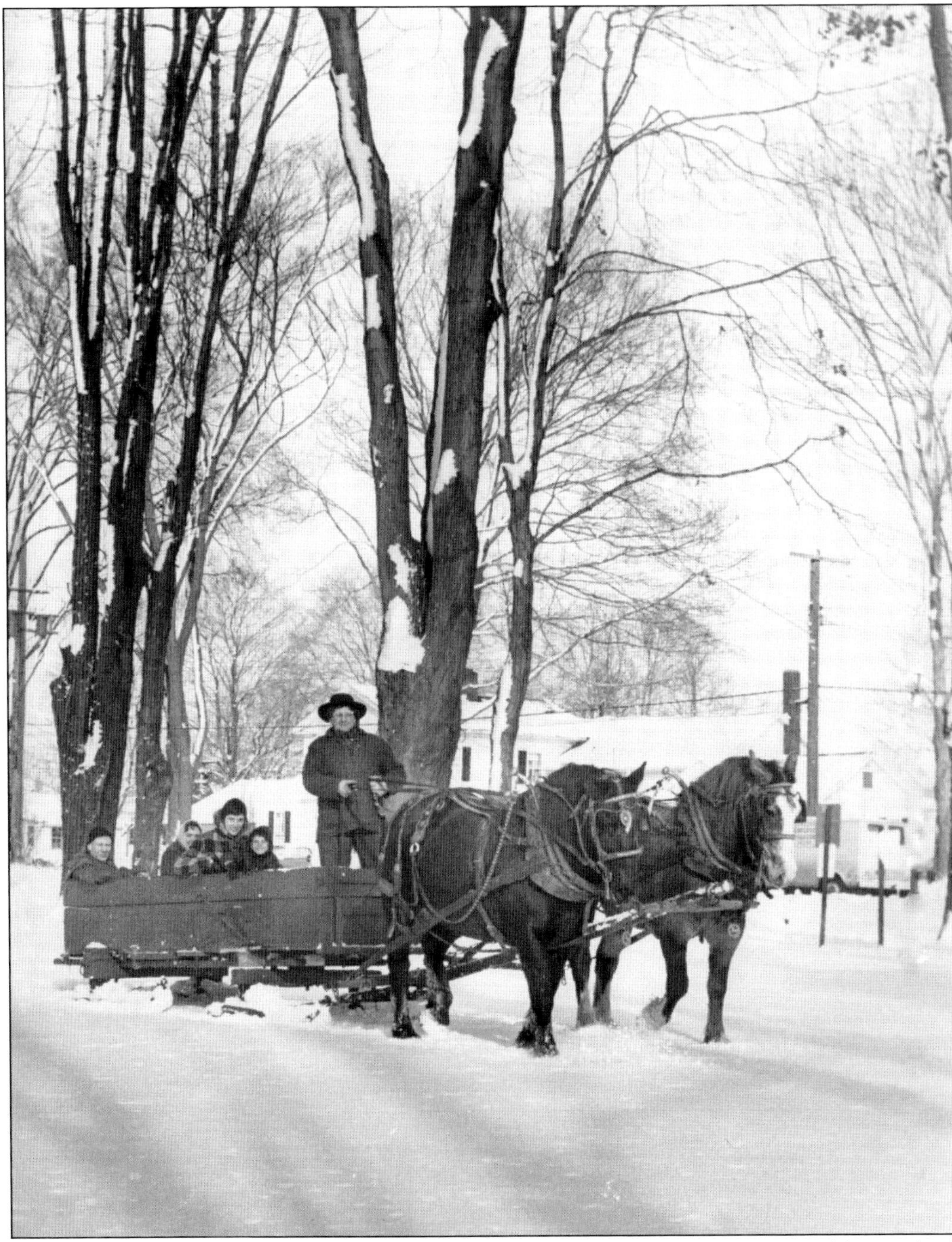

The *Cleveland Press* described this photograph thusly: "Amish man Roman Hershberger leads his prize-winning team of Percherons in bob-sled rides on Burton Square. The sled rides were organized by the Geauga County Historical Society." (Courtesy of Special Collections, Michael Schwartz Library, Cleveland State University.)

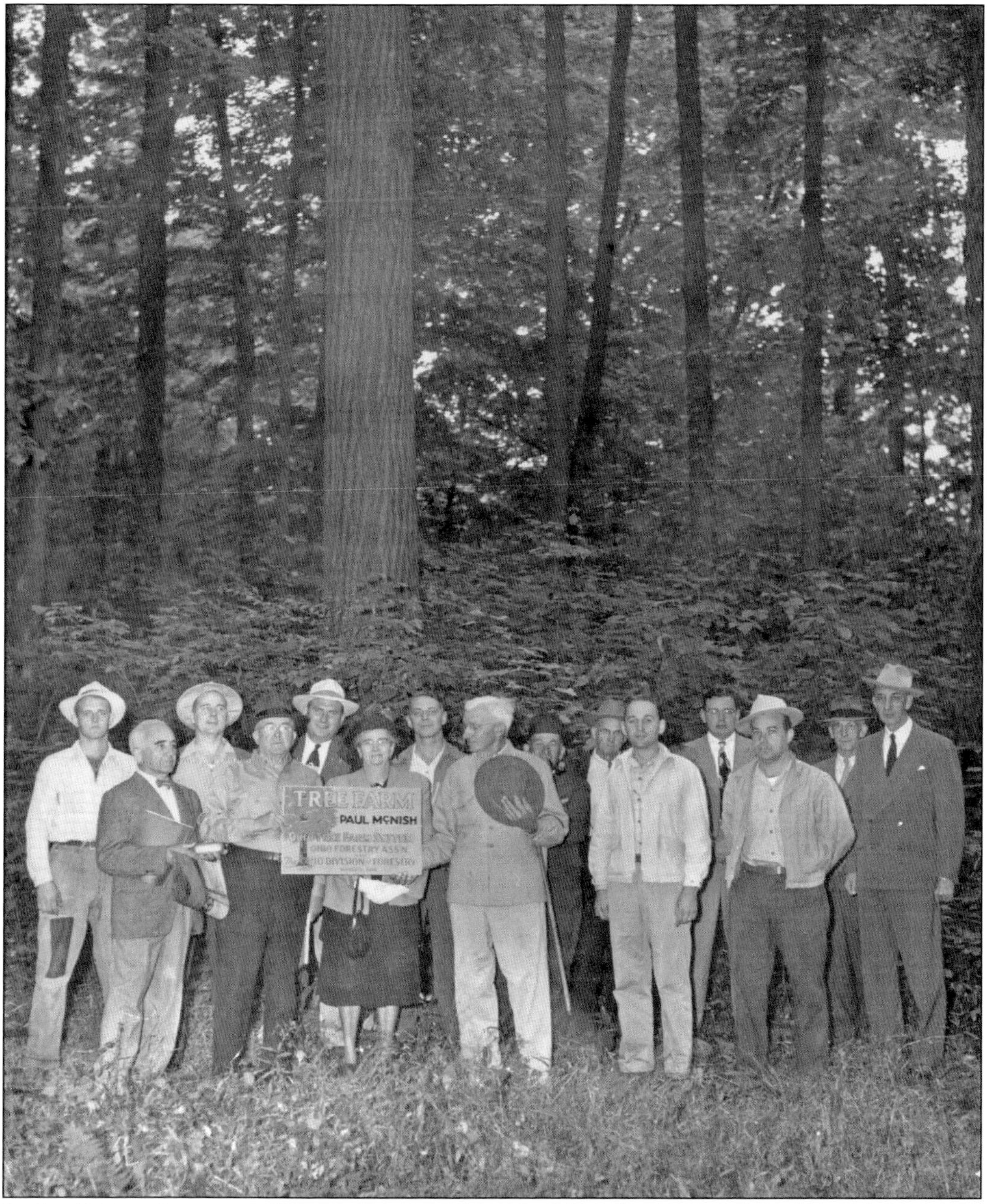

In the 1940s, a forest was planted on 32 acres of acquired land in honor of World War II veterans. While the town has always been passionate about nature, perhaps no Burton citizen was more enthusiastic about forest management and agriculture than Ture Johnson (back row, second from left), whose passion led him to join the Ohio Division of Forestry. (Courtesy of Burton Public Library.)

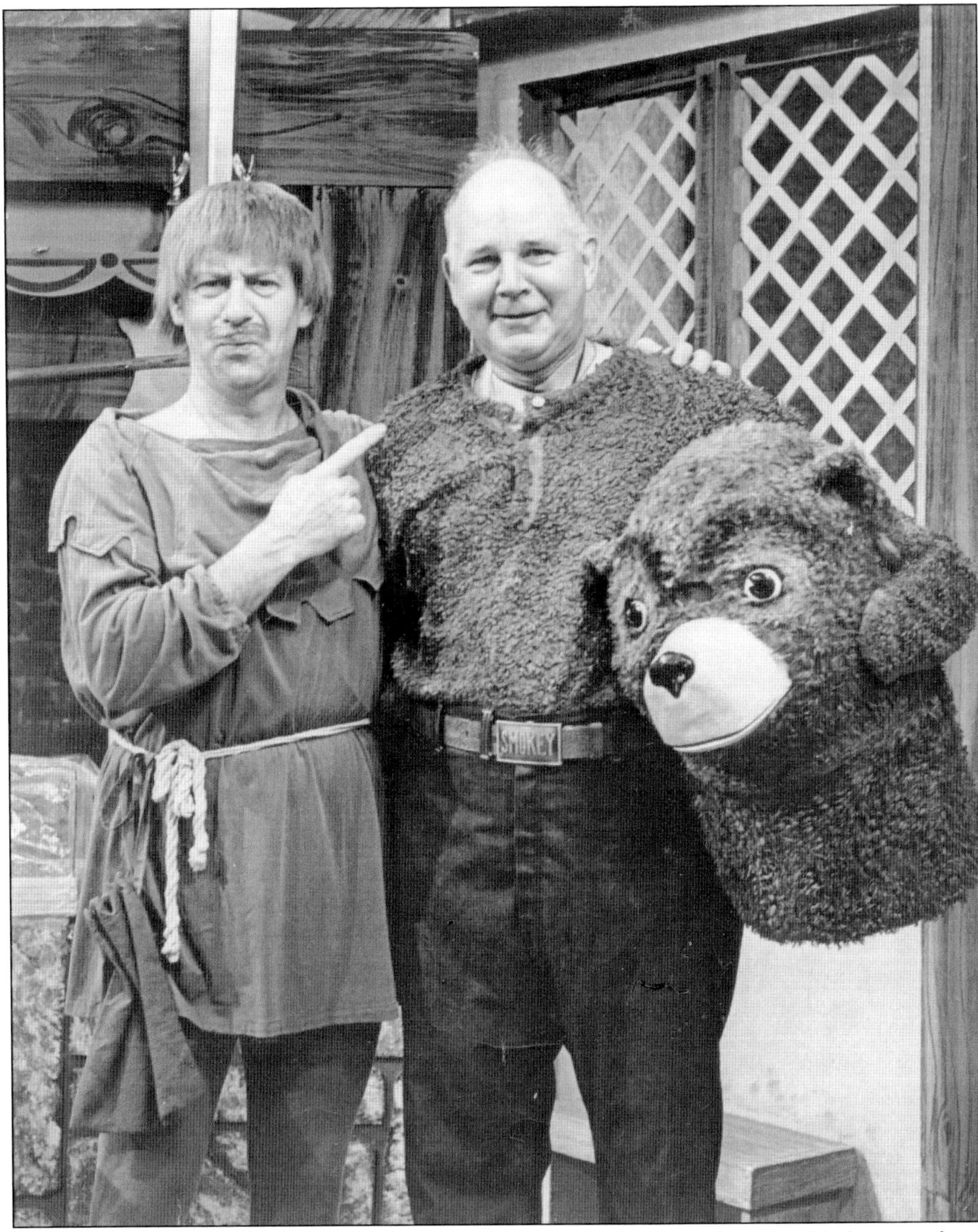

Ture Johnson appeared on the *Woodrow the Woodsman* television show in this bear outfit in 1964. Johnson was a natural guest for the program, as he had devoted many years to forestry and running the maple sugar production in Burton. J. Clayton "Clay" Conroy (left) was the lead actor on the show, whose character had originated on *Barnaby*, the hugely popular Cleveland-area kids program. *Woodrow the Woodsman* ran in Cleveland and Detroit intermittently from 1961 to 1972 and again from 1997 to 2000. (Photograph from the Ture Johnson Archives, courtesy of the Johnson family.)

Six

Worshipping, Shopping, and Doing Business

One of the very first things the citizens of Burton did was establish places to worship. Their religion was important to them, and they wanted to make sure the villagers conducted themselves in a manner befitting their Puritan ancestry. They welcomed Joseph Badger, the first missionary in the Western Reserve, to Burton in 1802, and he established such a reputation in the community that a plaque in Burton Park was placed in his honor more than a century after his arrival.

The Burton Congregational Church and the Methodist Episcopal Church were both holding regular services by 1808; they were the only two churches in Burton until the Church of the Disciples was founded 1848. Today, Burton has many churches of different faiths and has seen a few fade out of existence, such as the Finnish Church, which was open for part of the past century.

Not long after churches and schools opened, Burton turned towards practical matters and began to open stores. In 1802, J.S. Cleveland opened the first store, and others followed. By mid-century, Burton had a flourishing business district with hardware stores, hatters, and drugstores. In the latter part of the 19th century, the east and west blocks were laid out and filled with businesses. When one side burned in 1871, it was quickly rebuilt and is still used today. From businesses such as Parmalee Bros. Hardware and E.E. Dry Goods in the 1880s to Coffee Corners and Gunrunners, which are open today, the east and west blocks have been the centers of Burton's commercial district for well over a century.

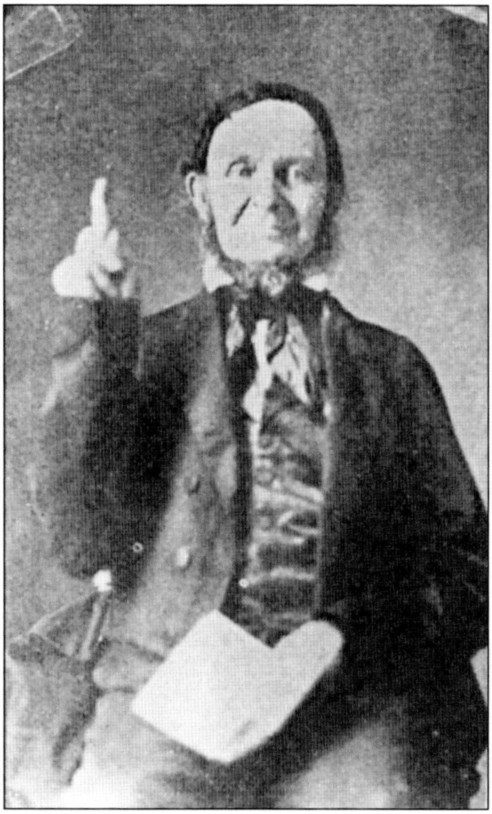

Rev. Luther Humphrey was the Burton Congregational Church's first minister, serving from 1815 to 1828. Humphrey was the cousin of abolitionist John Brown and corresponded with him up until two weeks before Brown's execution. He was also an early leader in the temperance movement and was one of the first ministers in the region to advocate abstinence from alcohol. (Courtesy of the Geauga County Historical Society.)

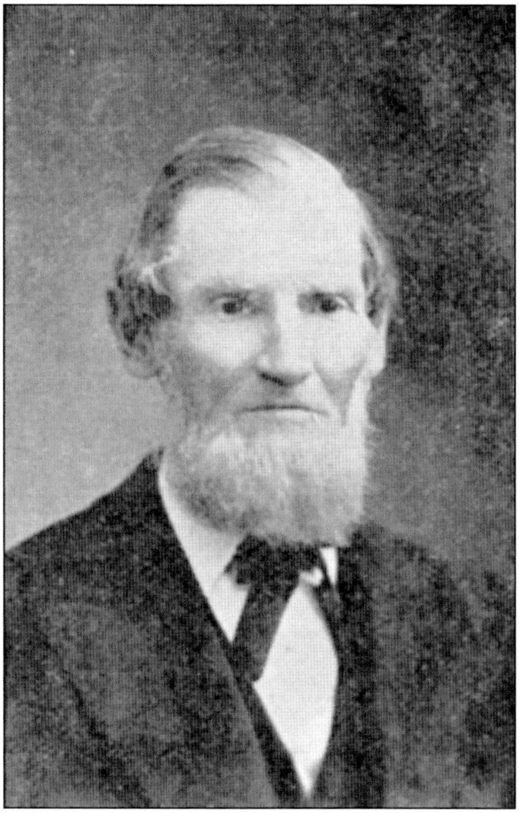

Rev. Dexter Witter was the second and fourth minister of the Burton Congregational Church, occupying the pulpit from 1829 to 1849 and again from 1857 to 1866. After graduating from Yale University, he moved to Burton and taught at the Burton Academy in 1824 and 1825. (Courtesy of the Geauga County Historical Society.)

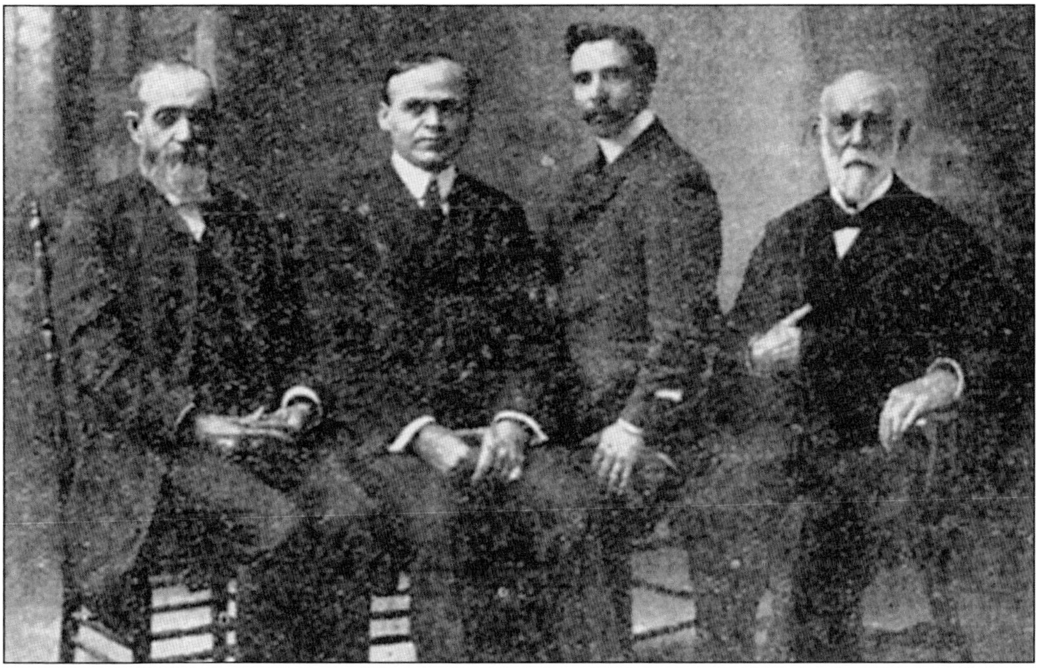

This group photograph shows four of the five ministers of Burton Congregational Church from 1875 to 1906. They are from left to right Rev. William B. Marsh (served 1886–1889), Rev. Elwell O. Mead (1889–1899), Rev. Benjamin A. Williams (1901–1906), and Rev. Charles Cutler (1875–1883). (Courtesy of the Geauga County Historical Society.)

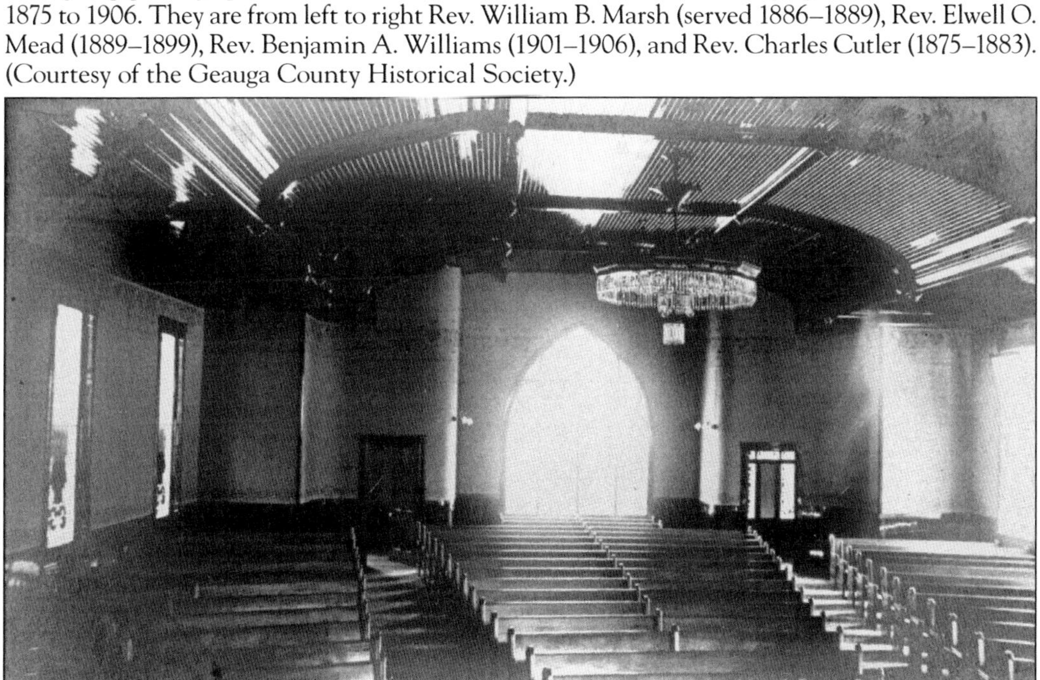

The Burton Congregational Church, seen here from the choir's viewpoint in 1900, was organized on August 22, 1808, by Rev. Enoch Burt, who was sent by a missionary society from Connecticut. It was the 10th Congregational church founded in Ohio and is one of the longest continuously churches running in the state. (Courtesy of Mary L. Wilson.)

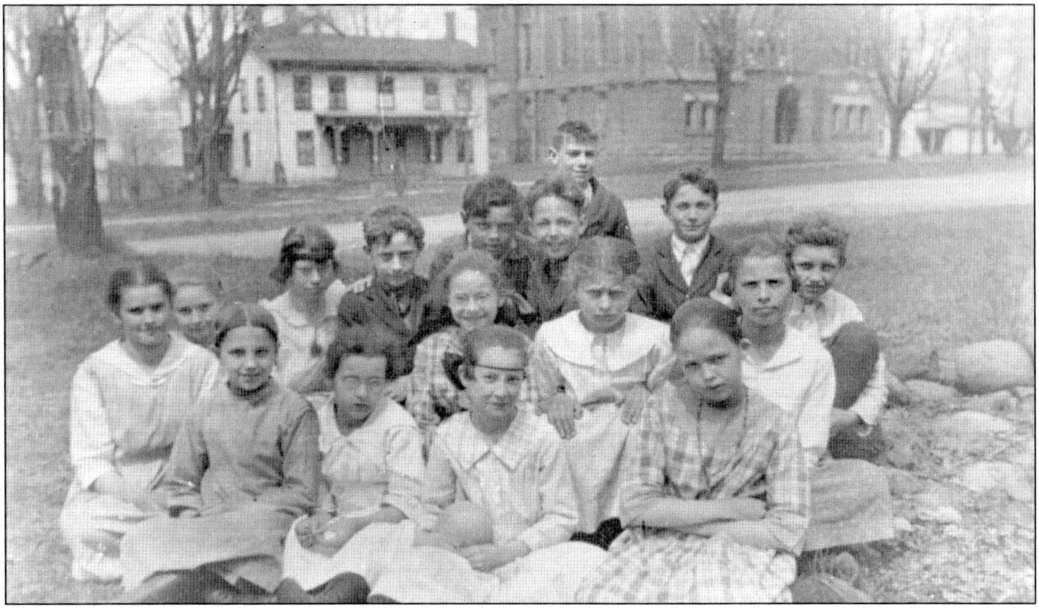

This group of children sits in Burton Park with the Congregational church and its parsonage in the background. The church was built in large part through member subscriptions at a cost of $4,000 and has had many additions and modifications since, including one move. (Courtesy of Burton Public Library.)

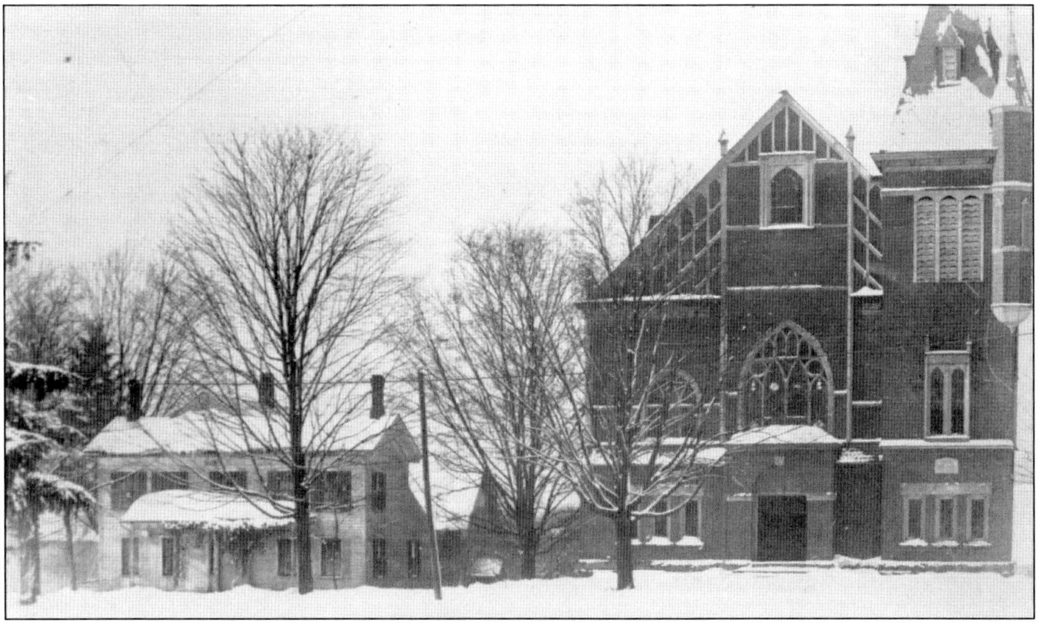

This mid-century photograph shows the Burton Congregational Church in modern times. From 1808 to 1836, the members of the church held meetings at the first Burton Academy, Peter Beal's Tavern, one of the early schoolhouses, and the second Burton Academy before erecting the current building in 1836. (Courtesy Special Collections, Michael Schwartz Library, Cleveland State University.)

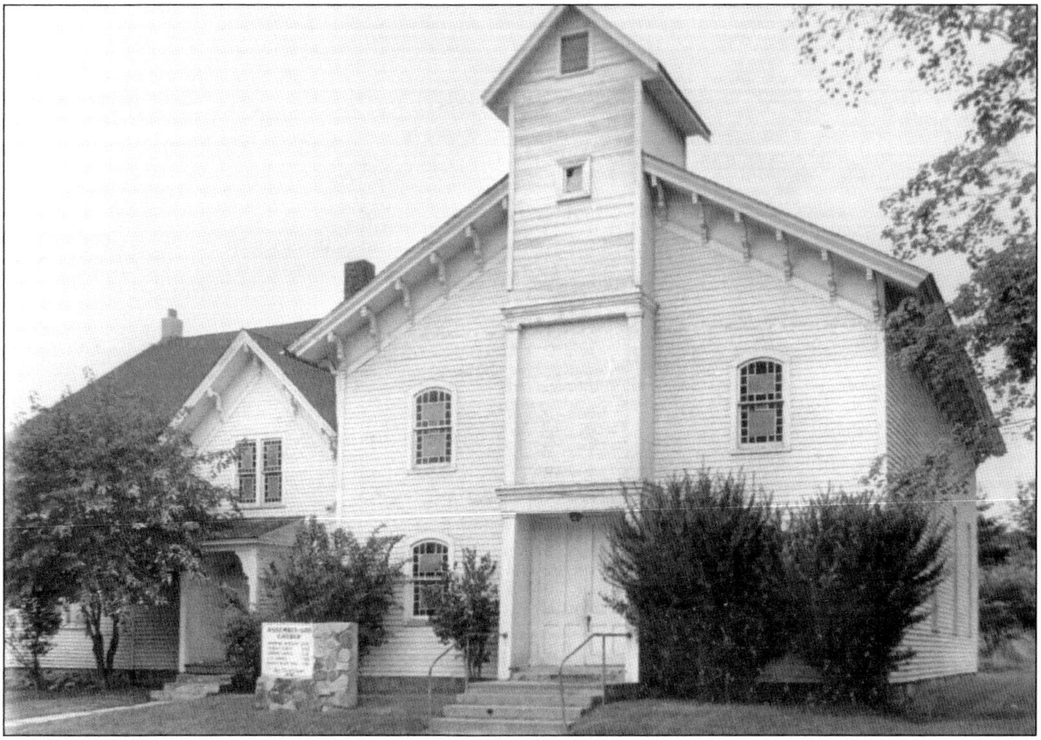

The Methodist Episcopal Church's beginning is not as clear as that of the Burton Congregational Church. Some sources set the date in 1811, while other reputable sources believe it was Burton's first religious organization, having been established in 1806. Regardless, the two churches were the only religious organizations in Burton until 1848. The Methodist Episcopal Church occupied this building for exactly 100 years until it was taken over by the Assembly of God congregation. The structure itself was erected in 1845 at a cost of $3,000. The church's first ministers were Reverend Charles and Reverend Ewens. The Methodist parsonage, most likely built in the 1880s, still exists as a private residence. Above is a 1909 postcard, and the photograph below was taken during a 1930s service. (Above, courtesy of the Geauga County Historical Society; below, Burton Public Library.)

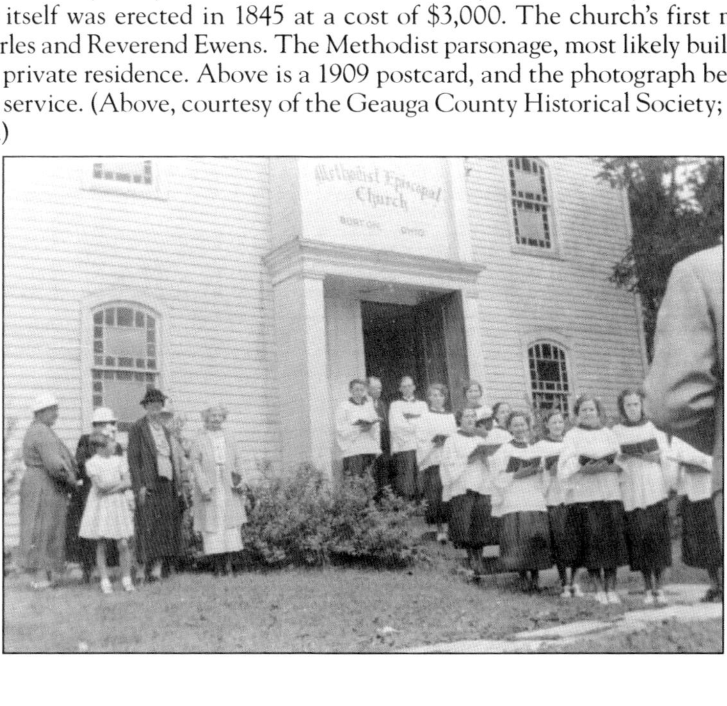

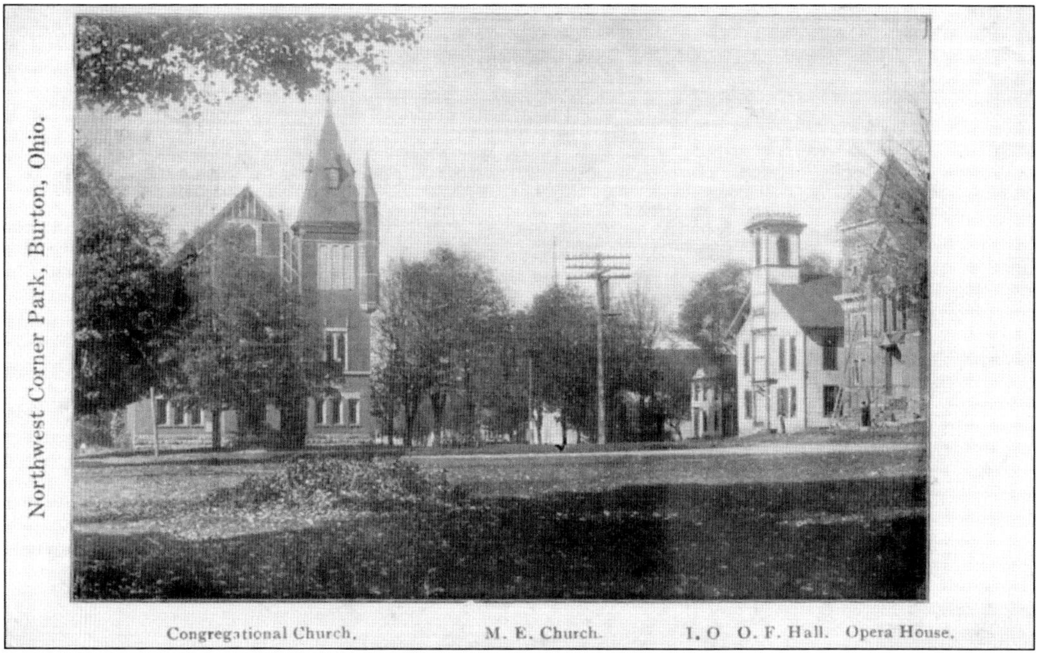

This early-20th-century postcard from Burton Park illustrates how close the Methodist Episcopal church and the Congregational church were to each other. (Courtesy of the Geauga County Historical Society.)

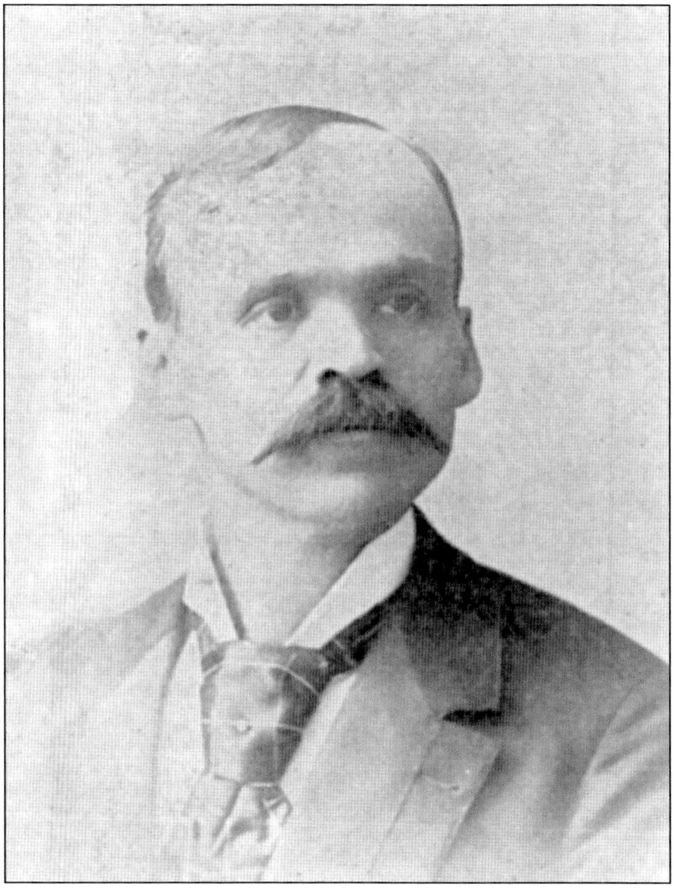

Rev. Elwell O. Mead was the 11th reverend of the Burton Congregational Church, serving the community from 1889 to 1899. He also authored a history of his church in 1894, one of the first Burton-specific histories. (Courtesy of the Geauga County Historical Society.)

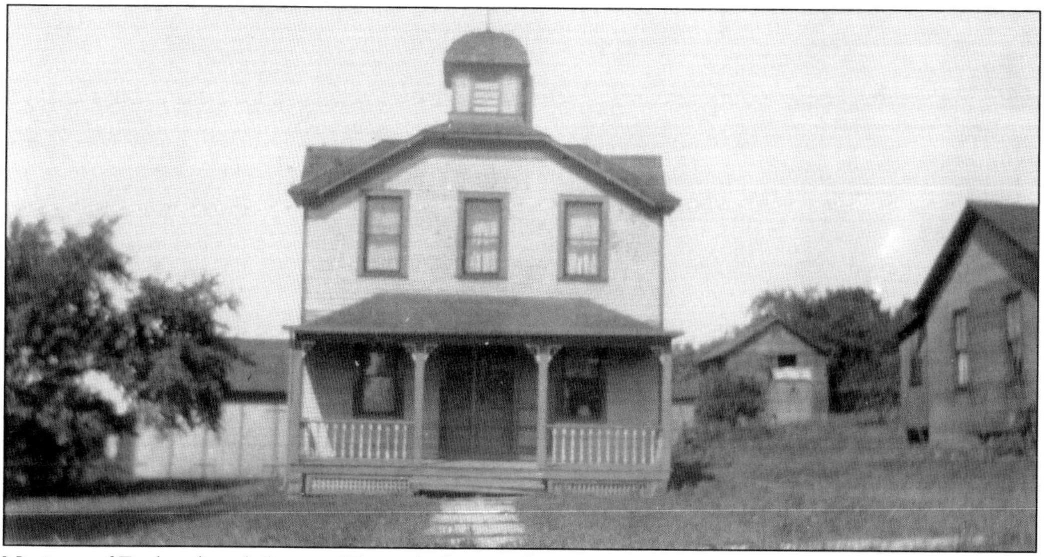

Natives of Finland and those of Finnish descent began to arrive in the area as early as the 1870s, mostly working in the railroad industry. A congregation existed as early as 1885 and joined the Suomi Synod in the early 1900s. The church reported a membership of 44 people in 1935, and it eventually closed in 1970. (Courtesy of the Geauga County Historical Society.)

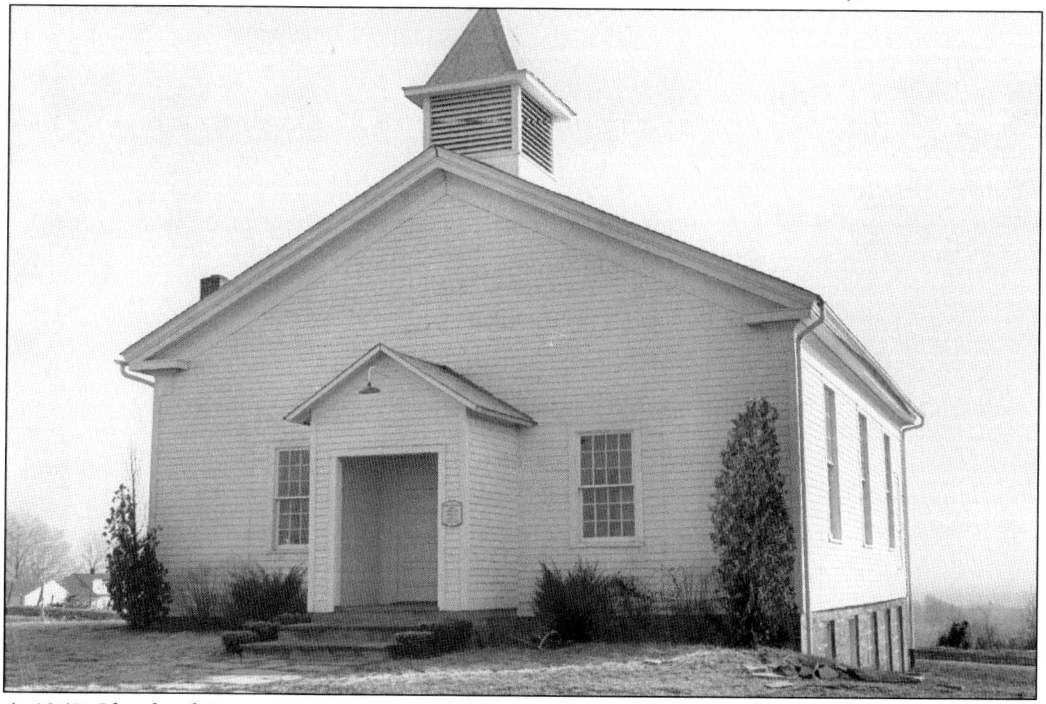

A 1969 *Cleveland Press* article reported that the First Lutheran Church conducted services in this 123-year-old church located on the Geauga County Historical Society grounds in Burton. The structure was erected in Auburn Township before being moved to Century Village. Pastor Rev. J. William Pearch jumped at the chance to use the old church when his congregation began looking for a new building. (Courtesy Special Collections, Michael Schwartz Library, Cleveland State University.)

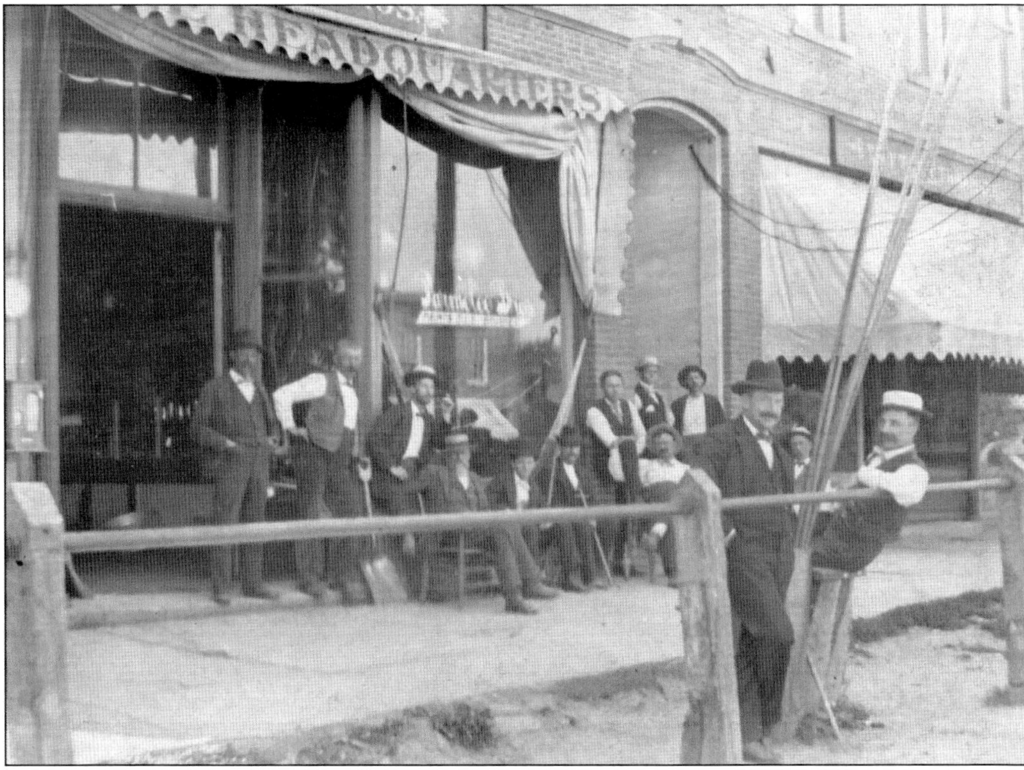

This early photograph shows the west block of Main Street. The stores in the background are Parmalee Bros. Hardware and most likely Tuttle and Thrasher, which featured clothing, boots, and shoes. (Courtesy of the Geauga County Historical Society.)

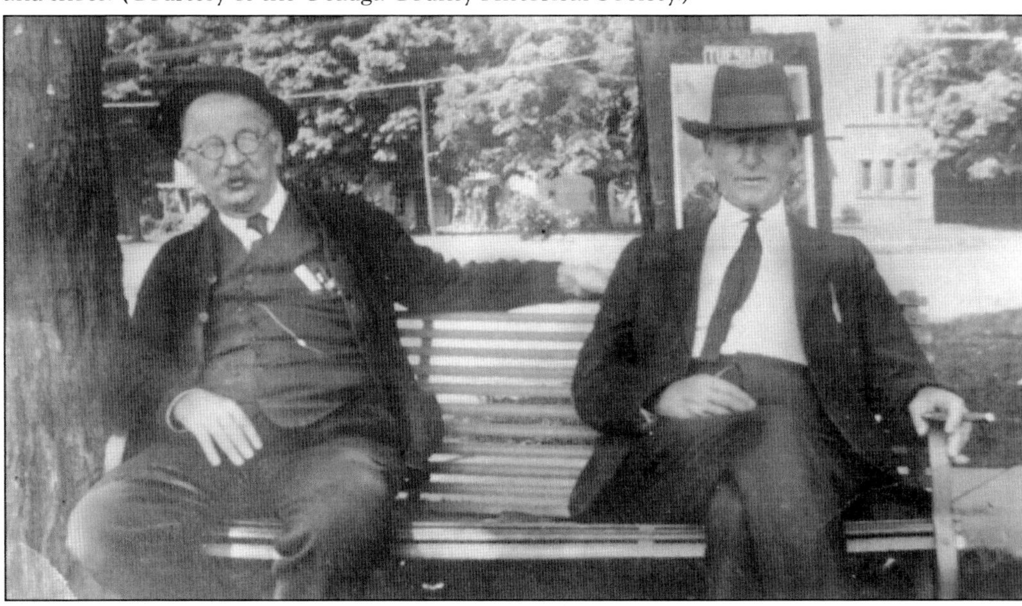

Here, the Parmalee brothers sit on a bench in Burton Park. Their hardware store was a fixture in Burton and a gathering place for the men of Burton for most of its existence. (Courtesy of the Geauga Historical Society.)

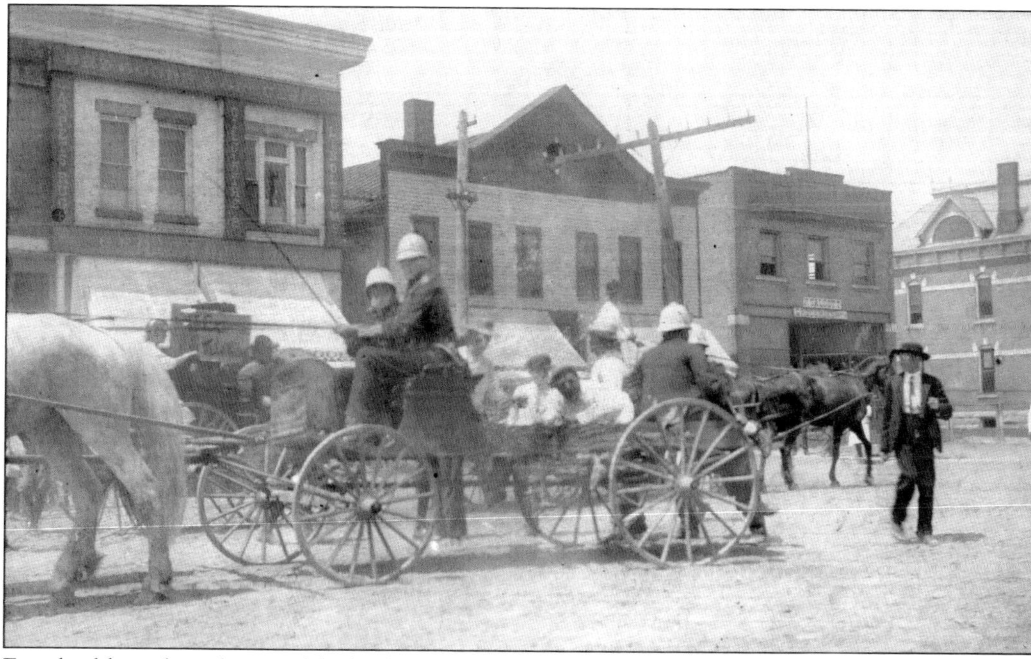

Four buildings line the west block of North Cheshire Street, which has been inhabited by several stores and businesses over the years. Other than the Parmalee Bros. and Tuttle and Thrasher, the west block has also been home to Scott & Burliegh, E.E. Nash, Cleveland and Crittendon, S.M. Dayton, and Talcott's. In these two photographs taken between 1900 to 1910, S.H. Welch and Talcott's are visible above, and Ludlow's and Welch's storefront are seen below. The storefront changed a bit during this time, and a few well-established stores did not survive the bank closing. Fred Talcott not only owned one of most remembered stores of the era, he also opened a miniature golf course in Burton Park in the 1920s. (Both, courtesy of the Geauga County Historical Society.)

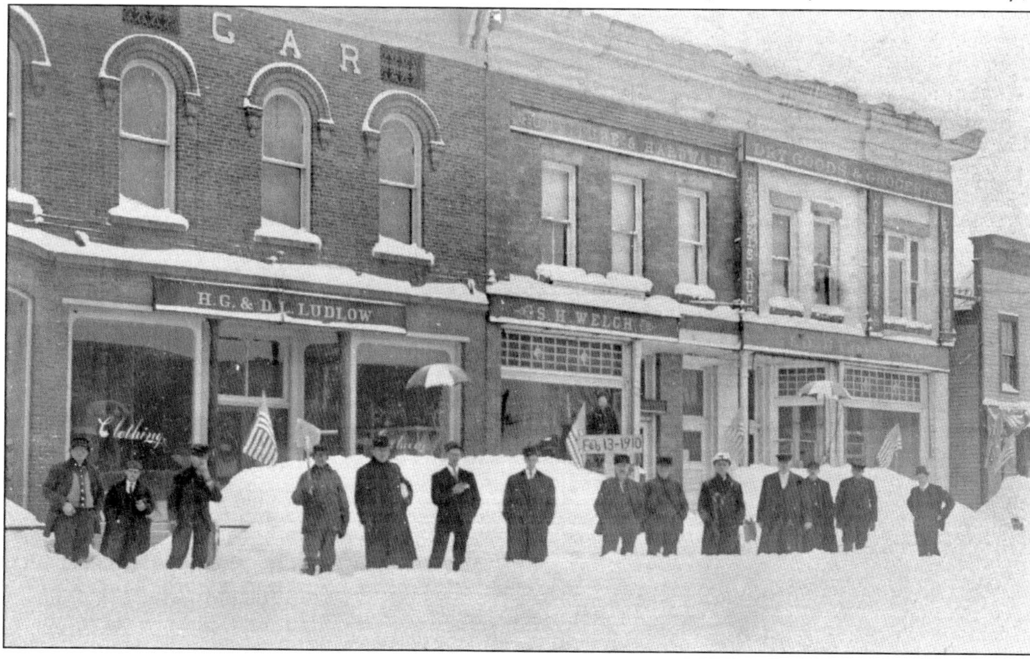

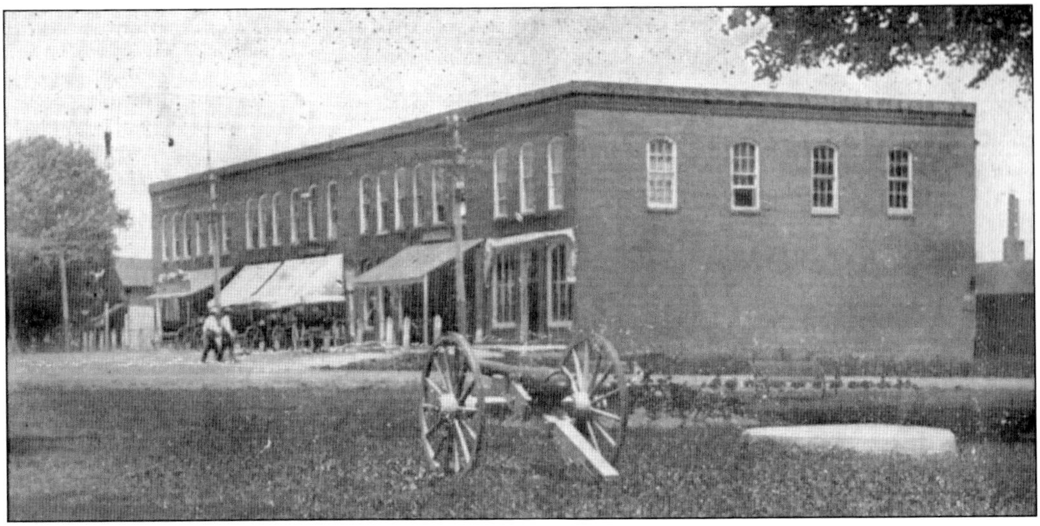

The east commercial block of North Cheshire Street consisted of seven separate storefronts. Before the fire of December 1871, it was a continuous wood building ending with a hotel. Newspaper reports at the time credited a Miss Wilmart with raising the alarm and bringing the citizens out into what was described as a howling storm with winds so bad it was difficult to hear other voices. Water froze onto anything it touched, which probably helped slow the spread of the fire. The damage was over $25,000, but Burton rebuilt, and the current structure has not changed significantly since it was erected in 1872 and 1873. (Both, courtesy of the Geauga County Historical Society.)

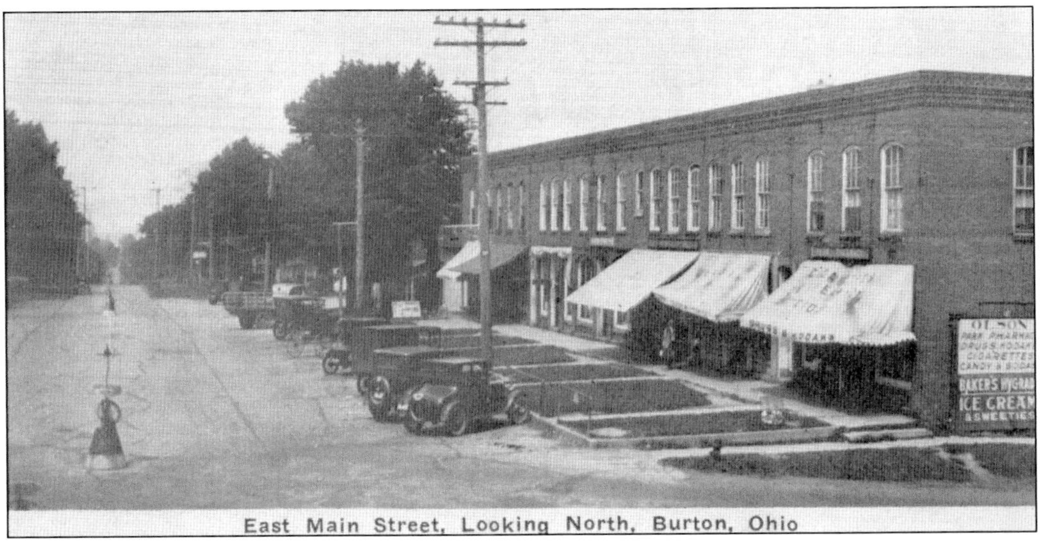

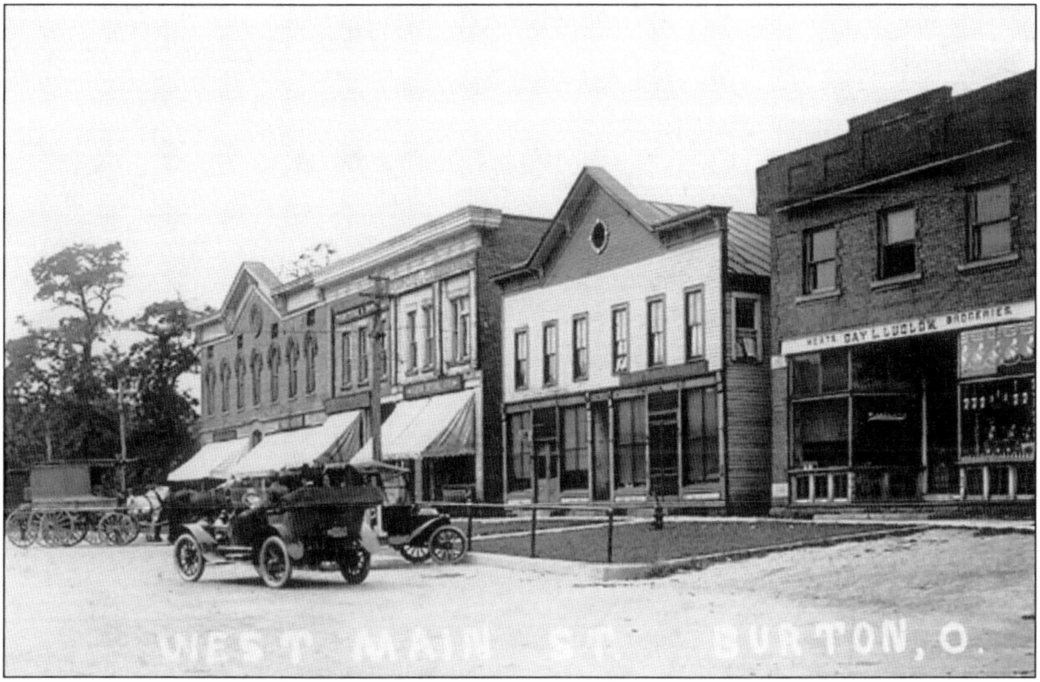

The commercial district of Burton has continued to evolve over the years. This photograph of the west block shows what seems to be an entirely different alignment of stores than the block had 10 to 15 years prior. (Courtesy of the Geauga County Historical Society.)

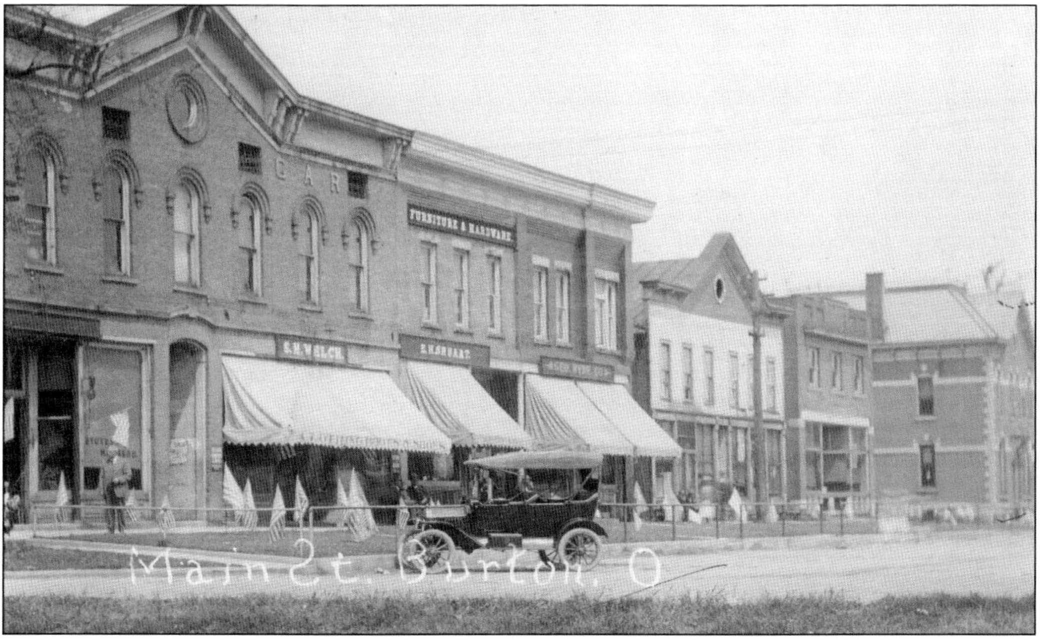

Another photograph from the same era also illustrates the changing landscape of the town's businesses. The collapse of Boughton, Ford & Co. is often blamed for the swift turnover in business establishments during this time in Burton's history. (Courtesy of the Geauga County Historical Society.)

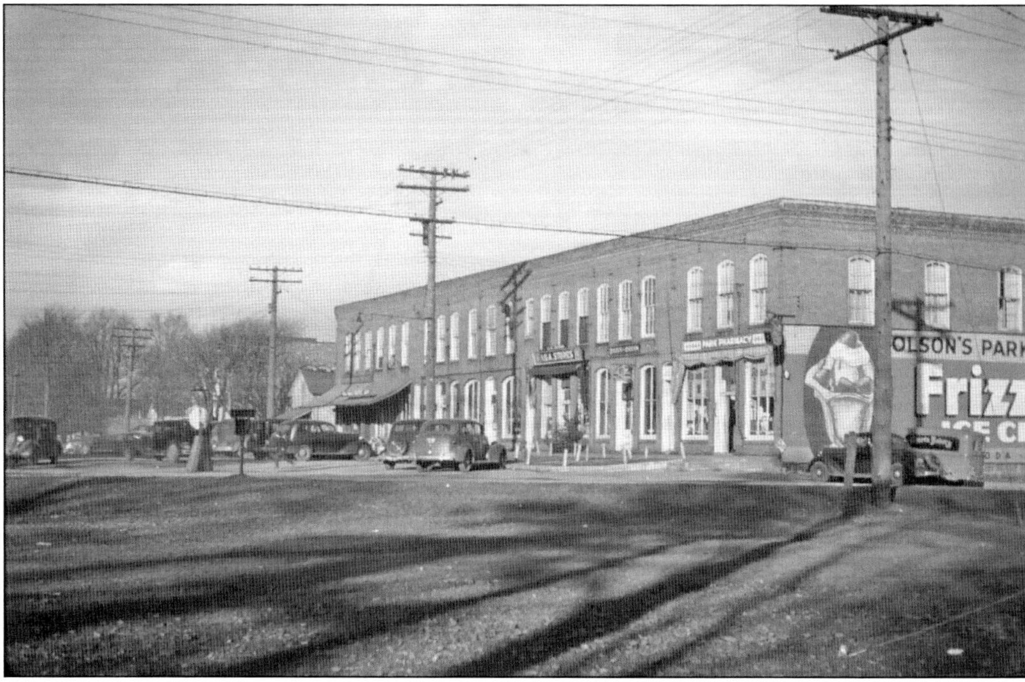

Although tenants have changed frequently through the decades, the east and west block buildings have stayed much the same. In these photographs are mainstays like the IGA grocer, Park Pharmacy, Dean's, the Full Gospel Mission, and Atlantic & Pacific. Although one horse and buggy is seen in the image below (perhaps belonging to the large Amish community on the outskirts of Burton), automobiles have taken over the street. (Courtesy of Elizabeth A. Cupp.)

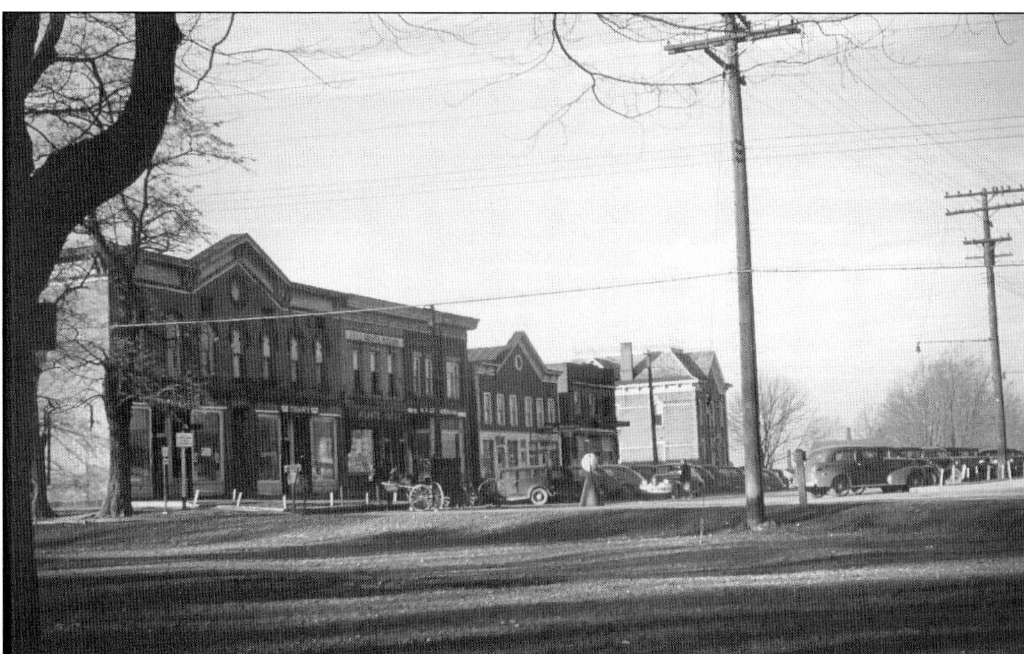

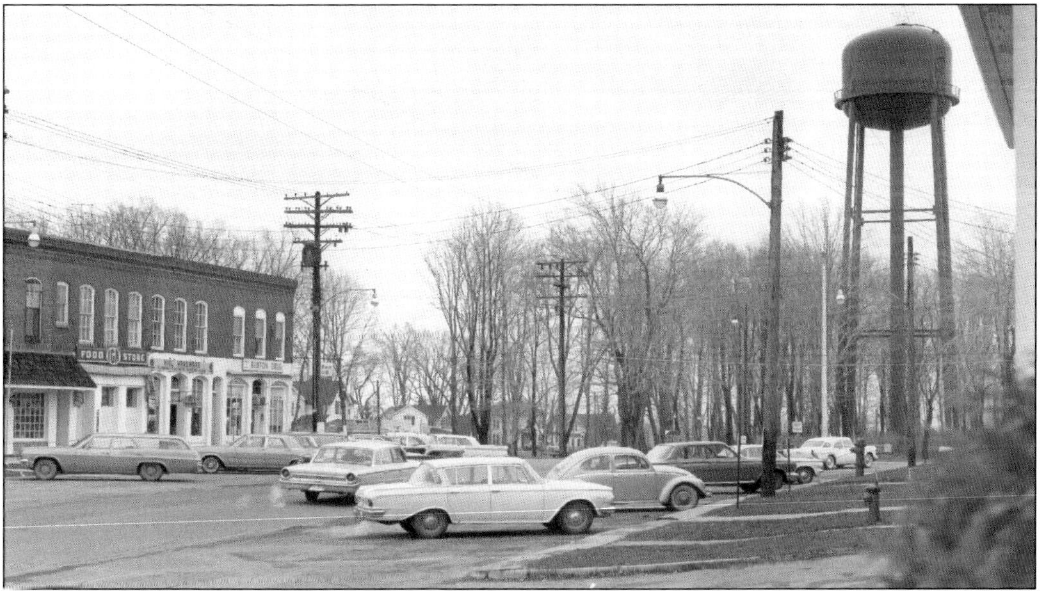

By the mid-1960s, the only business left from the photograph on the previous page was the IGA store, although the corner shop had simply changed its name from Park Pharmacy to Burton Drug. Today, the only old store remaining is Hill Hardware. (Courtesy of Joseph E. Cole.)

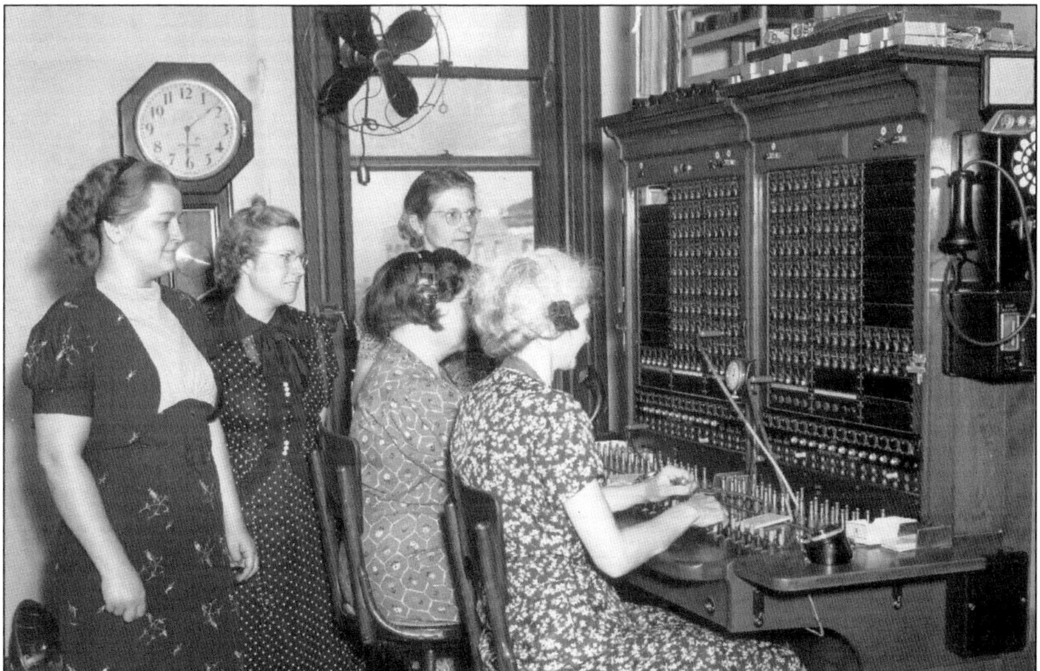

On November 23, 1877, the first phone lines in Ohio were installed in Burton. From the Baltimore & Ohio Railroad depot to Boughton, Ford & Co. two-and-a-half miles away, the phone lines were installed so the bank could get financial information from New York more quickly. Although it was bought out by Ohio Bell in 1927, the switchboard operated until 1939. (Courtesy of Elmer Bollinger.)

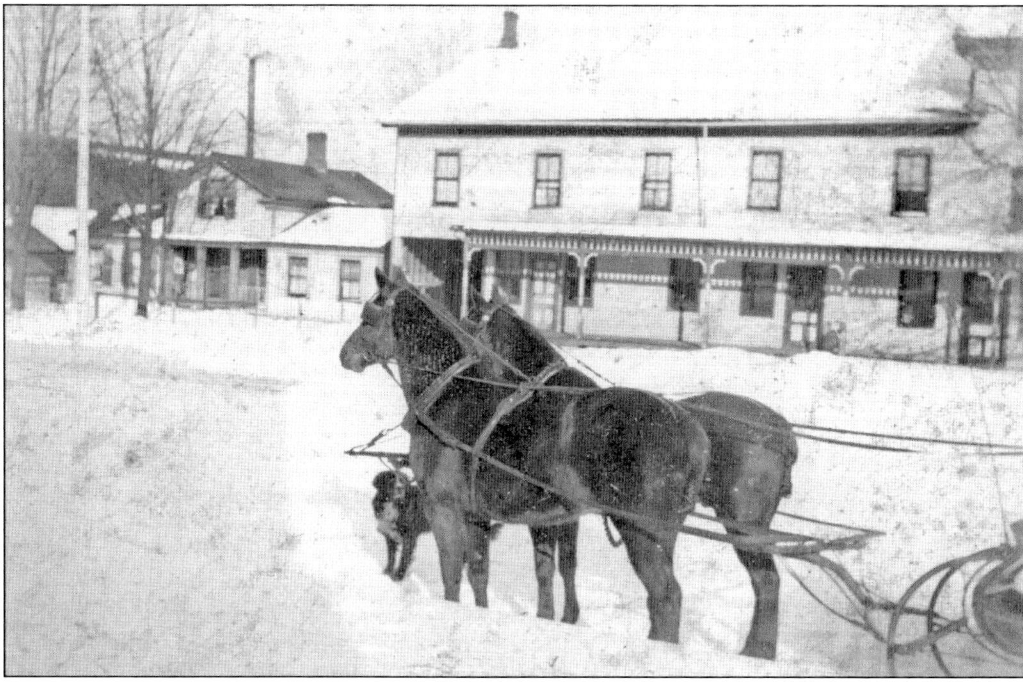

On the east side of Main Street, this establishment was first known as the Exchange Hotel was built in 1845. This photograph is from 1880, when it was known as the Brewster. (Courtesy of the Geauga County Historical Society.)

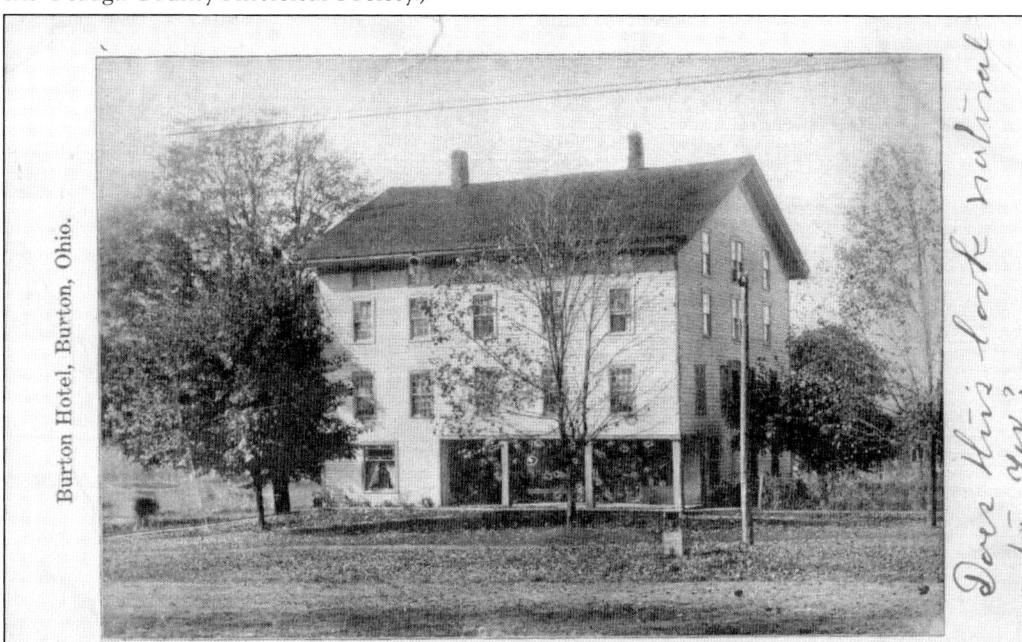

After several incarnations, including time as a boardinghouse for academy students and a temperance house, this building was bought by Will Dean and renamed the Dean Hotel. This 1908 postcard shows the structure around the time Dean bought it, just south of the Burton Public Library building. (Courtesy of the Geauga County Historical Society.)

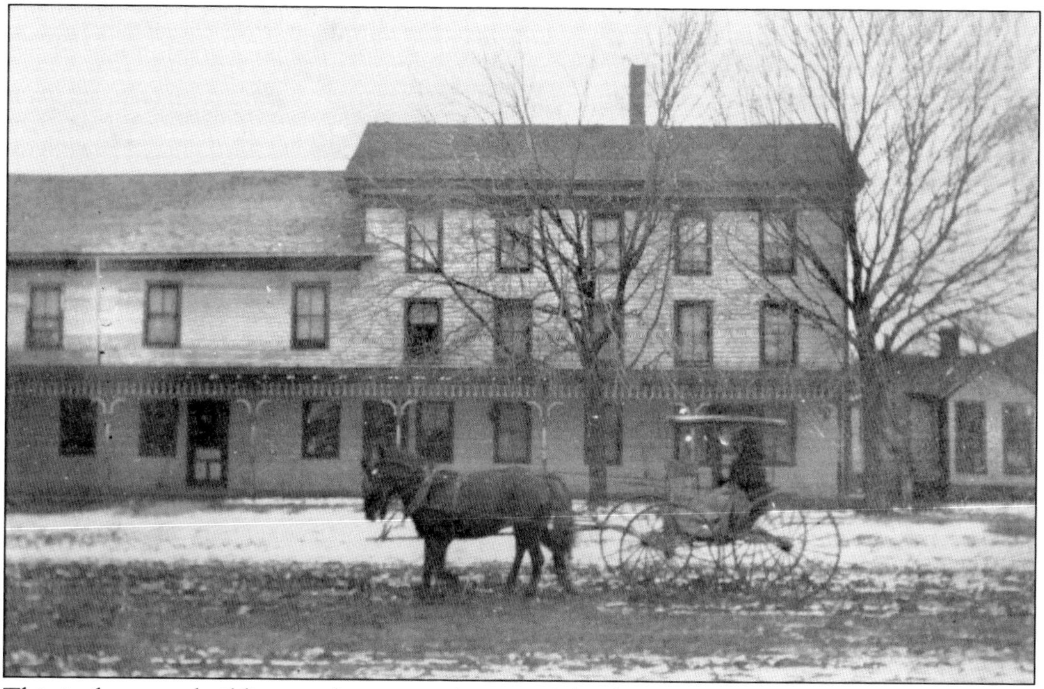

This is the same building as the one at the top of the facing page, page 98, referred to as the Burton House and also possibly the Baird Hotel. It was destroyed by fire in 1903. (Courtesy of the Geauga County Historical Society.)

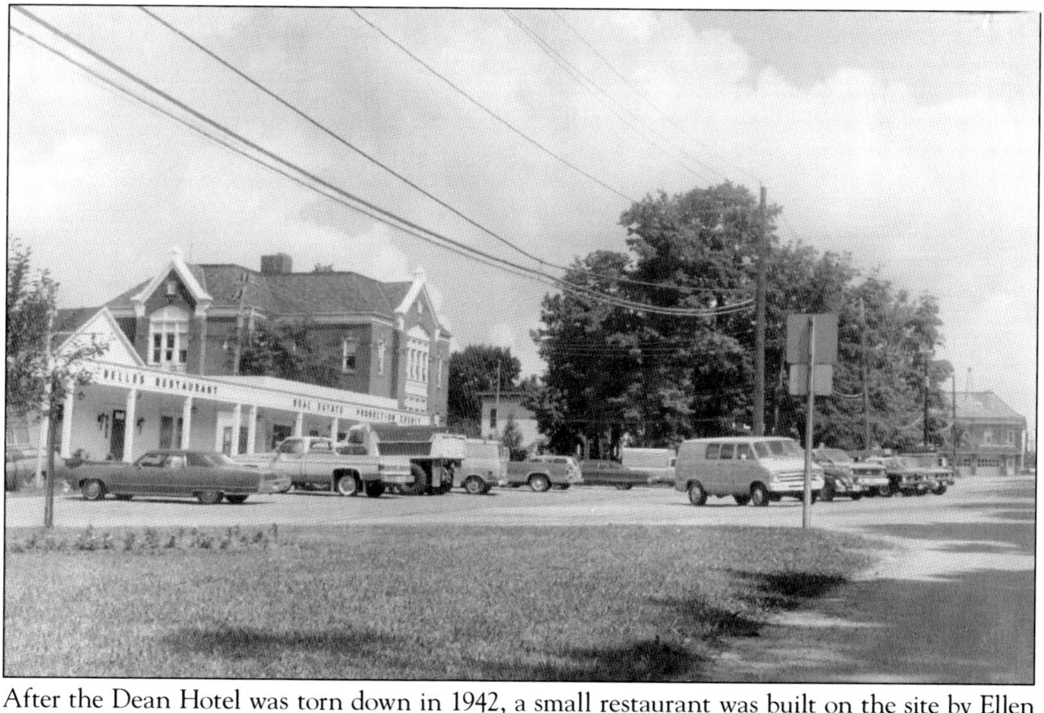

After the Dean Hotel was torn down in 1942, a small restaurant was built on the site by Ellen Hosmer and eventually purchased by Lillie Belle Kennedy. She sold it in the early 1970s, but Belle's Colonial Restaurant still operates on the square. (Courtesy of the Burton Public Library.)

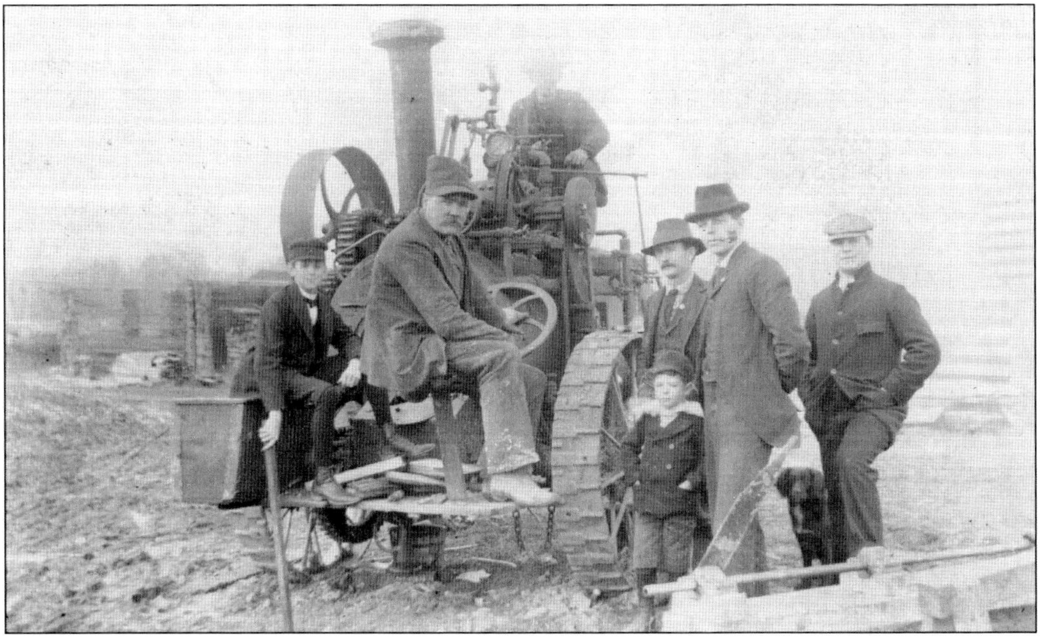

The Burton Electric Light Company, built in the mid-1890s, provided electricity to the area for many years. The group of men above includes E.J. Norton, Loyd Norton, Earl Bliss, Otis Burnett, Noel Hicks, Frank Laurence, Wally Aikens, and ? Vutte. Earl "E.C." Bliss opened the Burton Light plant in 1896. Below is an unidentified employee inside the Burton Light plant in the late 1890s. At the time, the operation was considered state of the art. (Both, courtesy of the Geauga County Historical Society.)

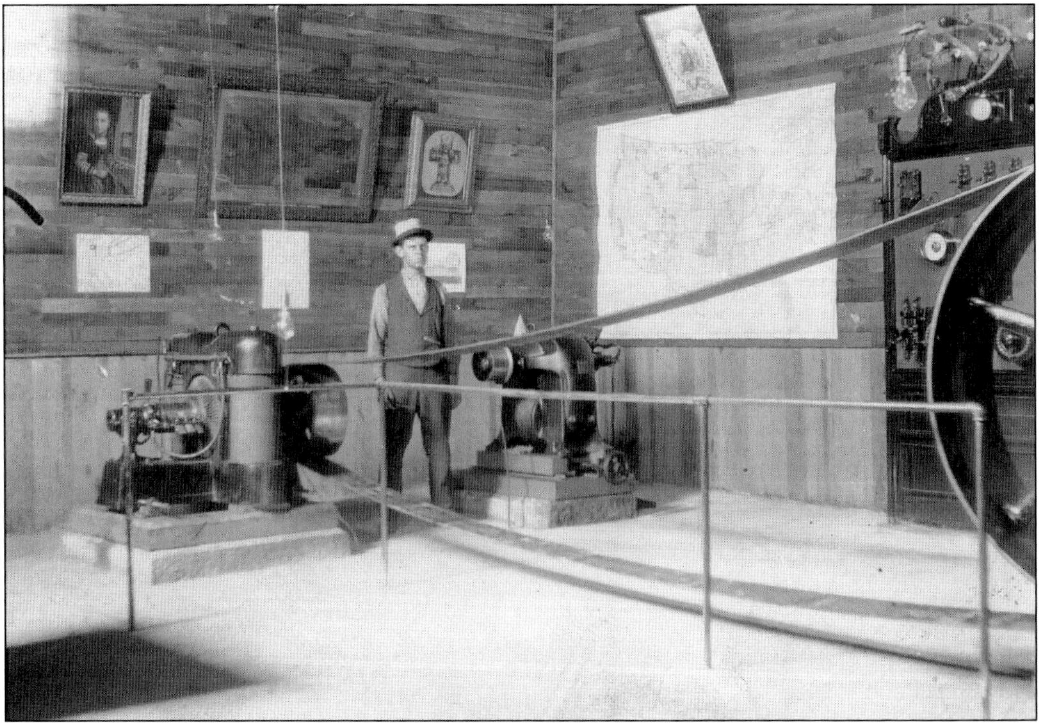

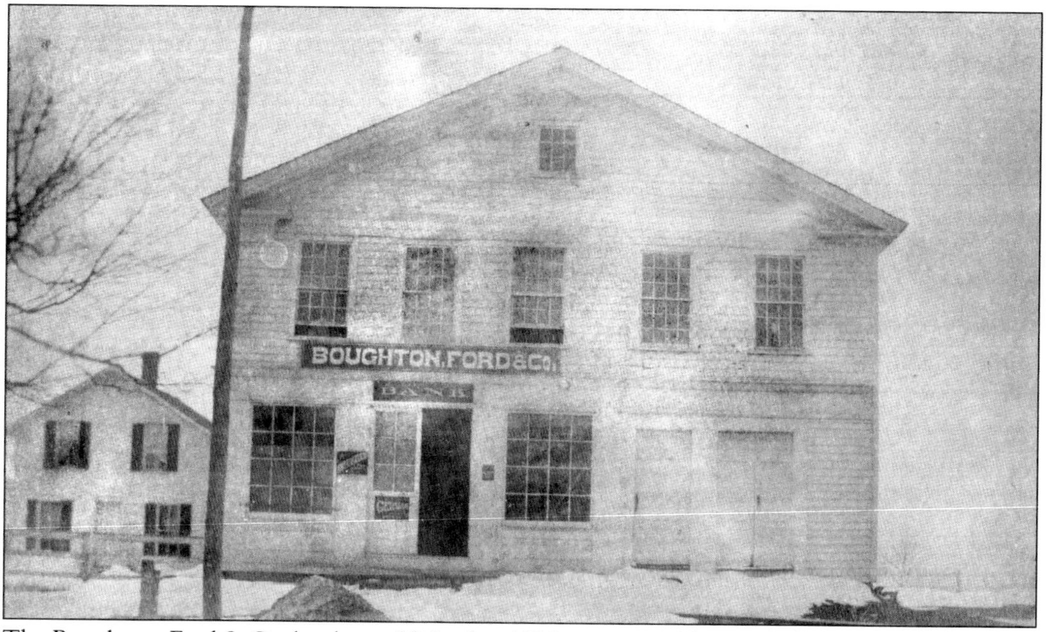

The Boughton, Ford & Co. bank, established in 1856, was one of the major financial institutions in the area for many years. Its sudden failure and closing in 1903 created hardship all through the area and was covered by the *New York Times*. (Courtesy of the Geauga County Historical Society.)

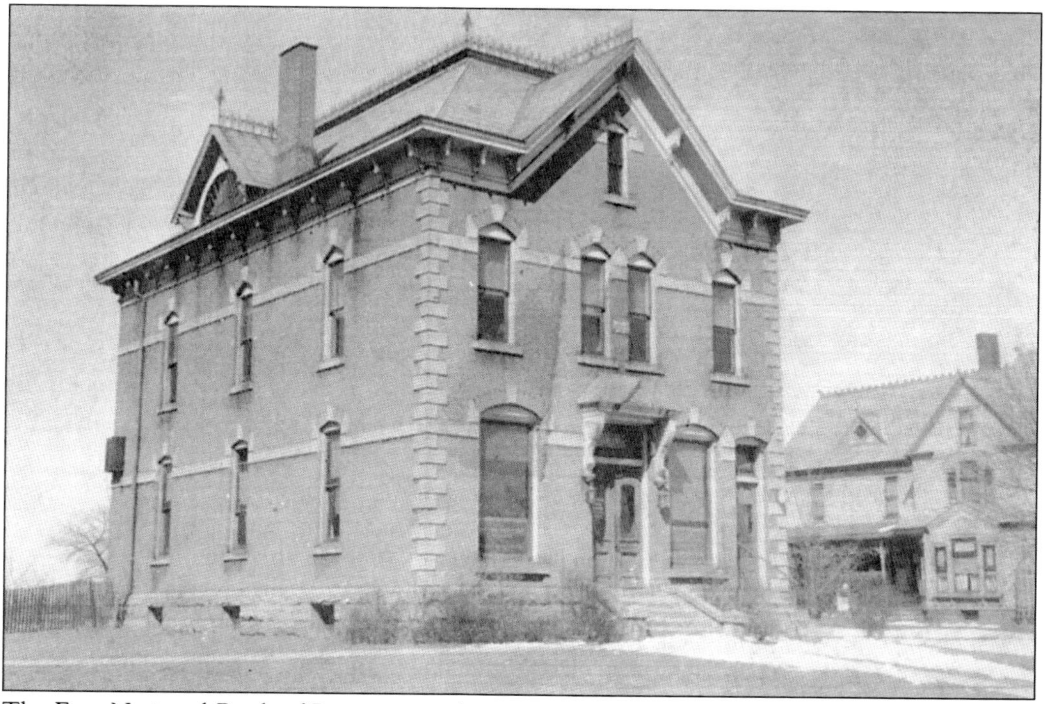

The First National Bank of Burton, seen here in 1917, was established in May 1902. After the Boughton, Ford, and Company Bank collapsed in January 1903, First National became the dominant financial institution in town. It was eventually bought by Huntington Bank. (Courtesy of the Geauga County Historical Society.)

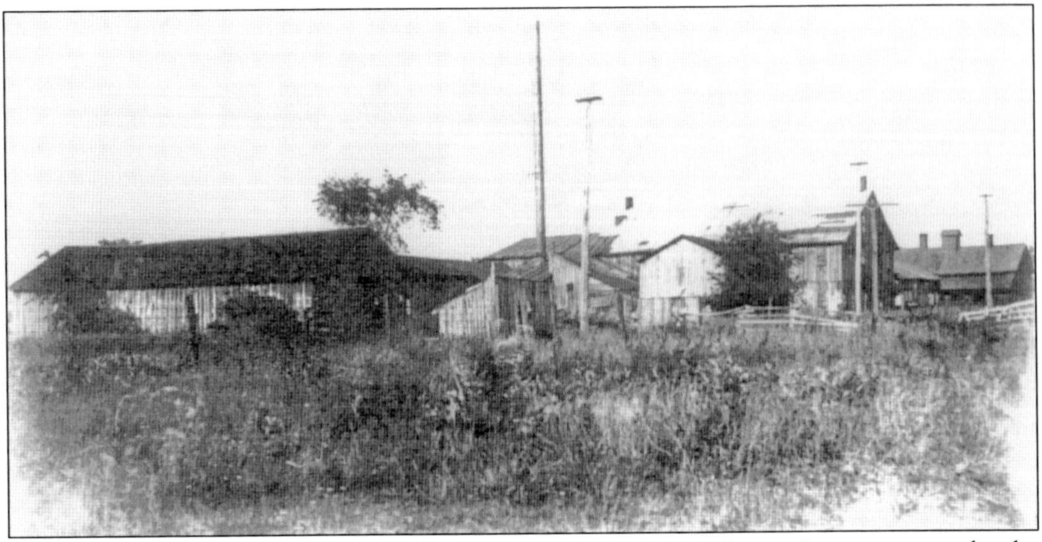

The Burton Handle Company was established in 1880 on Spring Street. It was purported to be the largest manufacturer of plows, cultivators, handles, bobsleds, horse rakes, and castings in the country. They were best known, however, as the manufacturer of the innovative bobsleds known as Burton Bobs. These bobsleds featured a knuckle joint, permitting each sled runner to move independently. This photograph was taken around 1900. (Courtesy of Wayne Hosmer.)

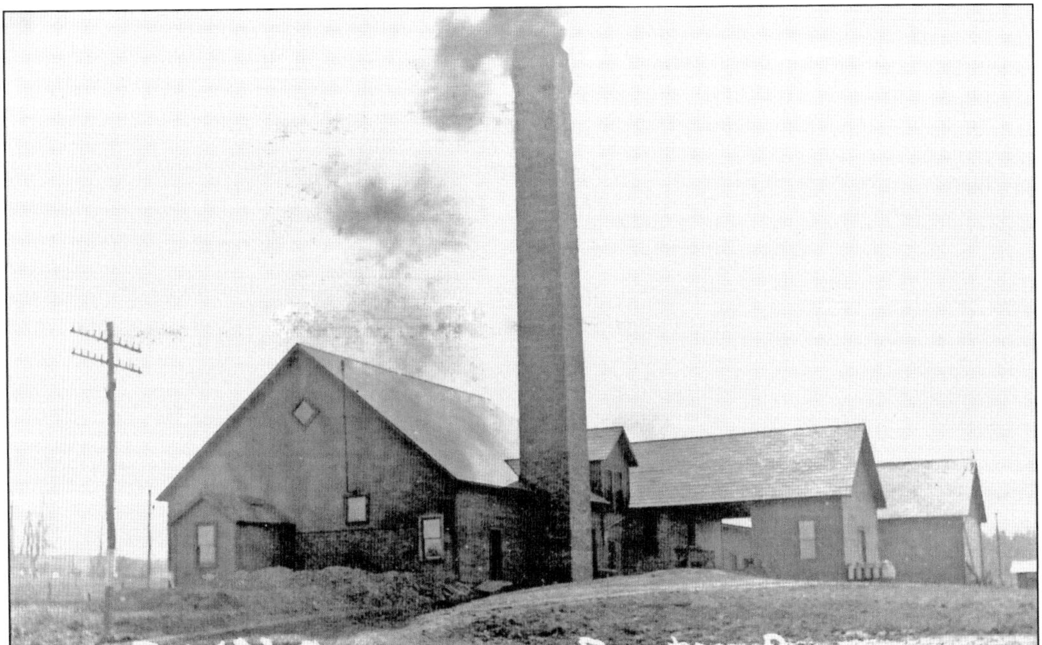

The Belle Vernon Creamery Company operated in Burton from 1901 to 1925. The creamery was capable of handling 75,000 pounds of milk a day. The Cleveland & Eastern Railroad (C&E) ran through the property. (Courtesy of the Geauga County Historical Society.)

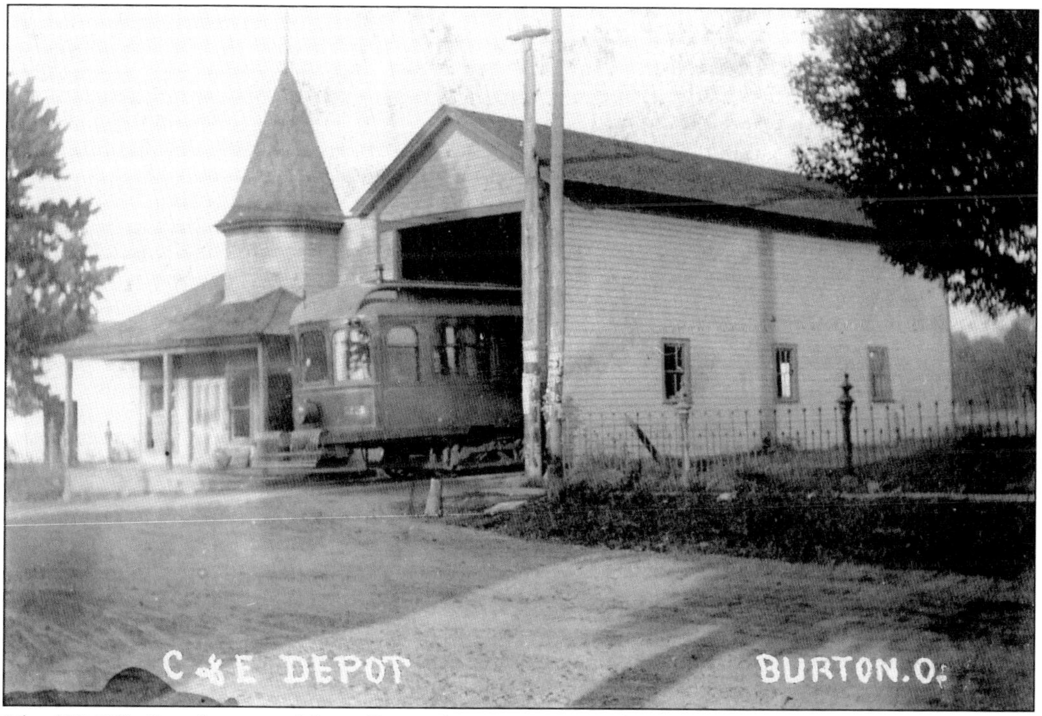

The C&E Railroad operated from December 1899 to March 1925 and played an important part in Burton's history. This photograph of a car barn is from around 1910. (Courtesy of Bill Jackson.)

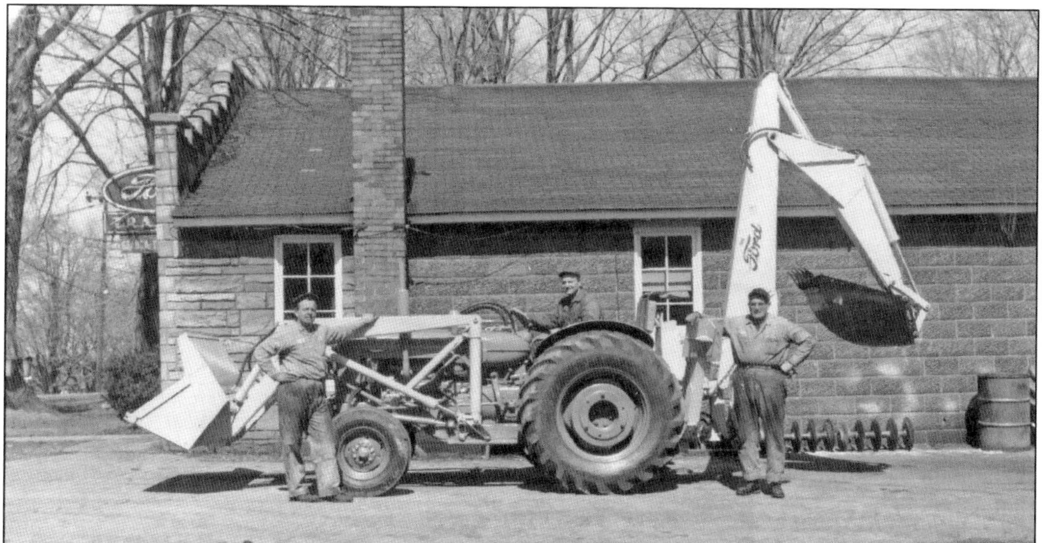

Jim Bahnick and Audre Blair, co-owners of Geauga Tractor Sales, stand in front of their store in 1962. Bahnick eventually bought Blair out and owned the store by himself for many years. (Courtesy of Thomas Briggs.)

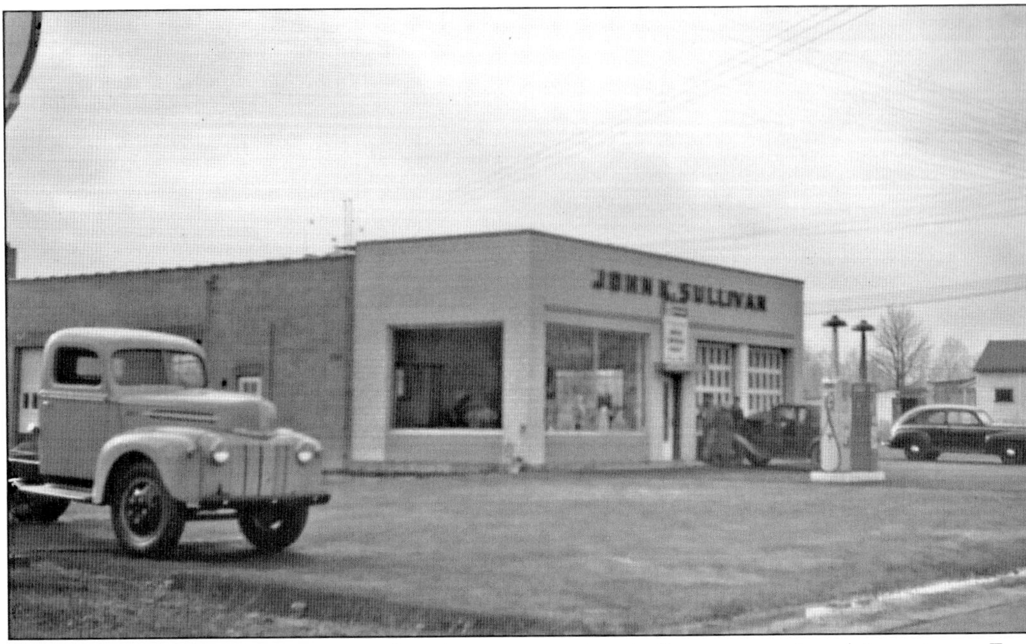

John K. Sullivan was long associated with transportation in Burton, owning this station, a Ford dealership, and Geauga Tractor Sales all at different times. (Courtesy of the Geauga County Historical Society.)

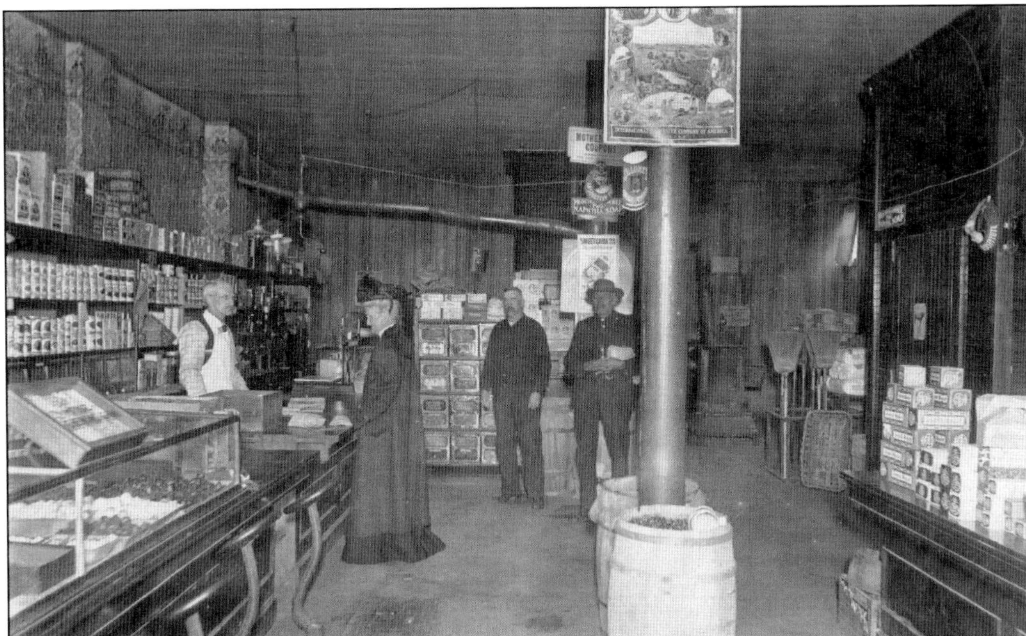

The Talcott Store was on the north end of the west block for years. Its slogan claimed that the store sold "exceptional service." (Courtesy of the Geauga County Historical Society.)

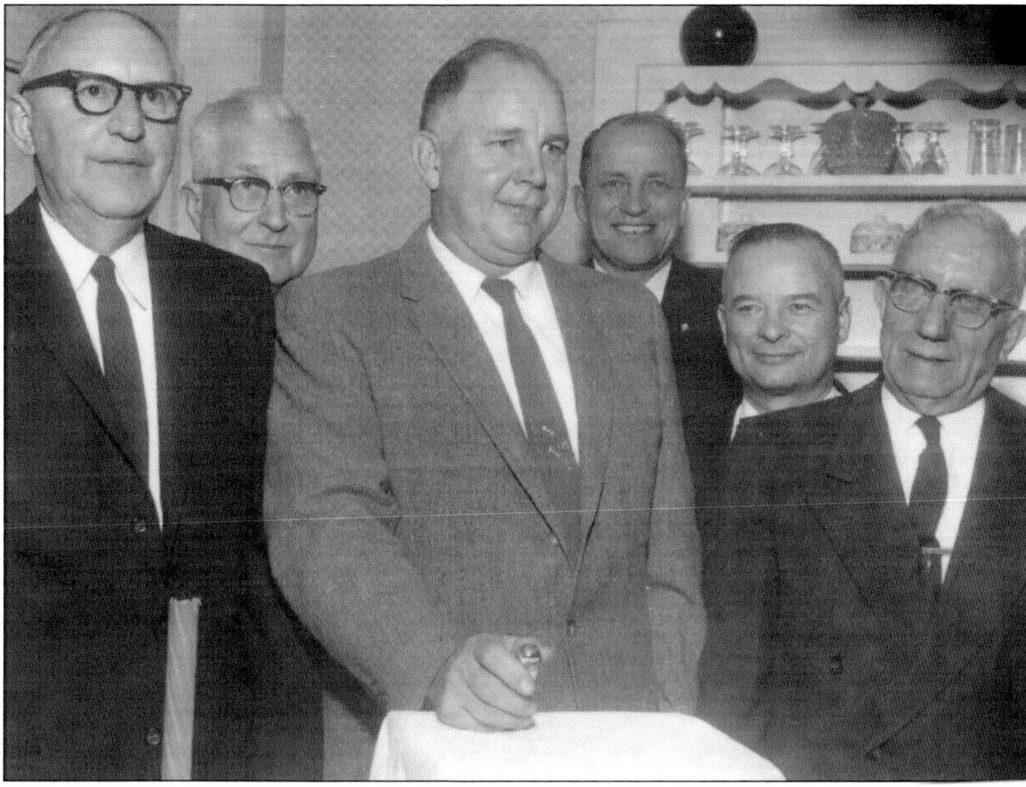

The Burton Chamber of Commerce has long been a positive influence in the village. Probably best known outside of Burton for running the Log Cabin Sugar Camp, the chamber promotes a positive, forward-thinking business environment and community spirit. Above, the chamber of commerce officers and directors in December 1961 included, from left to right, (first row) Theron Dean, Ture Johnson, and Al Vinecourt; (second row) B.J. Shanower, John Gander, and Fred Knisely. Shanower was mayor of Burton, and the Geauga County Historical Society library is named for him. Below, television personality Fred Griffith (left) poses with Charles Head, the president of the chamber, in 1979. (Both, courtesy of Joann J. Hiscox.)

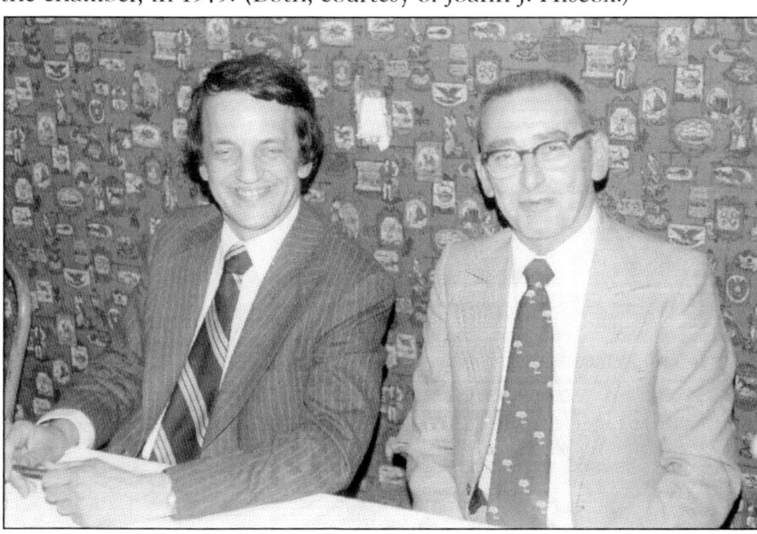

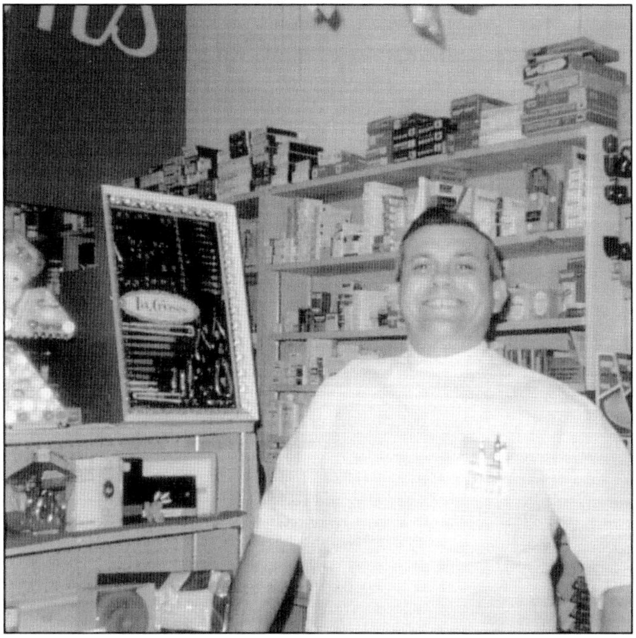

Carl Mowery, a Burton druggist in the 1960s, poses with a big smile in his workplace that carried a bit of everything. (Courtesy of Elizabeth A. Cupp.)

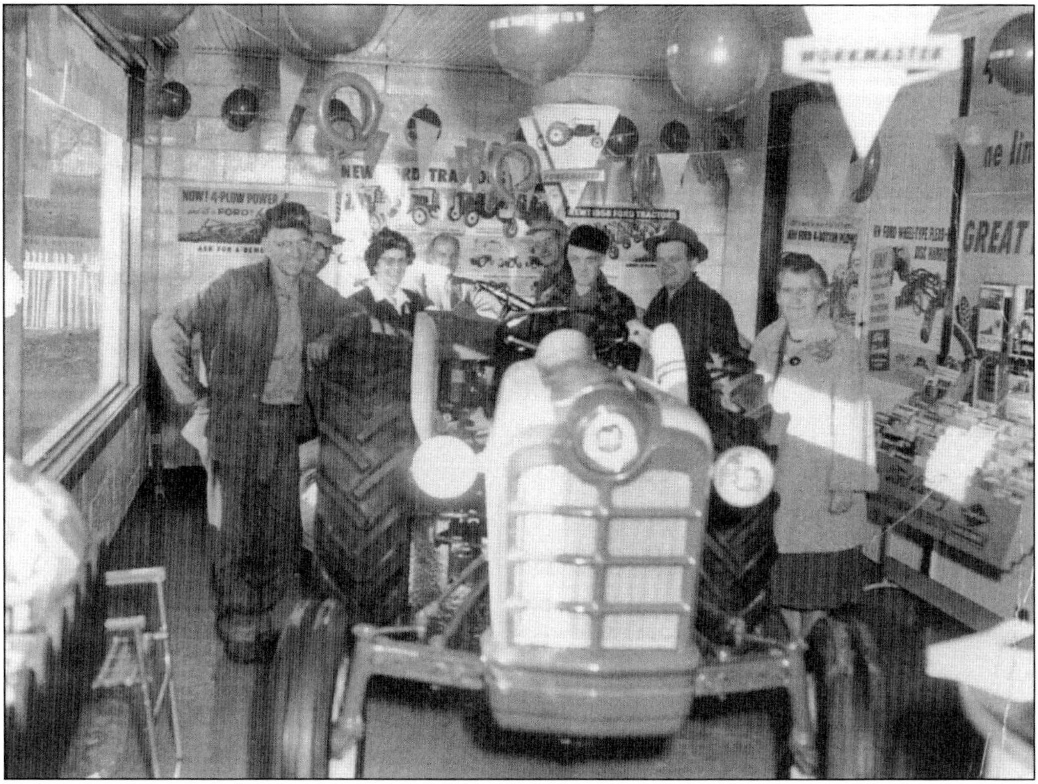

The interior of Geauga Tractor Sales is seen here in the spring of 1962 with longtime owner Jim Bahnick on the right. Originally owned by John K. Sullivan, who also owned a Ford dealership in the village, Bahnick is usually remembered as the owner. For years, his calendars dotted many a wall in Burton. (Courtesy of Thomas Briggs.)

Seven

School Days

The first settlers of Burton brought with them the New England tradition of the schoolhouse. As early as 1802, Sallie Miner held regular classes for children in a small room near the Umberfields' home. From then on, a schoolhouse was a permanent fixture in Burton. In 1803, the first building erected specifically as a schoolhouse was constructed. By 1805, a member of the Hickox family held classes in his store. The first frame school was built in the northwest corner of the town square in 1815.

In Burton's first decade, a petition was sent to the territorial government requesting the charter of a university in Burton, and the Burton Academy was born. The effort and expense of erecting that first building was a major undertaking for the young village, as it was known as the most impressive structure in the Western Reserve for some time. When it was moved to Hudson in the 1820s, against the wishes of most of the townspeople, it left a hole in Burton that was not filled until a second Burton Academy opened in 1845. The second academy stayed in Burton until it burned down in 1878. Burton set the educational bar high, sending the first students from the Western Reserve back east to attend Yale, including future governor Seabury Ford and Dexter Witter, who affected the religious mindset of the community more than anyone else during the mid-1800s.

Burton Central High School opened in 1868, with the top floor used as the high school and the bottom floor used for primary and intermediate classes. This school system continued, albeit with several changes, until the late 1960s, when Burton merged with other school districts and the high school was renamed Berkshire High School.

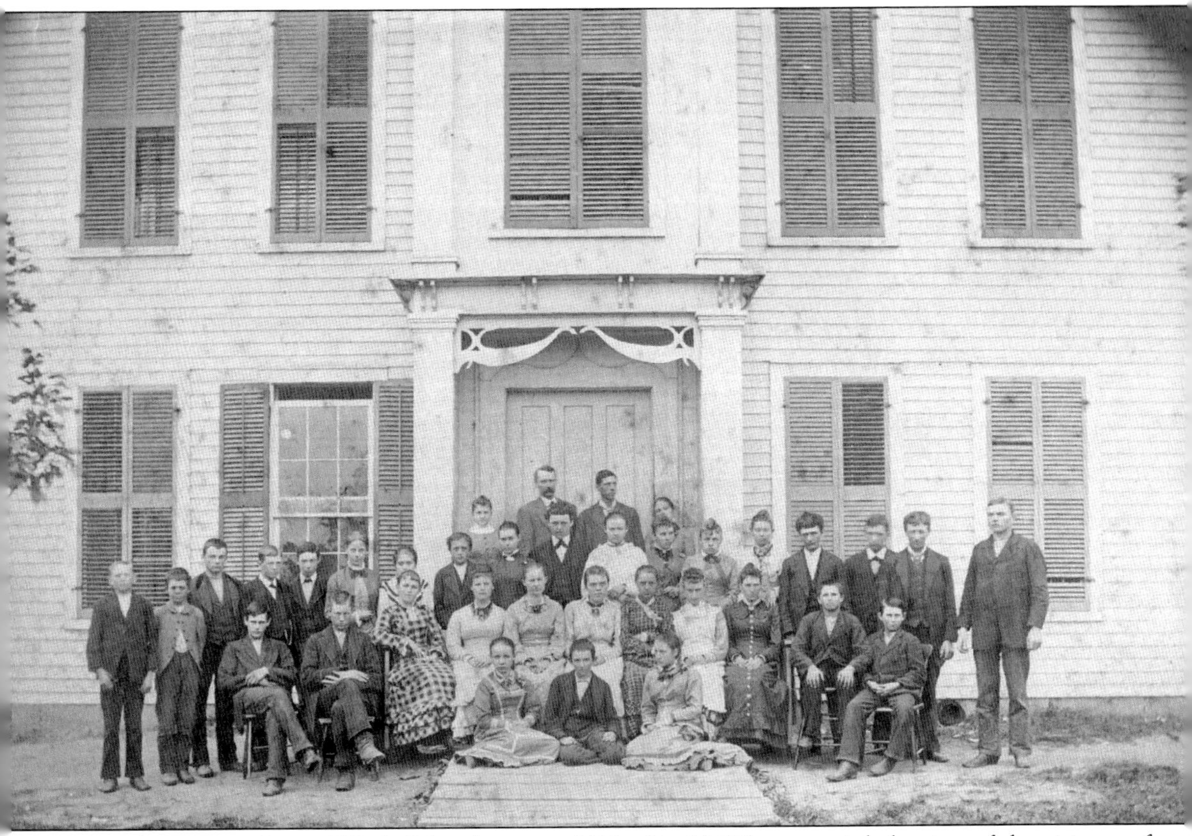

The Burton Central High School was established in 1866 by a special election of the citizens of Burton. The schoolhouse was built in 1868 for $4,000. It housed several grades of students until it was replaced in 1884. (Courtesy of the Geauga County Historical Society.)

The Burton High School class of 1893 consisted of only four members, pictured here in no particular order, Victoria Linton, Mary McNish, Susan Hotchkiss, and Cassie Lawyer. (Courtesy of the Geauga County Historical Society.)

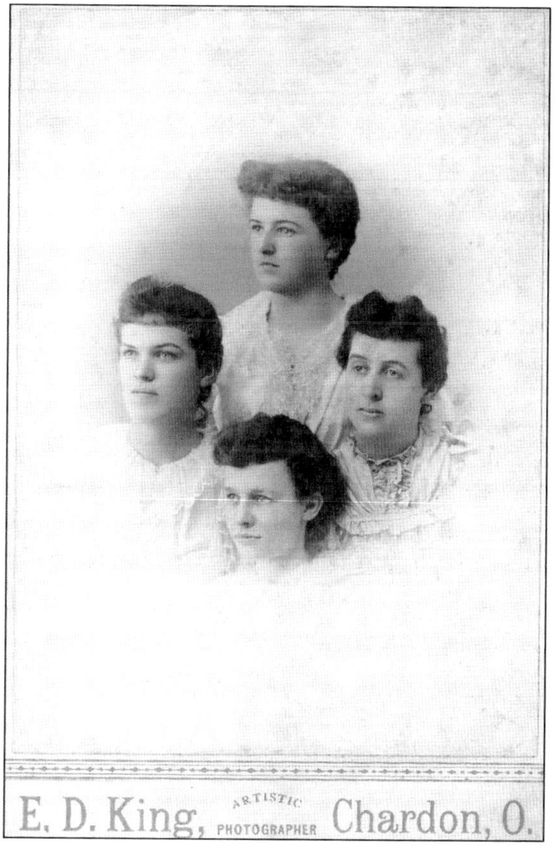

The 1896 graduating class included, from left to right, (first row) F. Ray Truman; (second row) Ethelyn Park and Emily Whitney; (third row) Austa Baird, Edith Taylor, Clyde Carlton, Carole McIntosh, and Fannie Martin. Unlike 1893, there are few men in this class. (Courtesy of the Geauga County Historical Society.)

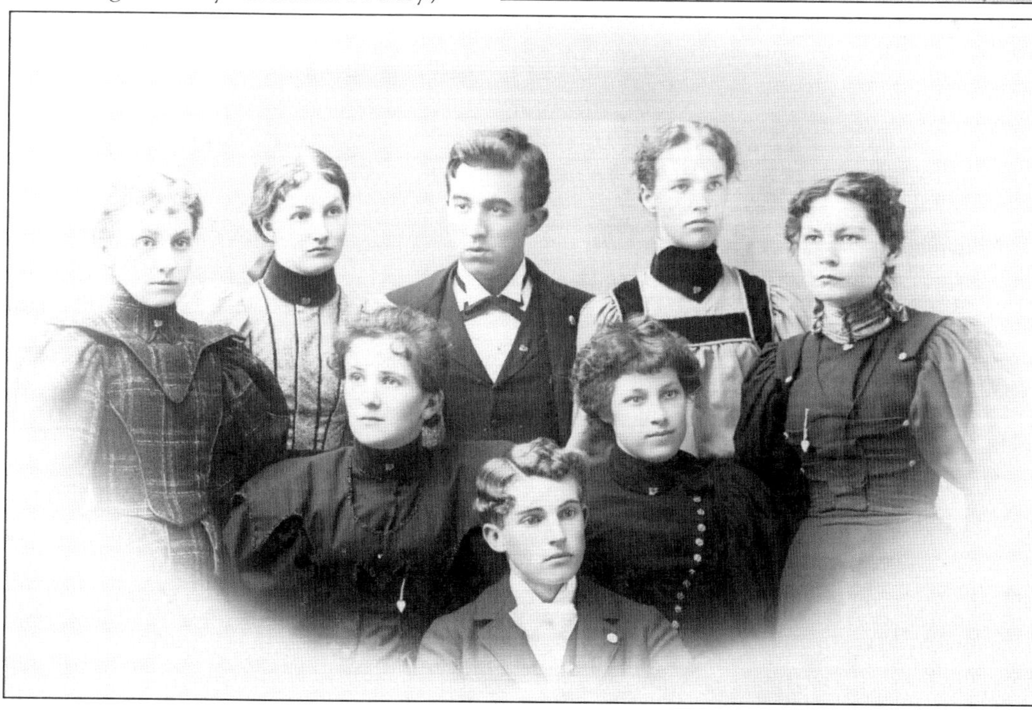

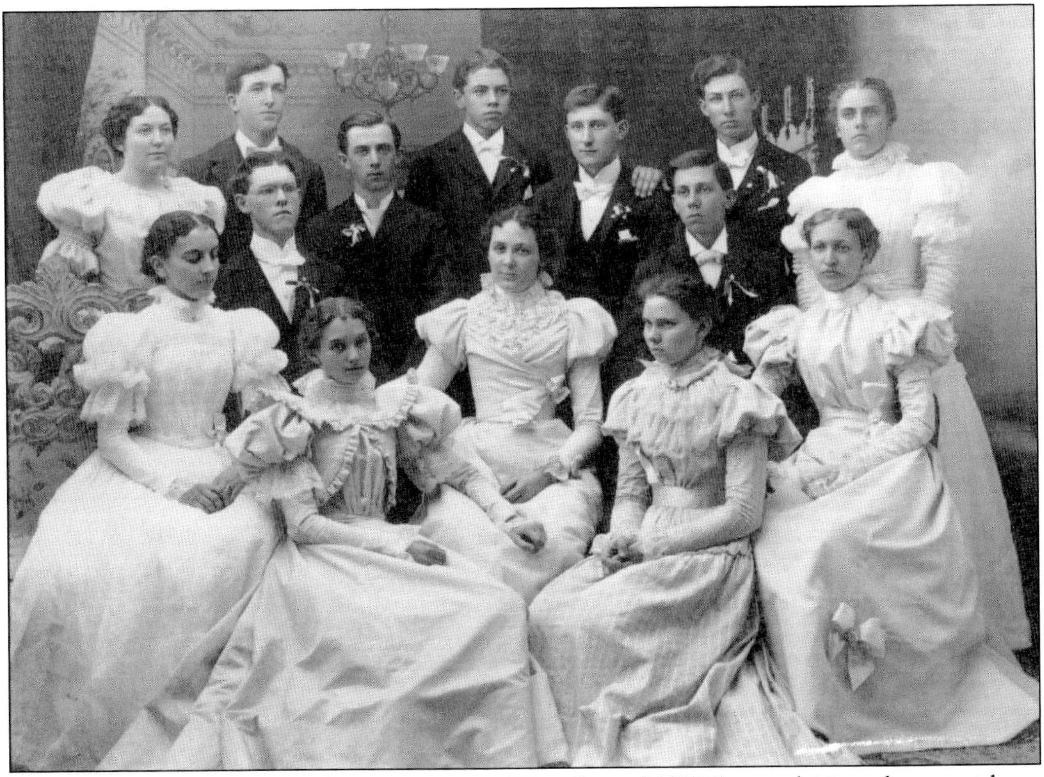

Graduating classes continued to grow in size. The class of 1897 featured 14 graduates with an equal split between men and women. (Courtesy of the Geauga County Historical Society.)

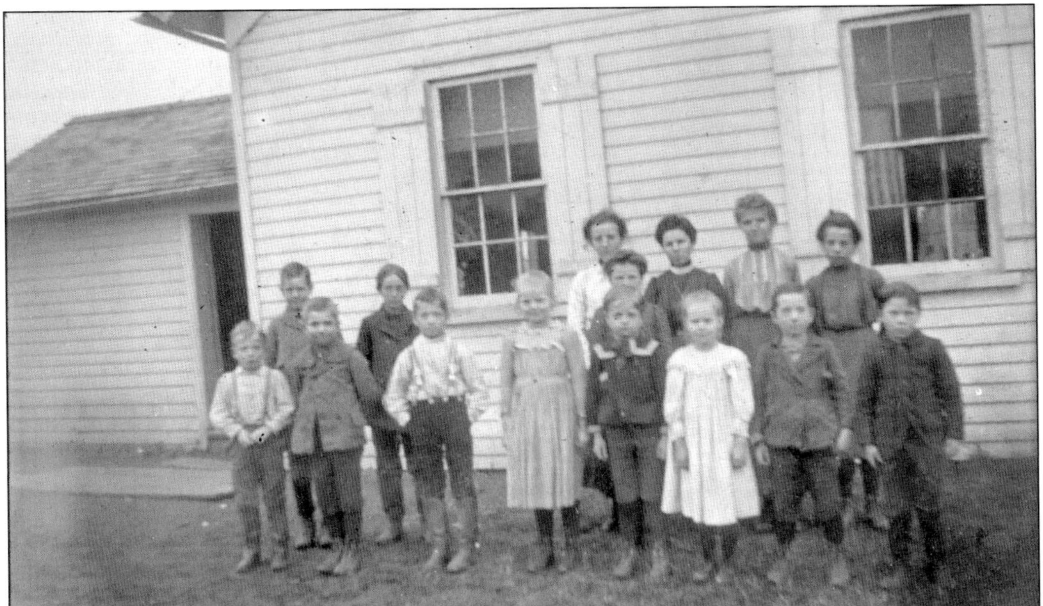

Teacher Bessie Baptie and a group of her students pose in front of the district school during the fall of 1902. (Courtesy of the Geauga County Historical Society.)

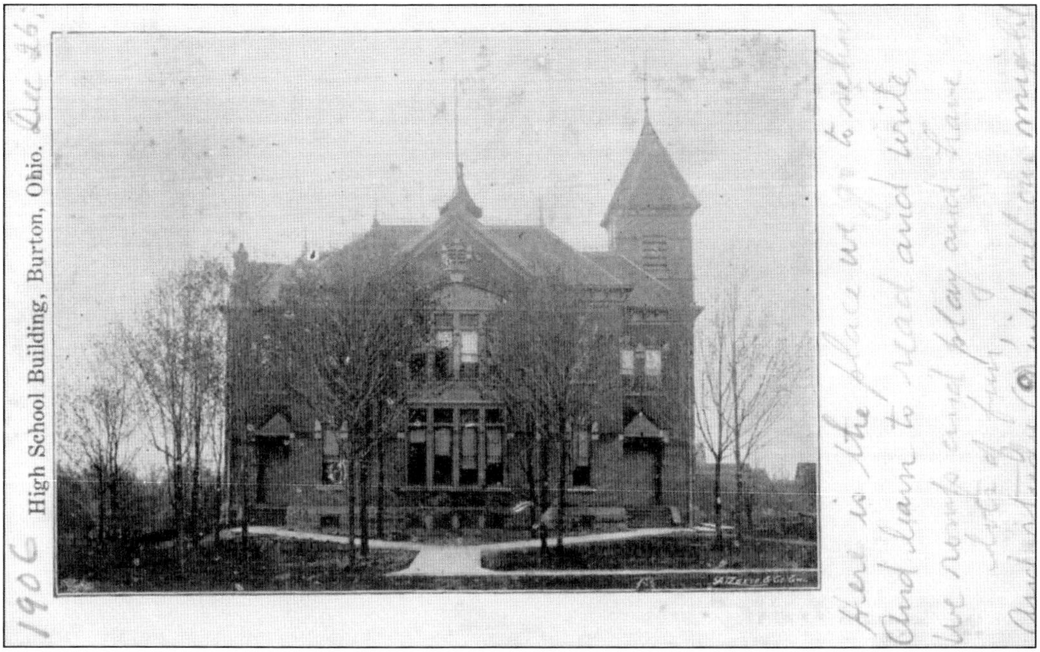

This postcard of Burton High School is dated "1906-12-26." According to the writer, "Here is the place we go to school and learn to read and write. We romp and play and have lots of fun, and study hard with all our might." This building, the second high school, was erected in 1884 and used until 1936. (Courtesy of Mary L. Wilson.)

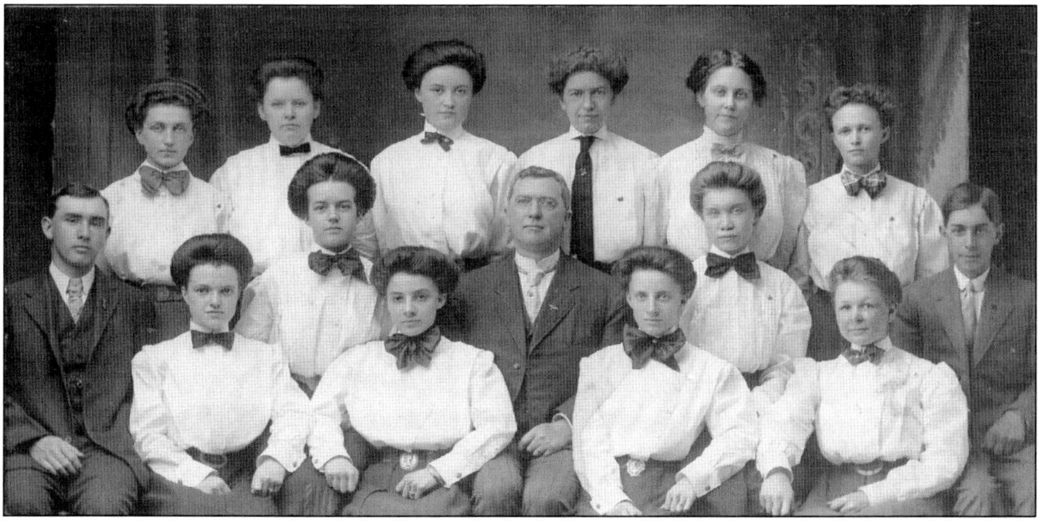

The Burton High School class of 1909 included Louise Silvernail, Flossie ?, Loveland Wells, Lottie Hyde Neilson, Hazel Hyde Farrell, Lena Shanower, Belle Ludlow Stuckey, Annabelle Pollack, Viette Merriman Mills, Aileen Canfield, Marion Welsh, Jean Patterson, and Mary Hale. Supt. L.V. Mills and teacher Miss Schmezik are also pictured. (Courtesy of the Geauga County Public Library.)

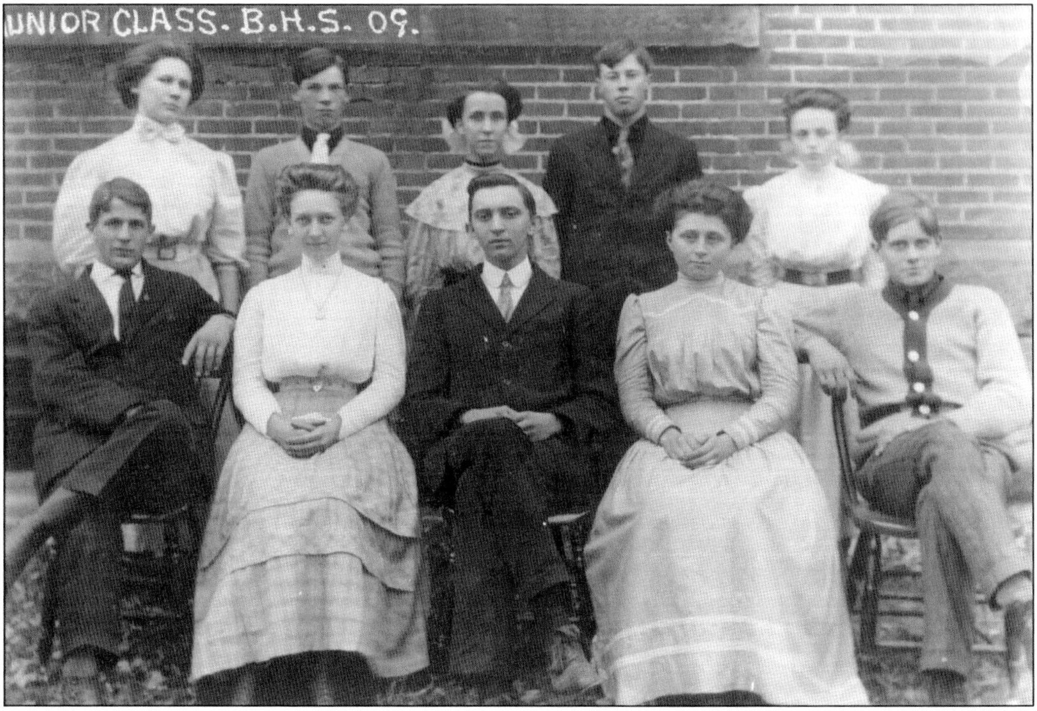

The Burton High School junior class photograph from 1909 shows a little informality sneaking into the dress of the students—a male student showed up for the photograph without a tie. (Courtesy of Helen Chelikowsky.)

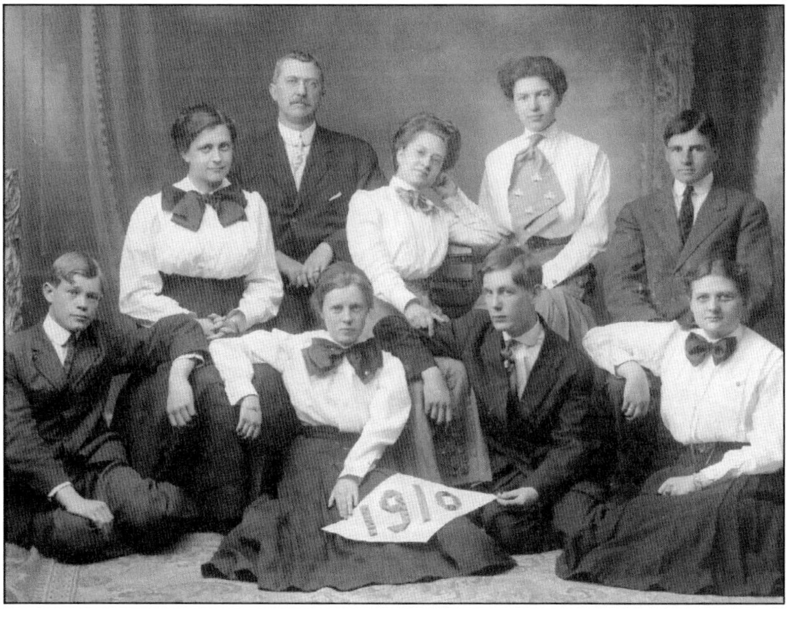

The class of 1910, taught by professor L.V. Mills, included Vera Smesik, Zelda Johnson, Fern Wakin, Forrest Smith, Malcolm Bond, Marjorie Olds, and Lloyd Farrell. (Courtesy of the Geauga County Historical County.)

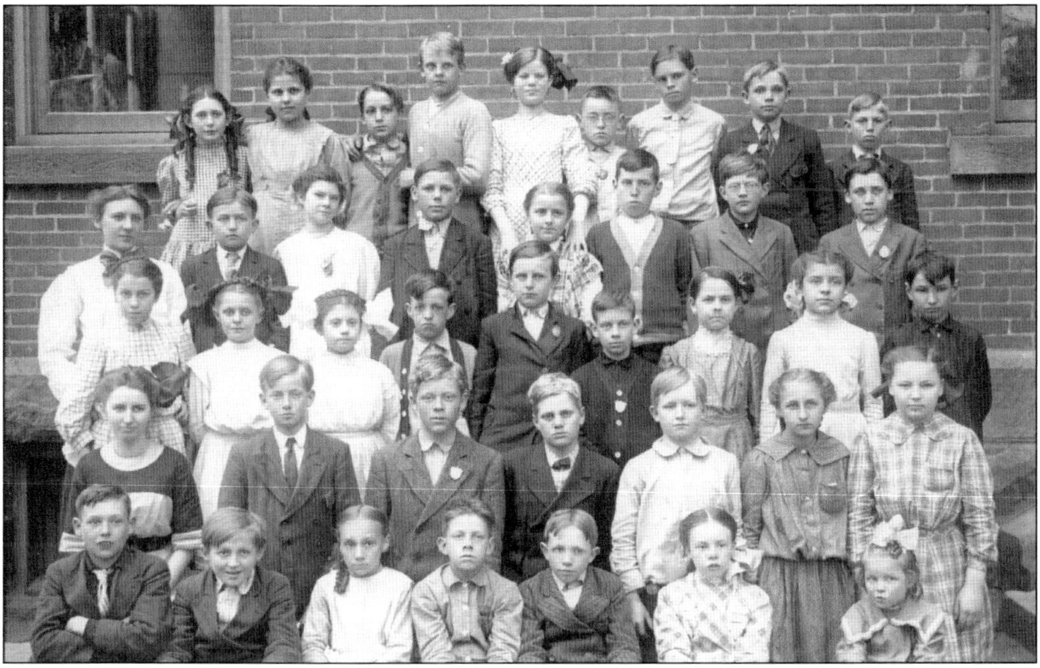

This 1910 class photograph shows that class sizes grew along with Burton's population. (Courtesy of Mary L. Wilson.)

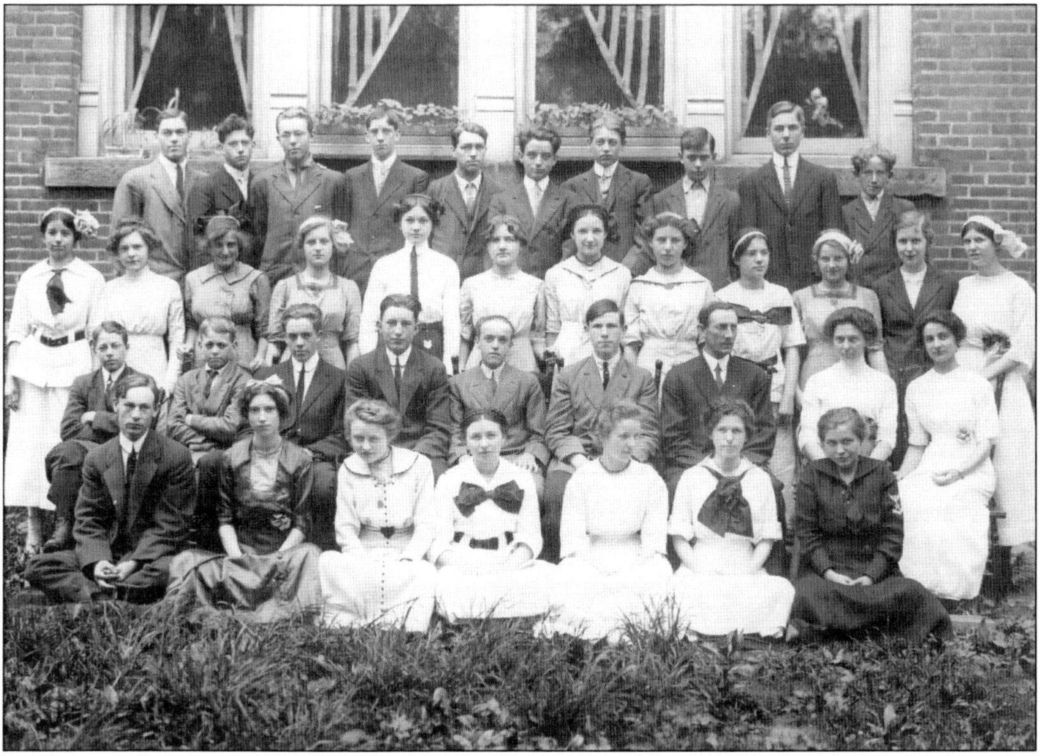

All the students of Burton High School pose in front of the school in 1910. (Courtesy of the Geauga County Historical Society.)

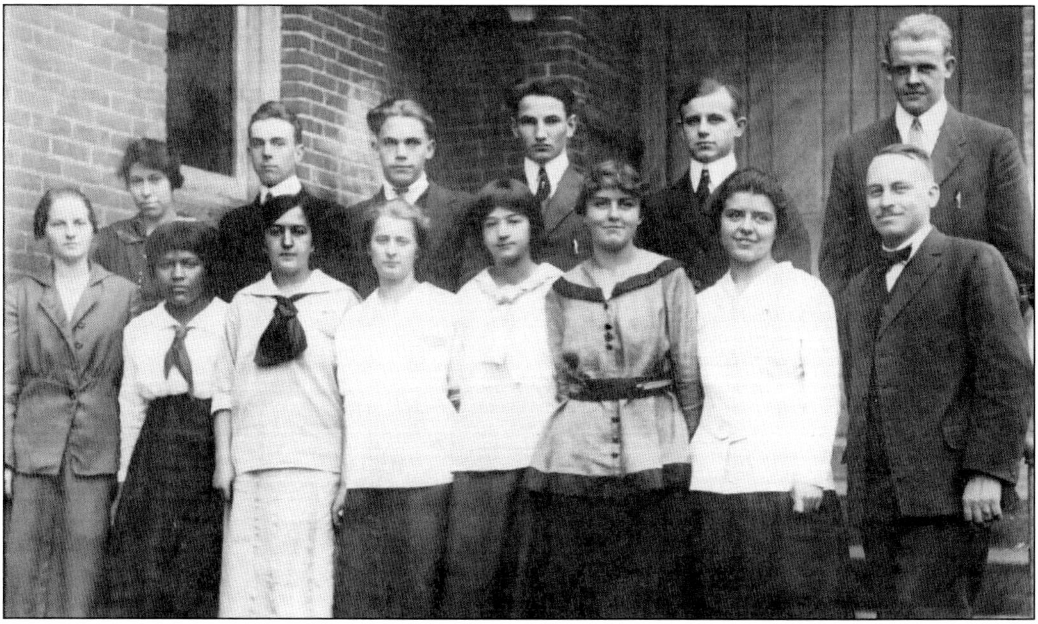

This class photograph from around 1915 includes teacher Miss Hendricks, Professor Hunter, Rend Riley, Marie Fisher, Charlotte Ferry, Olive Kline, Gertrude Ferry, Ella K. Welch, Alta M. Woodard, Emile Ojala, Bert Clapp, Raymond C. Linton, Wade P. Adams, and Stanley B. Hull. (Courtesy of Mary L. Wilson.)

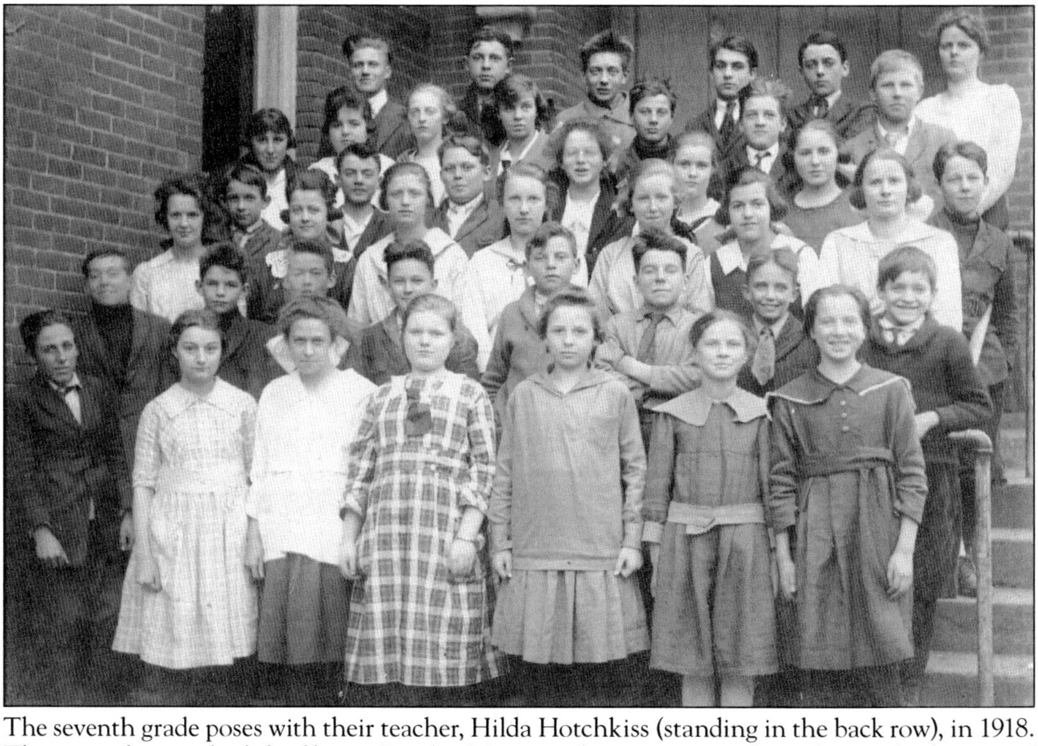

The seventh grade poses with their teacher, Hilda Hotchkiss (standing in the back row), in 1918. The young boy to the left of her is Stanlae Merritt, who wrote several articles on the history of Burton later in life. (Courtesy of Geauga County Historical Society.)

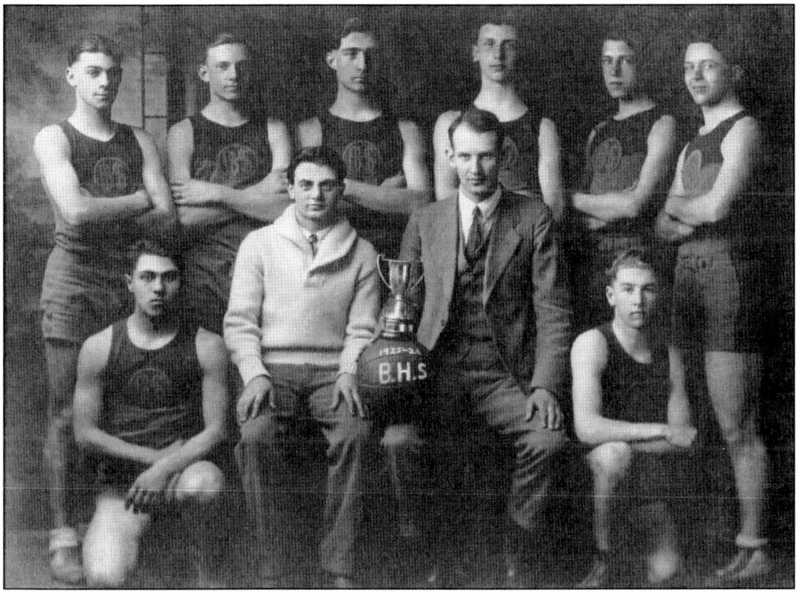

The 1925–1926 Burton basketball team included, from left to right, (first row) Lisle Bartholomew, manager John T. Humphrey, coach Frank Cox, and Charles Blake; (second row) captain Robert R. Gould, Ward Lawrence, Roger Hull, Lester Newcomb, Charles Gould, and Roland Osborn. (Courtesy of Geauga County Historical County.)

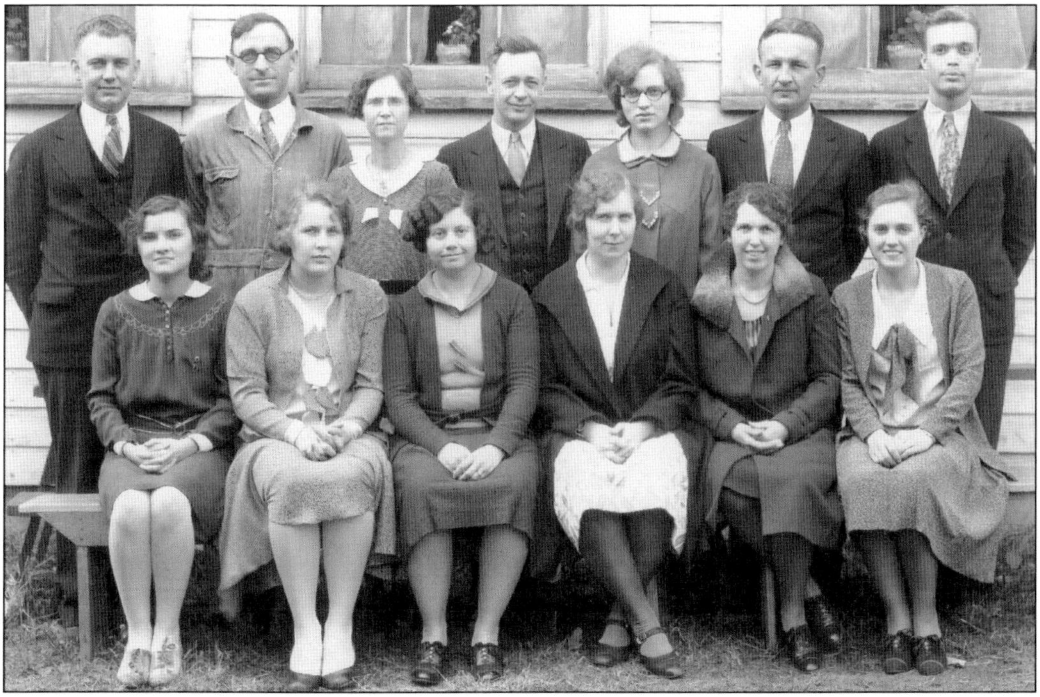

The 1929–1930 Burton School faculty and staff included, from left to right, music teacher Raymond Dehnbostle, Martha Cochran, M. Donald Owen, janitor Newt Stucky, Margaret B. Thrasher, Elizabeth Nye, Supt. Paul H. Calvin, Helen Hotchkiss, Jane Carlton, Mona Hodges, Jim Darsie, Carolyn Baptie, and Thelma Wagner. (Courtesy of the Geauga County Historical County.)

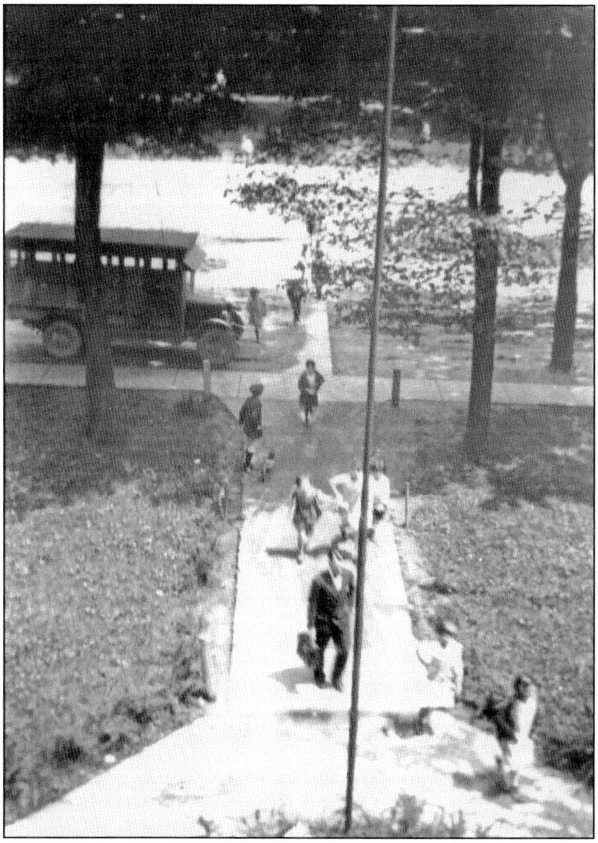

Seen here is the entrance to Burton High School in the 1930s. This building, the second school, has housed the Burton Public Library since 1936. (Courtesy of the Geauga County Library.)

The 1935–1936 seventh-grade class included Norbet Fritz, Gordon ?, Lawrence C., Edward M., Lawrence H., Karl Goff, Charles Sheets, Donny ?, Joyce Kenney, Ira G., Sophie Korowacki, Rose Dietz, Norma D., Vivian Gardner, Ruth McNish, Maczine K., Paul Clark, Mary Smith, June M., teacher Margaret B. Thrasher, Jeannette Grosvenor, Gertrude Olsen, Earl Miller, Ralph S., Burt Popp, and Bobby Owen. (Courtesy of the Geauga County Historical Society.)

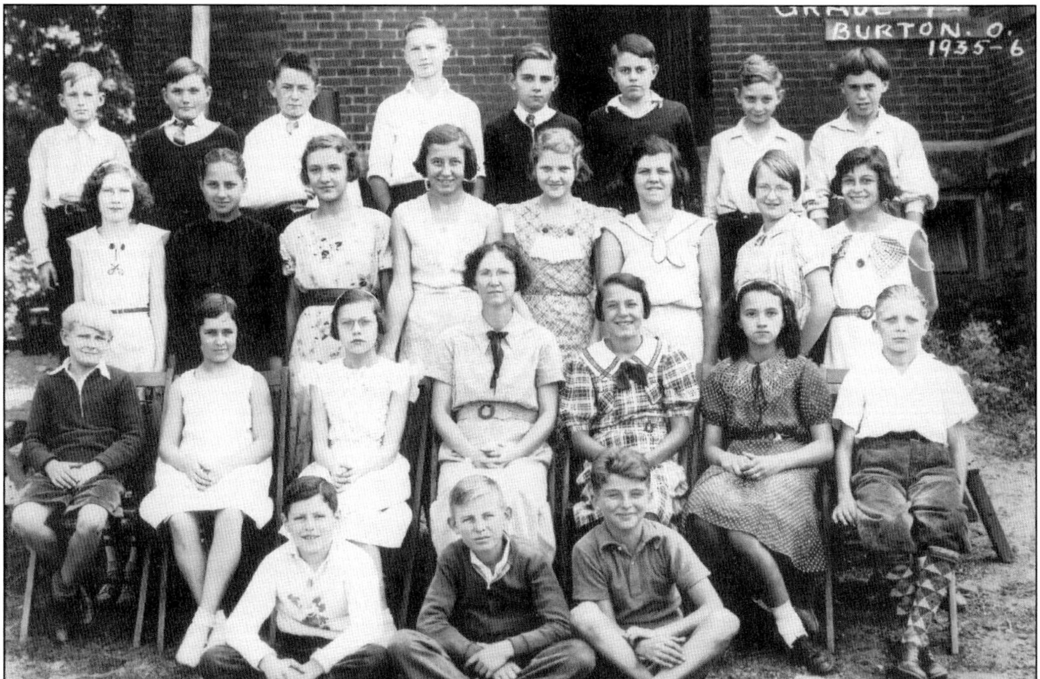

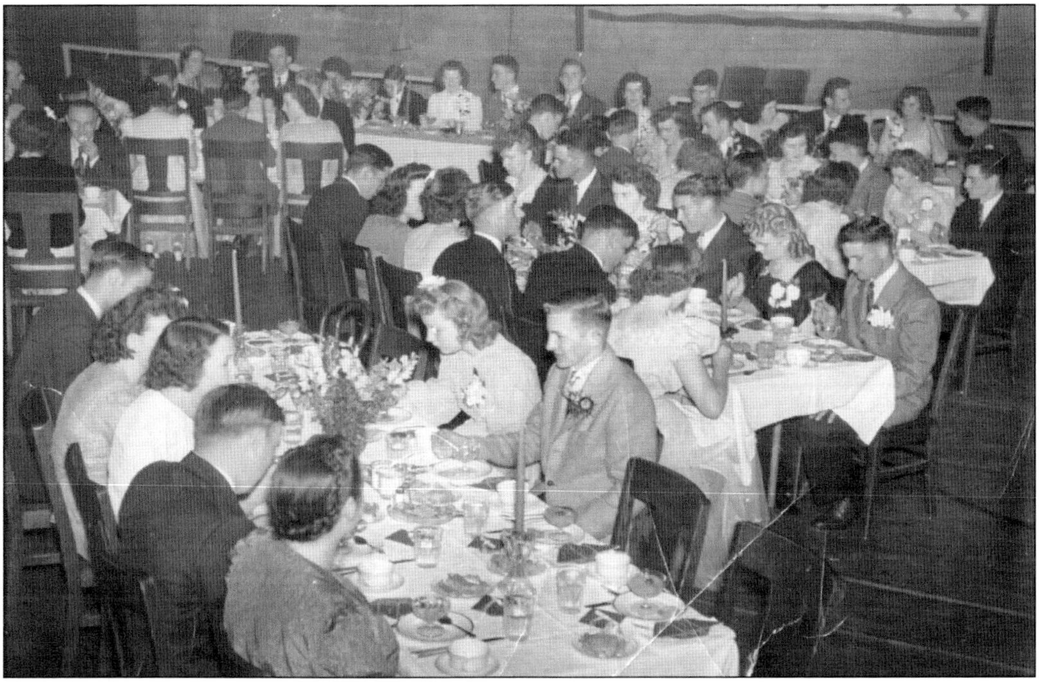

Some of the attendees of the Junior-Senior Prom in May 1944 pictured here include Otto Horwath, Helen Coats, Roy Coats, Carol Taylor, Pat Johnson, Frank Malensek, Olive Samuel, Frank Samuel, June Riffle, Paul Wilhelm, Hazel Rose, Calvin Wilson, Harold Hope, Mrs. and Rev. Eugene Hibbard, and Ruth Morgan and her brother. (Courtesy of Jacqueline Samuel.)

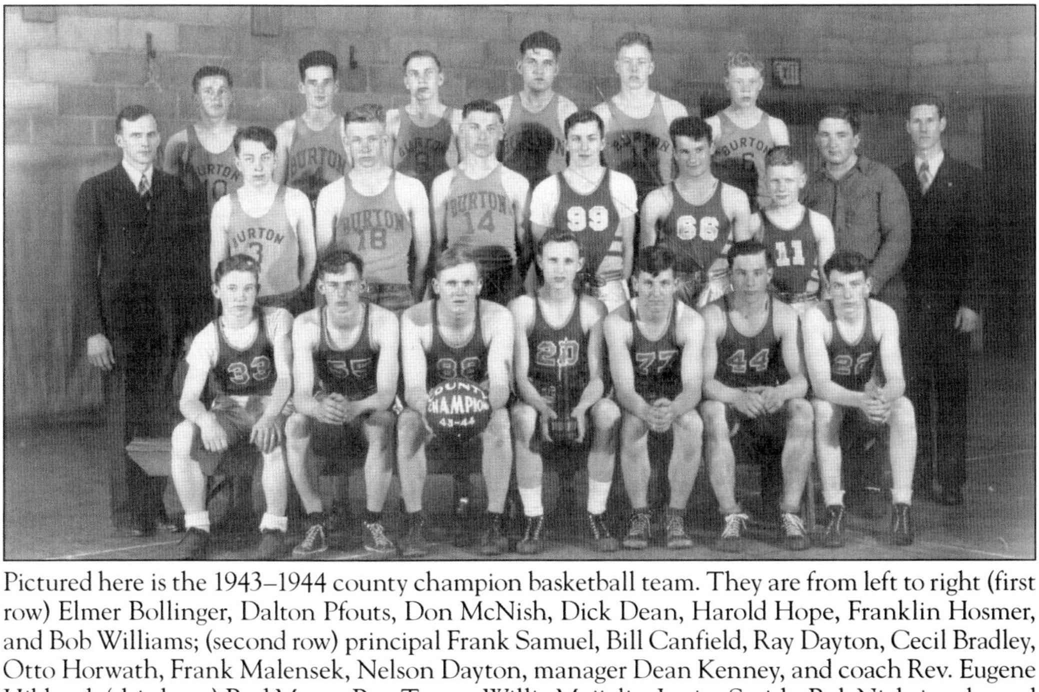

Pictured here is the 1943–1944 county champion basketball team. They are from left to right (first row) Elmer Bollinger, Dalton Pfouts, Don McNish, Dick Dean, Harold Hope, Franklin Hosmer, and Bob Williams; (second row) principal Frank Samuel, Bill Canfield, Ray Dayton, Cecil Bradley, Otto Horwath, Frank Malensek, Nelson Dayton, manager Dean Kenney, and coach Rev. Eugene Hibbard; (third row) Bud Myers, Ben Texter, Willie Maijalia, Junior Smith, Bob Nightingale, and Gould Van Deweel. (Courtesy of Jacqueline Samuel.)

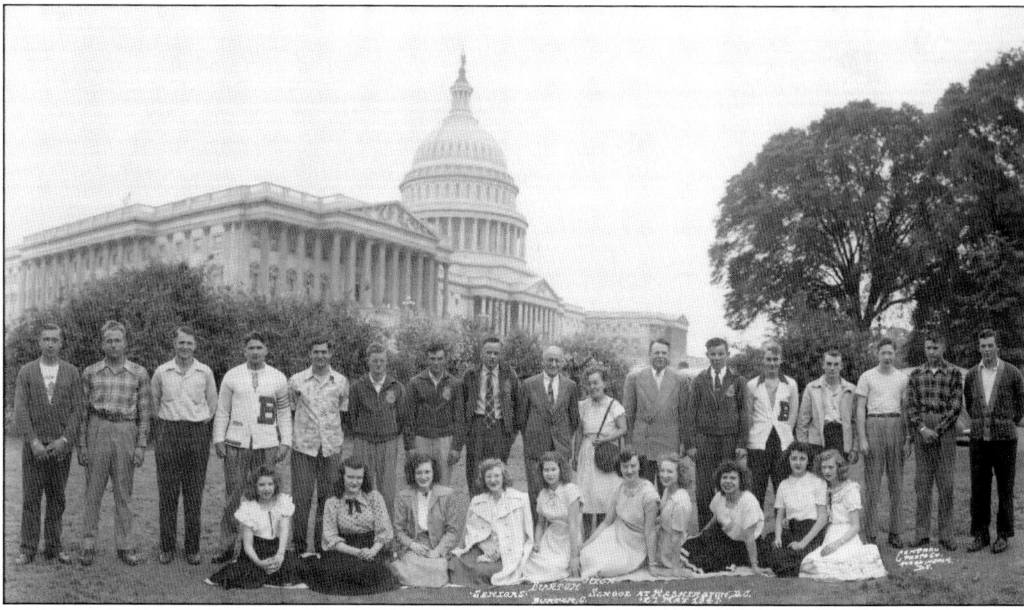

The 1948 Burton High School senior class poses on a trip to Washington, DC. (Courtesy of the Burton Public Library.)

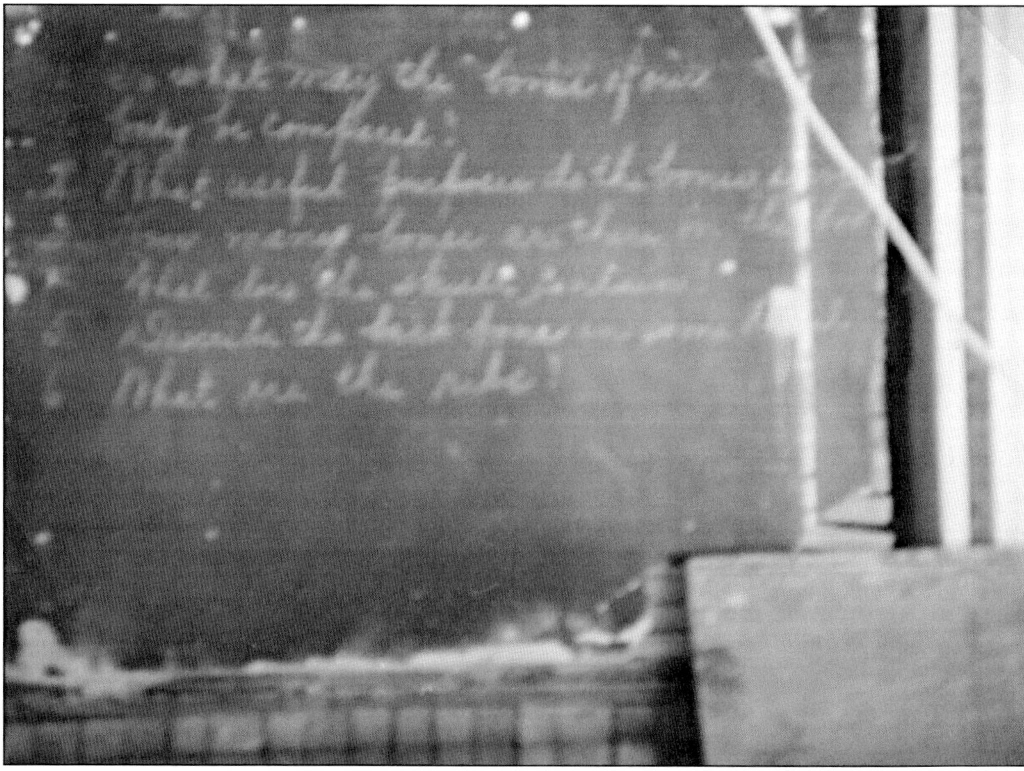

This blackboard with a lesson still on it was found during a 1981 renovation of the library, which was the school building until 1936, dating this lesson back to the mid-1930s. (Courtesy of the Burton Public Library.)

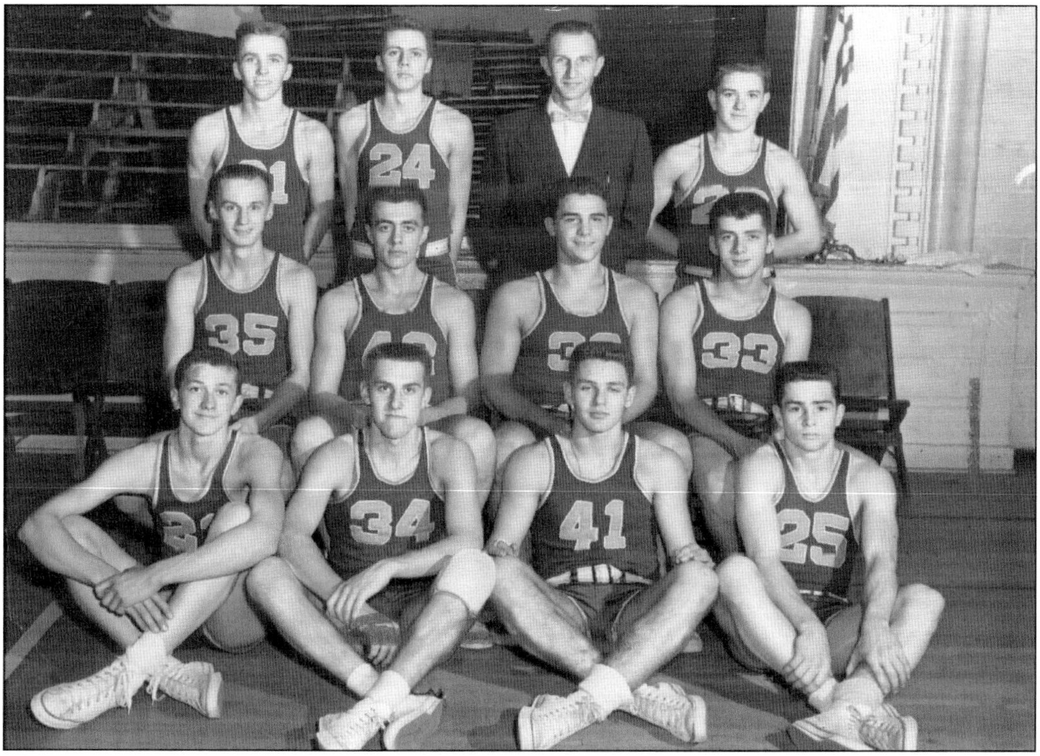

The 1956 Burton High School basketball team was comprised of, from left to right, (first row) Fred Hering, Charlie Green, Tom Polomsky, and Ken Blair; (second row) Jim Burzanko, Bob Potter, Russ Artwell, and Tom Wells; (third row) Rod Milhof, Butch Brininger, coach Bill Bradley, and Bob Bollinger. (Courtesy of Special Collections, Michael Schwartz Library, Cleveland State University.)

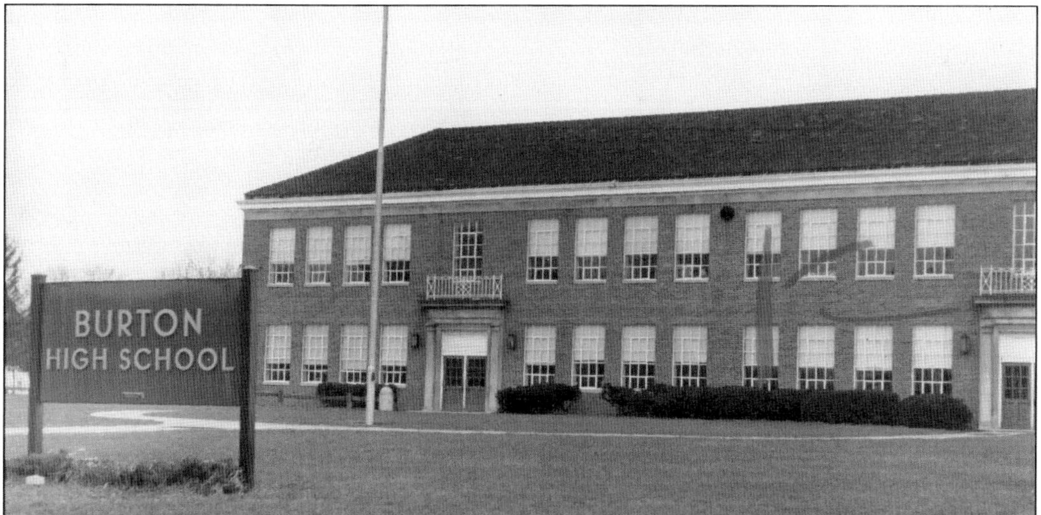

Burton High School is seen here on a pleasant spring afternoon in May 1965 just a few years before the school system merged with neighboring districts. (Courtesy of Special Collections, Michael Schwartz Library, Cleveland State University.)

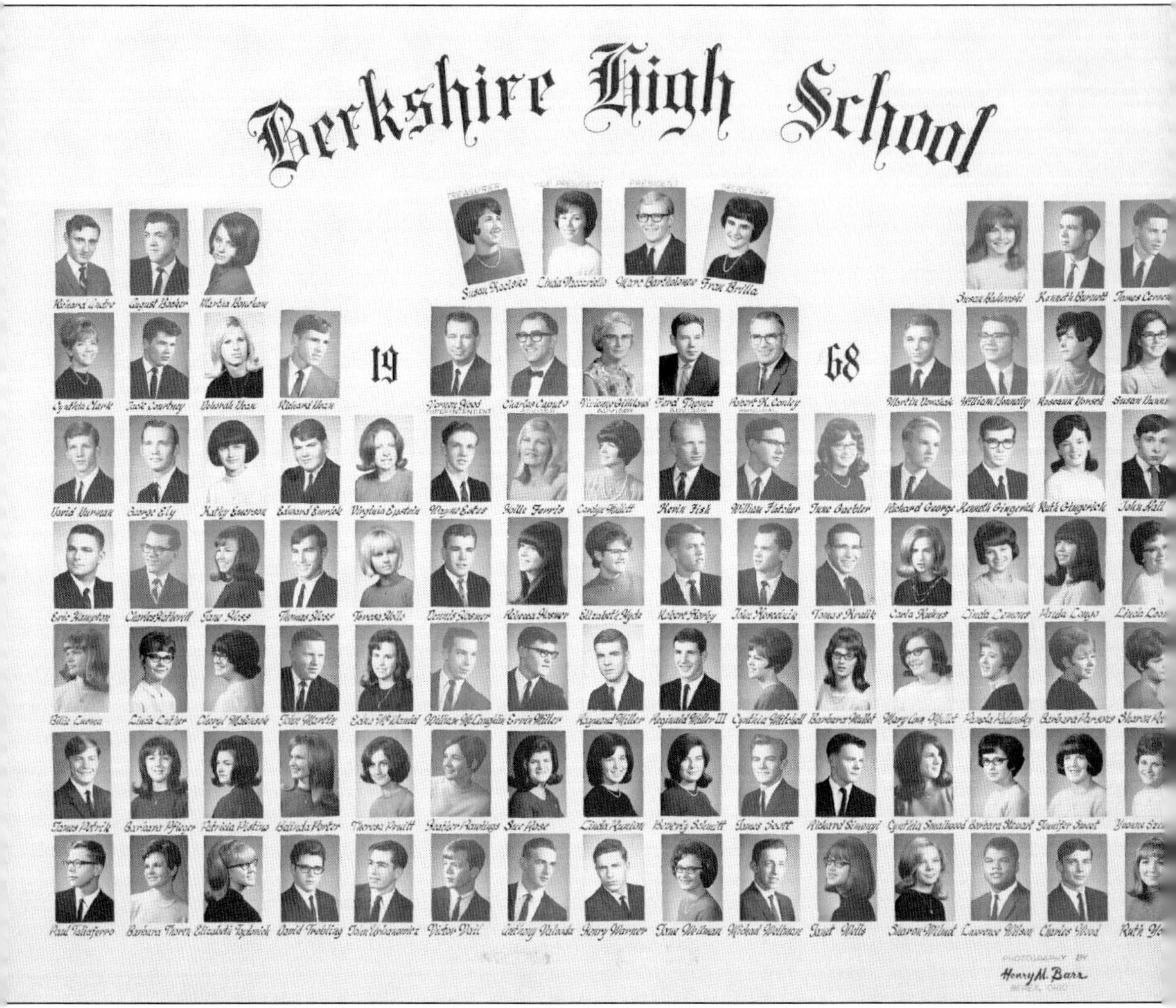

In 1967, students from Burton attended Burton High School and rooted for the Maple Leafs. In 1968, they found themselves joined by students from parts of Claridon and Troy Townships and rooting for the Badgers. Unlike most American high schools, Berkshire High School is composed of grades 7 through 12. The school is built on the site of the former home of Seabury Ford. (Courtesy of the Burton Public Library.)

Eight

Century Village Museum

Century Village is a unique historical hamlet located just south of Burton Village Park. Initially known as the Geauga County Historical and Memorial Society, the museum began in 1940 when the famed Hickox Brick was purchased by Congresswoman Frances Bolton and donated to the Geauga County Historical Society. Lottie Doolittle Fox, G.B. Fox's wife, and a close friend of Ms. Bolton, facilitated the gift to the county. In the 70 years since the museum's modest inception, it has grown considerably and currently contains 22 historically authentic buildings, more than 20,000 artifacts, and a working farm with a sugar bush for making maple syrup.

Century Village is a living museum—a portrait of Burton from a long-gone era. It is a fully restored and authentic representation of a Western Reserve Village from around 1798 and spans more than 200 years of history. For decades, it has been a popular destination for area teachers, providing guided tours and educational programs to students so they can experience firsthand how their ancestors lived. Every year, the living museum sponsors pioneer school, allowing schoolchildren to learn how to make a variety of items, ranging from root beer to woven belts. Century Village is also utilized for scholarly research at the Shanower Library.

The museum also boasts numerous interesting and entertaining events that appeal to a wide demographic. Every year, Century Village Museum is host to several festivals, such as the wildly popular Apple Butter Festival, and special events, including a Civil War reenactment. It is run by the Geauga County Historical Society, whose mission is to "ensure that the history of Geauga County is preserved for the education and appreciation of present and future generations."

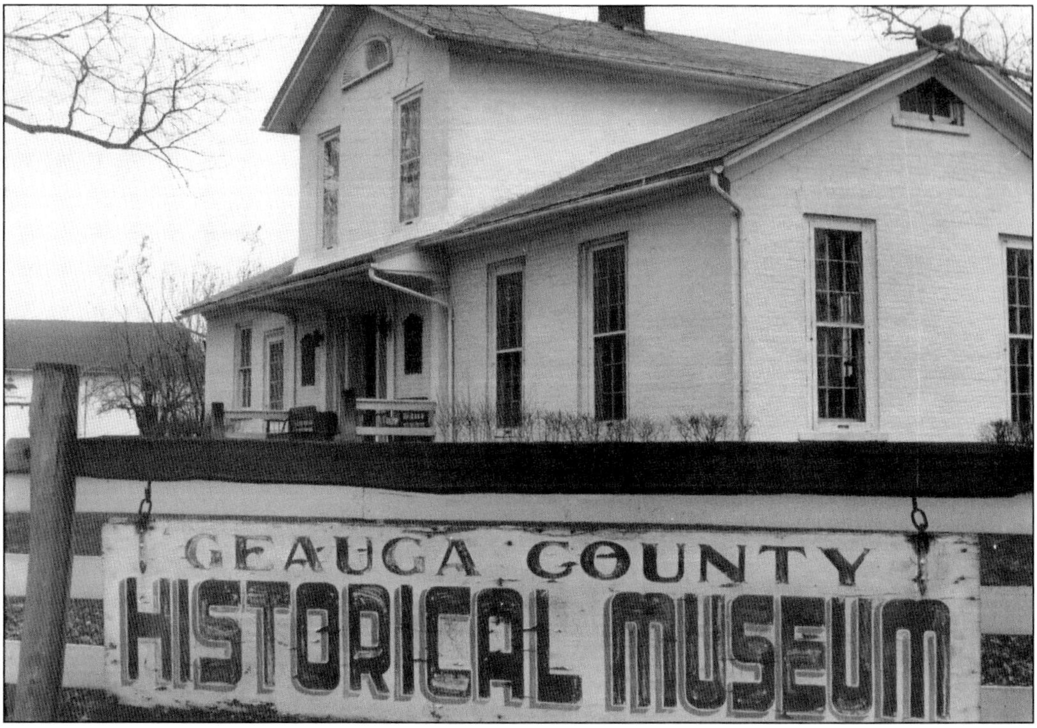

The Geauga County Historical Society was organized in 1873 to help promote and preserve the history and artifacts of Geauga County. For some time, the historical society was dormant, but it was reorganized in 1938, after which it embarked on its crowning achievement: the establishment of the Geauga County Historical Museum. The museum, a recreation of Burton Village, came to fruition in 1941 and now is known as Century Village. (Courtesy of Special Collections, Michael Schwartz Library, Cleveland State University.)

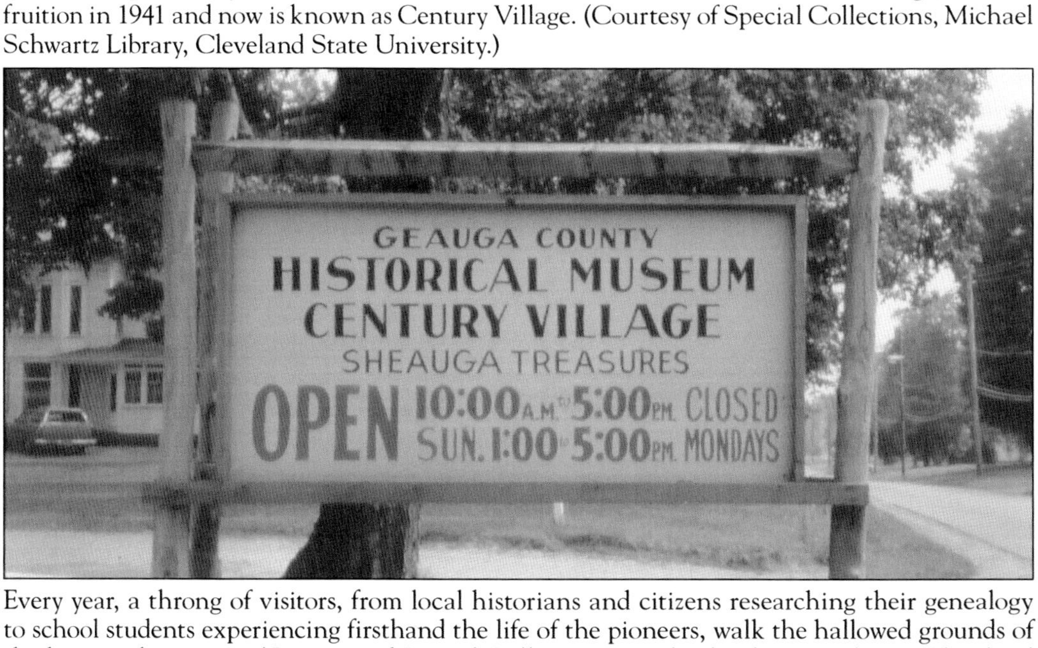

Every year, a throng of visitors, from local historians and citizens researching their genealogy to school students experiencing firsthand the life of the pioneers, walk the hallowed grounds of the historical museum. (Courtesy of Special Collections, Michael Schwartz Library, Cleveland State University.)

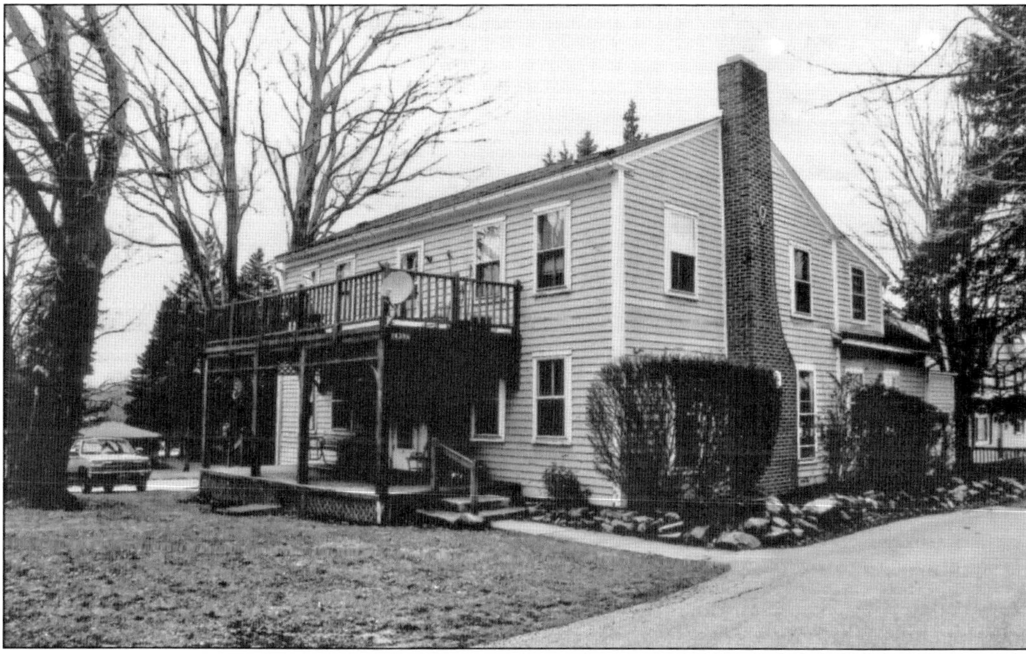

This Cook house is on North Cheshire Street. Built in 1807 by John Cook, the son of Marimon Cook, a former deacon of the Burton Congregational Church, the Cook House was operating as the Cottage Hotel in the early 1900s and was later the home of famed poet Fred J. Gould. Today, it is known as the VanDeweel house with the initials visible on the chimney. (Courtesy of Special Collections, Michael Schwartz Library, Cleveland State University.)

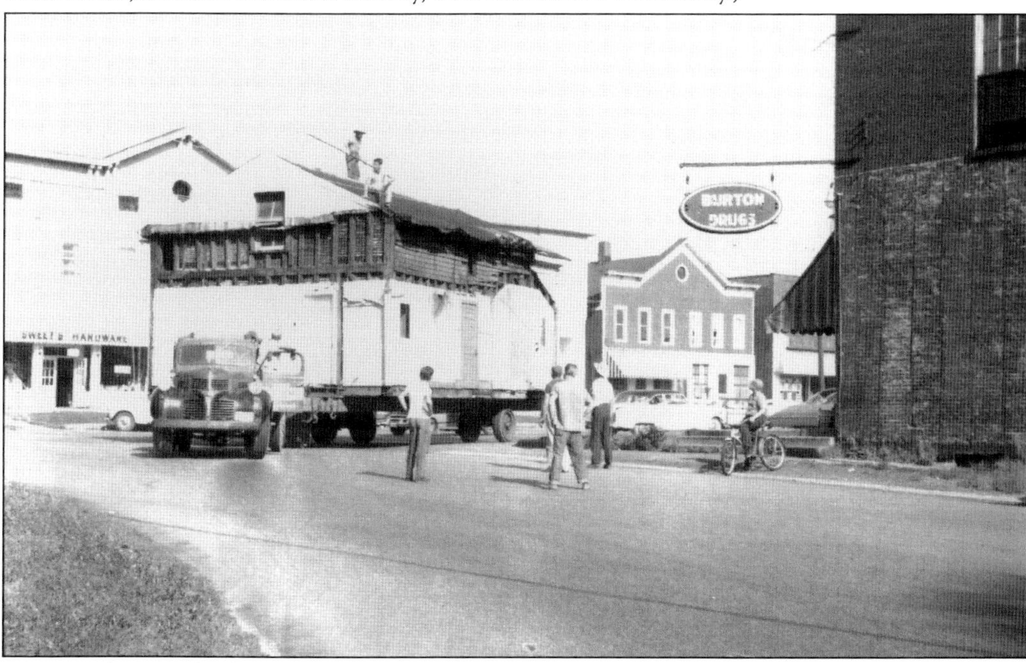

In 1959, the Brookside Building was transported down Main Street to Century Village, where it was converted into the general store and became a popular destination for visitors of all ages. (Courtesy of Geauga Historical Society.)

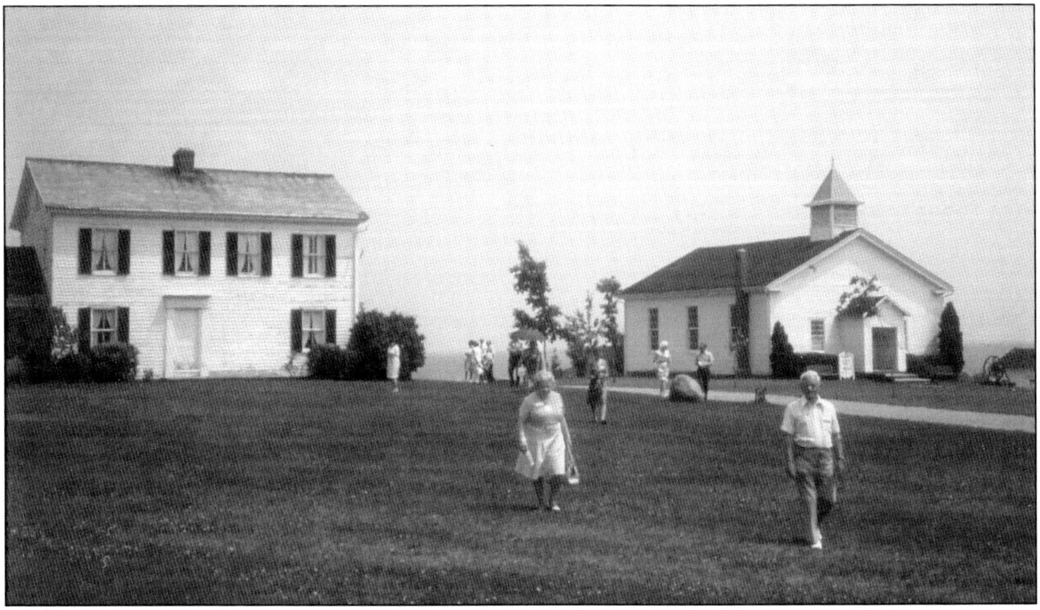

The acquisition, restoration, and preservation of historic homes and buildings are of fundamental importance to the mission of Century Village. One such structure is the Boughton house, seen in the background of this photograph. George Boughton, a native of Canfield, built this Greek Revival–style home in 1834. Boughton started the Boughton, Ford, and Company Bank in 1871 along with H.H. Ford, George H. Ford, and R.N. Ford. (Courtesy of Special Collections, Michael Schwartz Library, Cleveland State University.)

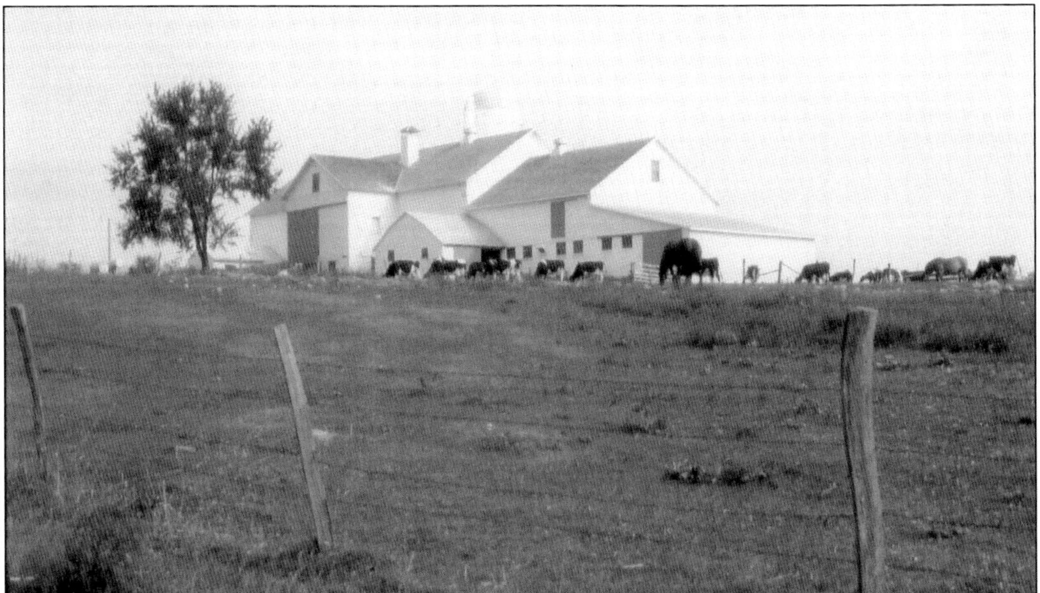

In the summer of 1975, a barn was raised on the grounds of Century Village. A team of men had to take down the barn piece by piece then raise it once more on the grounds of what is now the Century Village Museum. (Courtesy of Special Collections, Michael Schwartz Library, Cleveland State University.)

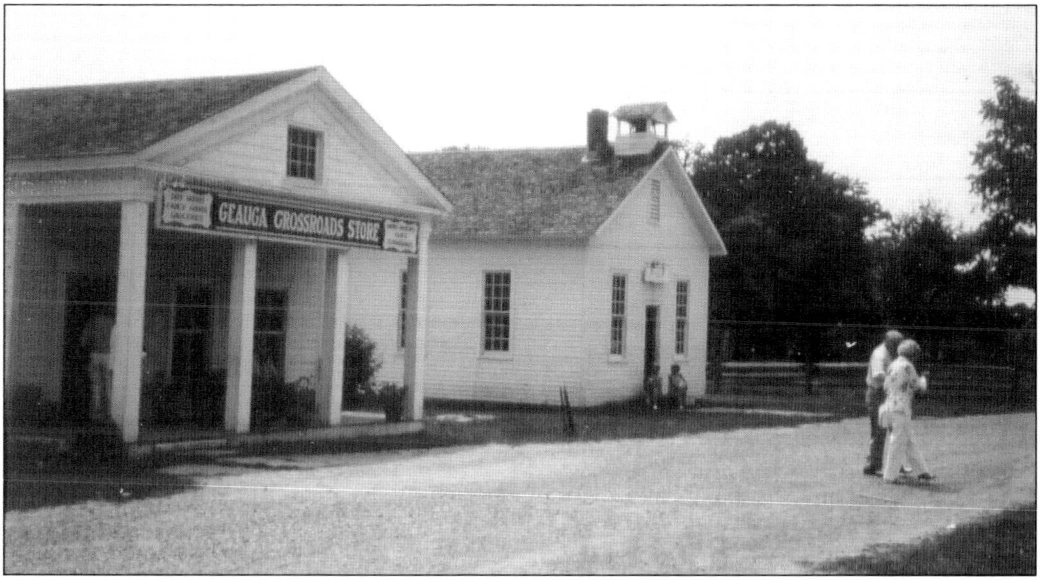

Visitors to Century Village can find gifts aplenty at the Crossroads General Store, including staples of any resident's diet: maple syrup and apple butter. The general store is just one of many buildings moved to or re-created for Century Village. There are over 20 buildings on the grounds, including an authentic 19th-century schoolhouse and the Munson Town Hall, which now serves as the Shanower Library. (Courtesy of Special Collections, Michael Schwartz Library, Cleveland State University.)

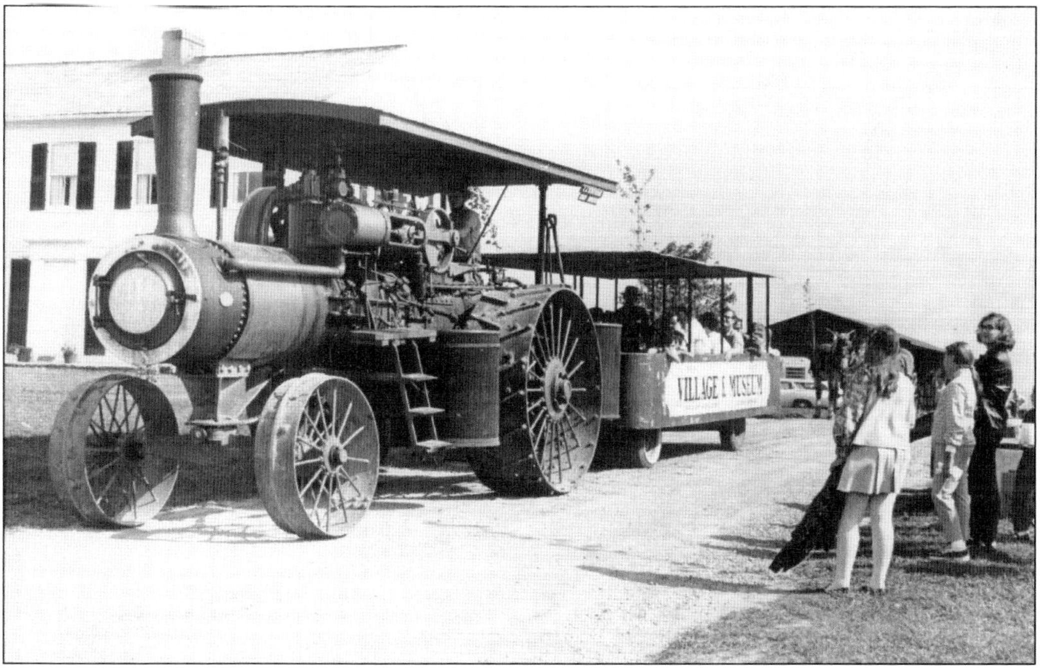

Work vehicles like steam tractors, as seen here in 1969, played a major role in the lives of the village people in the 19th and early 20th centuries. Steam tractors were utilized for threshing purposes, particularly for wheat and oats. (Courtesy of Special Collections, Michael Schwartz Library, Cleveland State University.)

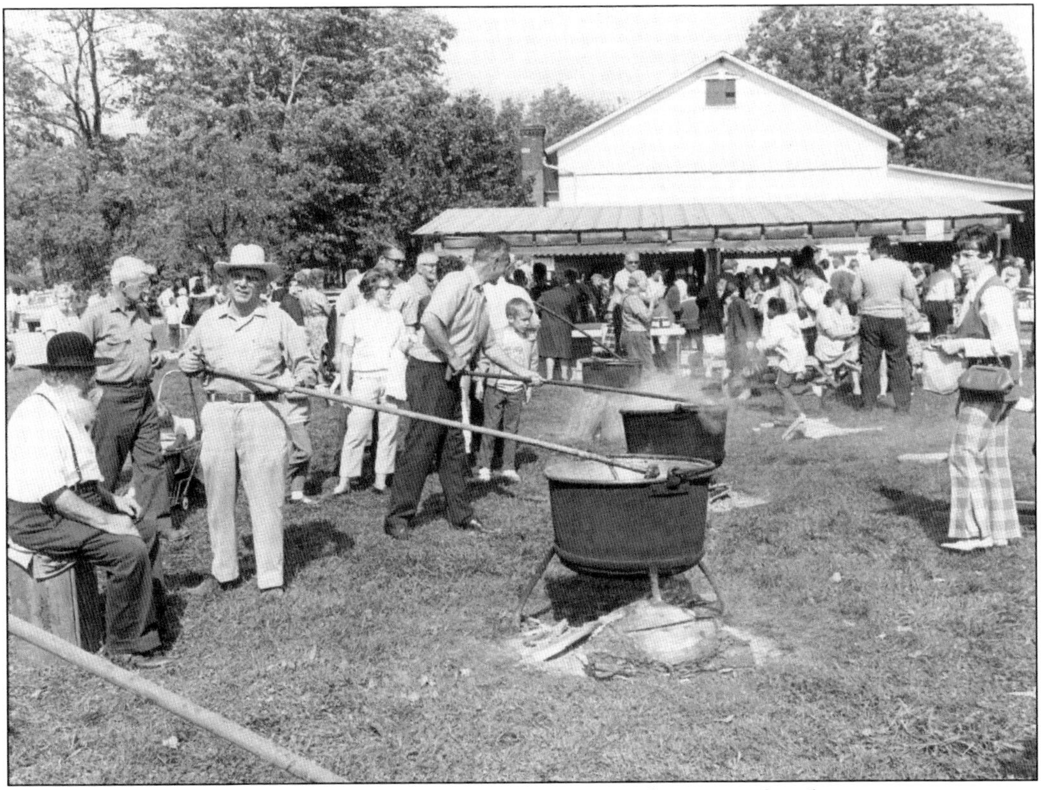

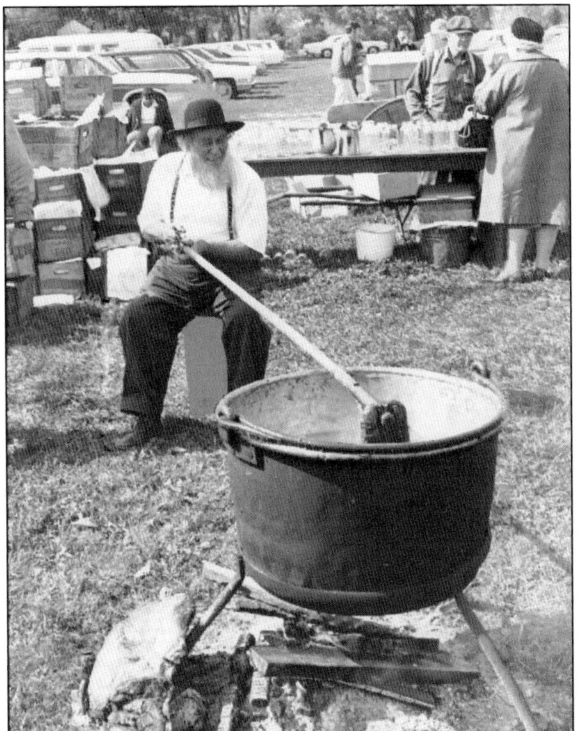

Nothing signifies the commencement of another autumn in Burton quite like the Apple Butter Festival. The delicate art of butter churning is always on display at the festival on the grounds of Century Village. For over 60 years, locals and visitors have enjoyed tradition and savored the aromas and flavors of the cinnamon-tinged apple butter cooked using century-old methods in huge copper kettles over open fires all day long. (Courtesy of Special Collections, Michael Schwartz Library, Cleveland State University.)

Early in Burton's history, many families peeled plenty of apples in preparation for the long and arduous winter, making apple butter an essential part of the pioneer diet. Its concentration of sugar gave it a much longer shelf life than applesauce, and it would not spoil over the rugged winter months. (Courtesy of Special Collections, Michael Schwartz Library, Cleveland State University.)

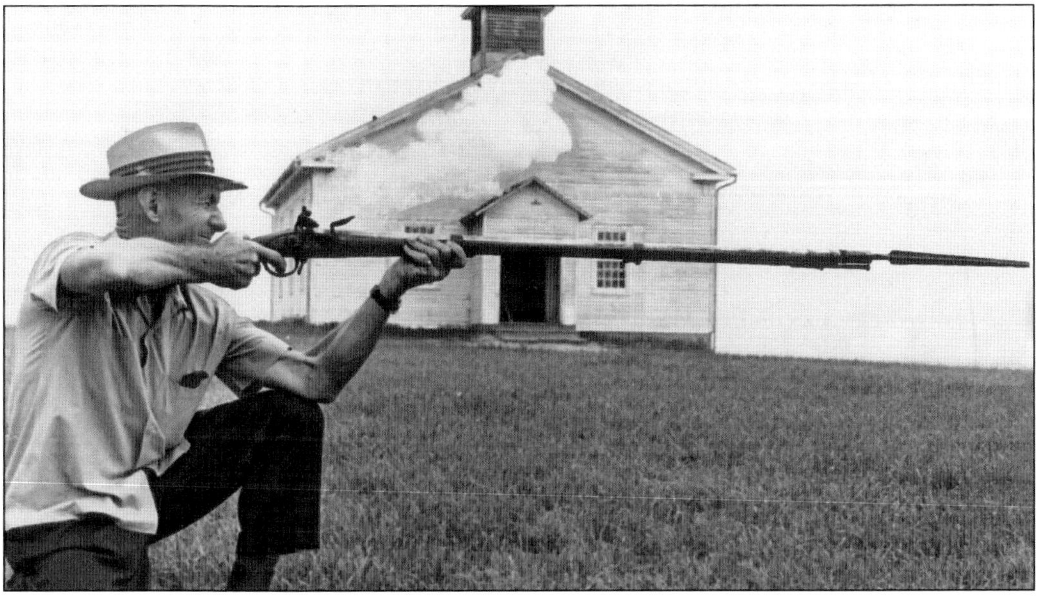

An unidentified man shoots at an unseen target during rifle practice on Geauga County Historical Society grounds in July 1964. Sights such as these are not unusual, as Century Village plays host to Civil War reenactments and numerous unique festivals every year. (Courtesy of Special Collections, Michael Schwartz Library, Cleveland State University.)

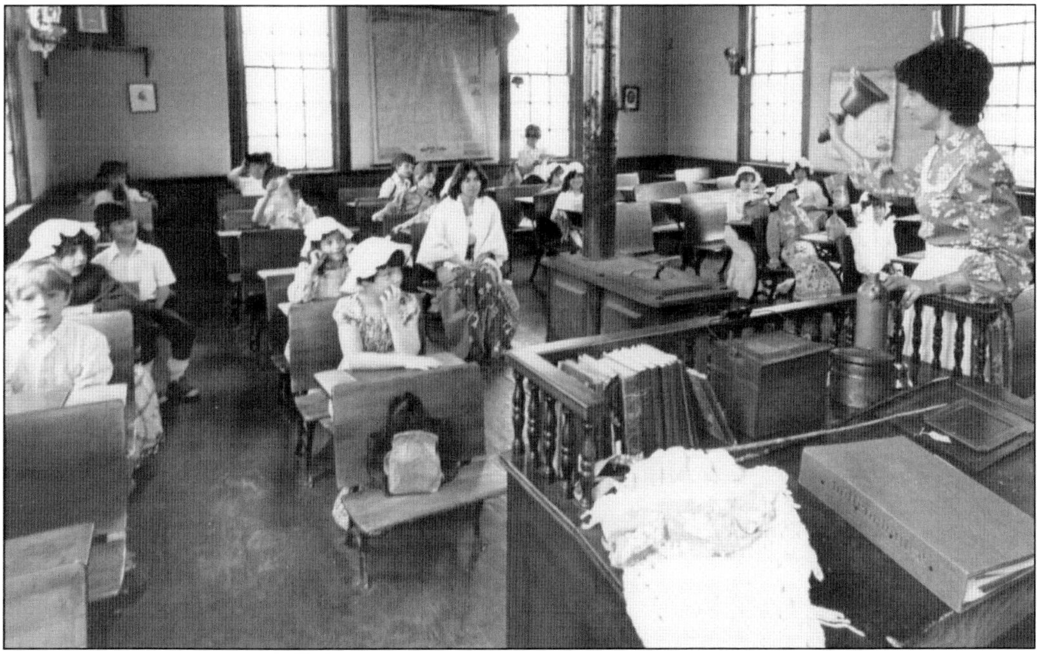

Local schoolchildren participate in pioneer school at Century Village. Starting in 1973, the historical society sponsored pioneer school to teach local youngsters firsthand how the pioneers lived. The children learn to make an assortment of goods, including root beer, cornbread, apple head dolls, old-fashioned medicine, woven belts, and other staples of pioneer living. Amish blacksmiths also teach the children how to shoe horses. (Courtesy of Special Collections, Michael Schwartz Library, Cleveland State University.)